A2 Revise PE for AQA

second edition

by

Dennis Roscoe

Jan Roscoe

JRP

CREDITS

A2 Revise PE for AQA
second edition

by
Dennis Roscoe
Jan Roscoe

Jan Roscoe Publications Ltd
An imprint of Heath Books Ltd

Text copyright to Dennis Roscoe, Jan Roscoe, Bob Davis, graphics copyright to Jan Roscoe Publications.

All rights reserved. No part of this publication may be reproduced, or transmitted in any form or by any means, electronic or mechanical, including photocopy, recording or any information storage and retrieval system, without permission in writing from the publisher.

First edition published in 2010 by Jan Roscoe Publications.
Second edition October 2017.

Heath Books Ltd
Willow House, Willow Walk
Sutton
Surrey
SM3 9QQ
United Kingdom

tel: 020 8644 7788
fax: 020 8641 3377
email: orders@heathbooks.co.uk

A Catalogue record for this book is available from the British Library.

ISBN   978-1-911-24100-3.

Cover designs by Roscoe Rutter.

Published via Adobe InDesign, CorelDraw 10.410, Adobe Illustrator 9.0, Smartdraw 6.0, laid out and typeset by Dennis Roscoe

Printed and bound by

Hobbs the Printers Limited
Brunel Road
Totton
Hampshire
SO40 3WX
United Kingdom

tel: 023 8066 4800
fax: 023 8066 4801

email: estimating@hobbs.uk.com

A2 REVISE PE FOR AQA

INTRODUCTION

This 'A' level PE book has been written to address the changes in content and style of the AQA Level 3 Advanced Year 2 GCE Physical Education (7582) syllabus which commenced in September 2017.

These Physical Education syllabuses are multi-disciplinary in nature, covering applied anatomy and exercise physiology, skill acquisition and sports psychology, and historical and contemporary studies. These subject areas have generated a substantial quantity of specialist literature each with its own specific language. At times you may be overwhelmed by the amount of material covered, however this book addresses the problem of dealing with copious notes by summarising the content of the subject matter and attempting to explain in simple language what are sometimes complicated concepts or issues.

Practice questions are provided at the end of each chapter, and answers can be downloaded by going to the following link: http://www.jroscoe.co.uk/downloads/a2_revise_pe_aqa/ on the JRP website. The answers will amplify the subject matter and provide clues as to how the exam itself should be approached. A continuing feature is that there will be a number of multiple choice questions on each exam paper, and we include a small number of such questions at the end of each chapter along with the practice questions. There is also a requirement that the final exam questions on each section of the syllabus shall include an essay type answer worth 15 marks. This allows students to express their ability and knowledge in the context of properly written language (prose) with attention to grammar and punctuation. Question assessment guidelines and use of terminology are included immediately before the index section in this book.

Materials are presented in a concise and visual approach for effective and efficient revision. Modern terminology, nomenclature and units have been used wherever possible. At the end of the book there is a comprehensive index for easy reference.

Please note that students are recommended to have a clear understanding of the content as outlined in the AQA specification and not rely solely on this guide.

HOW TO USE THIS REVISION GUIDE

The ideal use of this Revision Guide would be to purchase it at the start of the course and relate each of the summary pages to the specific areas of the syllabus as an aide memoire. The inclusion of specific questions and full answers (to be found on the following link: http://www.jroscoe.co.uk/downloads/a2_revise_pe_aqa/) provide a means of self-testing. Each chapter has its own link specified on the questions pages. Don't be tempted to find out the answers before attempting a question.

In reality, whole examination questions contain a much broader content than those given in this guide. Examiners will attempt to examine more than one small area of the syllabus within the context of one full question and therefore it is important that you revise all aspects of your syllabus.

The main use of the Revision Guide should be during the final revision period leading up to your examinations, as it should help you to understand and apply concepts i.e. link summary content with examination question.

The aim of this book is to provide an aid that enhances syllabus analysis, and to raise your level of success in examinations.

THE QUALITY OF AUTHORS

The authors are experts in the physical education field and have considerable experience in teaching 'A' Level Physical Education. They have written examination syllabuses, and have set and marked examination questions within this subject area and taught at revision workshops throughout the UK. Much of the material within this book has been thoroughly student tested.

The authors hope that this Revision Guide will prove useful to staff and students. Jan Roscoe Publications will welcome any comments you would wish to make about the book's utility or layout. Thank you for using this work.

Dennis Roscoe
Jan Roscoe

CREDITS

ACKNOWLEDGMENTS

The authors wish to thank Bob Davis for his contribution in the Historical and Contemporary Issues elements of this book. Thanks are also due to Helen Roscoe-Rutter and David Roscoe-Rutter for their contributions as cover designers and photographers, Debbie Francis of Heath Books as proof reader, and Lois Cresswell, Jenny Pacey, Helen Roscoe-Rutter and Osian Jones for their patience as photographic models. The authors wish to thank members of the Belgian Olympic Athletics Squad for permission to use their images. **Dennis Roscoe -** *Editor*

ACKNOWLEDGMENTS FOR GRAPHICS

p. 14 figure 1.4 Caterine Ibarguen Rio Olympics 2016, Erik Van Leewen/Wikipedia.org,

p. 16 figure 1.7 S. Kuvona/Shutterstock.com,

p. 18 figure 1.11 Espen E/Shutterstock.com, figure 1.13 Maxisport/Shutterstock.com,

p. 27 figure 2.4 Carefusion.com, p. 28 figure 2.5 photographee.eu/Shutterstock.com,

p. 31 figure 2.12 Sir Mo Farah Michealpuche/Shutterstock.com, p. 32 figure 2.13 maxriesgo/Shutterstock.com,

p. 40 figure 3.1 Avevizavi/Shutterstock.com, p. 42 figure 3.6 Snap2Art/Shutterstock.com,

p. 43 figure 3.7 Mitch Gunn/Shutterstock.com, figure 3.8 Chris Van Lennep/Shutterstock.com,

p. 45 figure 3.11 Physical Education and the Study of Sport 5e, ISBN 978072343750,

p. 46 figure 3.12 Physical Education and the Study of Sport 5e, ISBN 978072343750,

p. 50 figures 3.21 Yann Caradec/Wikipedia/Flickr.com, p. 54 figure 3.26 Sergey Nivens/Shutterstock.com,

p. 56 figure 4.2 Praissaeng/Shutterstock.com, p. 61 figure 4.8 Sergey Melodia plusphotos/Shutterstock.com,

p. 63 figure 4.15 fibromyianewtoday.com, p. 66 figure 4.20 Chuck Wagner/Shutterstock.com,

p. 74 figure 5.11 Mikael Damlder/Shutterstock.com, p. 84 figure 5.29 Pinterest,

p. 87 figure 6.3 Simone Biles Rio Olympics 2016, A. Richardo/Shutterstock.com,

p. 89 figure 6.6 Dmitry Morgan/Shutterstock.com,

p. 95 figure 6.23 Wth /Shutterstock.com, p. 96 figure 6.26 Wikimedia Commons.org,

p. 103 figure 7.4 Laura Trott, Rio Olympics 2016 J. Ernesto/Alamy, Max Whitlock Rio Olympics 2016 Lilyana Vynogradova/Shutterstock.com, Jack Laugher Rio Olympics 2016, Mitch Gunn/Shutterstock.com,

p. 106 figure 7.10 Ligfo/Shutterstock.com, figure 7.11 maradon333/Shutterstock.com,

p. 109 figure 7.15 Shahjehan/Shutterstock.com, p.110 figure 7.17 Jimmy48 photography/Shutterstock.com,

p. 110 figure 7.18 Dame Jessica Ennis-Hill, Anton Ivanov/Shutterstock.com, p. 114 figure 8.2 @katewalsh11

p. 125 figure 9.4 Richard Hobson/istockphoto.com, p. 126 figure 9.5 Michael Dabell/istockphoto.com,

p. 131 figure 9.14 Toby Creamer/istockphoto.com, PGL, Purdue9394istockphoto.com,

p. 137 figure 10.3 Air Images/Shutterstock.com,

p. 138 figure 10.4 Sport England, figure 10.5 StreetGames.org,

p. 138 figure 10.6 David Beckham Everett Collection/Shutterstock.com,

p. 140 figure 10.9 GB Women's hockey team Rio Olympics 2016, BOA/Andy Ryan,

p. 141 figure 10.11 well photo/Shutterstock.com, p. 142 figure 10.12 Dina Asher-Smith, Wikimedia Commons.org,

p. 144 figure 10.14 domhnall doda/Shutterstock.com, figure 10.15 The Olympic Park/Flickr,

p. 149 figure 11.2 Nicola Adams Wikimedia Commons.org. figure 11.3 Usian Bolt Wikimedia Commons.org,

p. 150 figure 11.5 webphotographer/istockphoto.com, p. 153 figure 11.1 Vlad/Shutterstock.com,

p. 154 figure 11.12 UEFA 2016 Alberto Girotto/ Shutterstock.com,

p. 158 figure 12.2 Maria Sharapova Leonard Zhukovsky/Shutterstock.com,

p. 159 figure 12.3 Marcos Mesa Sam Wordley/Shutterstock.com,

p. 160 figure 12.4 Sir Bradley Wiggins Yoann Morin/Shutterstock.com,

p. 161 figure 12.6 Andrew Safonov/Shutterstock.com, figure 12.7 Diane Modahl Wikimedia Commons.org,

p. 165 figure 12.9 Dwain Chambers Maxisport/Shutterstock.com, p. 166 figure 12.10 Hillsborough Kenny1/Shutterstock.com,

p. 173 figure 13.2 Loughborough University Sports Technology Institute, p. 174 figure 13.3 sylv trob1/Shutterstock.com,

p. 175 figure 13.4 gamesetmap.com, p. 176 figure 13.5 Elvar Palsson/Coda Coza/WikipediaCreative Commons2.0/Flickr,

p. 177 figure 13.6 DayOwl/Shutterstock.com, p. 179 figure 13.10 Ben Jeayes/Shutterstock.com.

All other photographs or graphics are by Helen Roscoe-Rutter, David Roscoe-Rutter, Jan Roscoe, Dennis Roscoe, Bob Davis or other free sources.

We have made every effort to trace all copyright holders, but if any have been inadvertently overlooked, the publishers will be pleased to make the necessary arrangements as soon as possible. We have also used current web-site and other URL information which is accurate at the date of going to press, but may be subject to changes made by owners and authors.

AS/A1 Revise PE for AQA

HIGH QUALITY PHOTOS

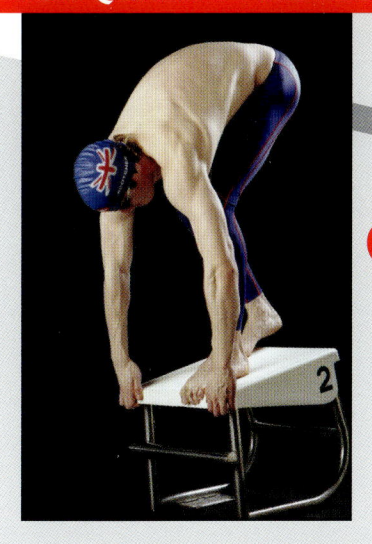

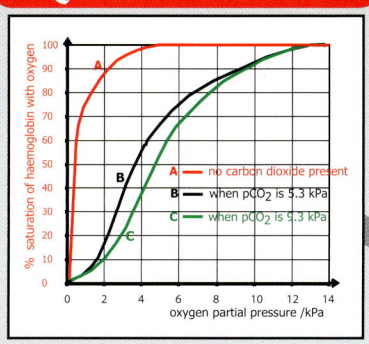

ROSCOE et al
AS/A1 Revise PE for AQA
ISBN 978-1-901-42485-0

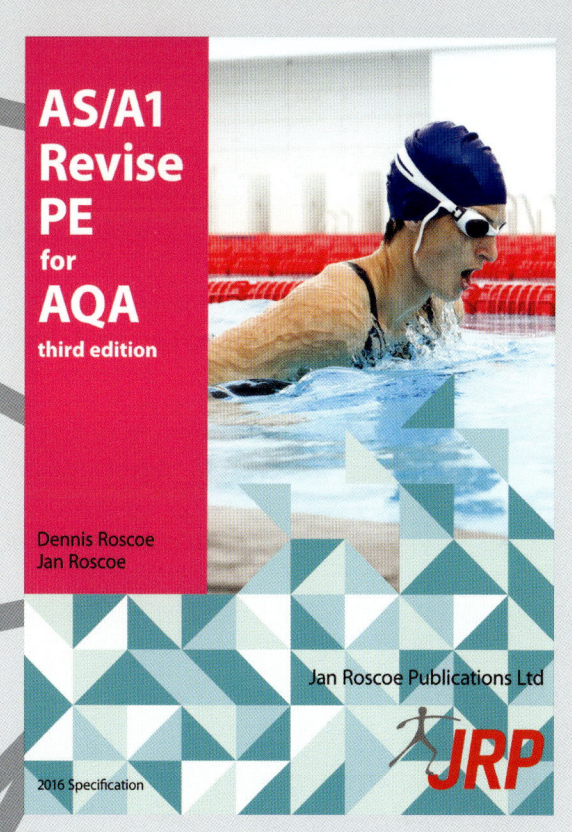

QUALITY GRAPHS

REVISION SUMMARY NOTES

Disadvantages of the part method
- Transfer from part to whole may be ineffective.
- Highly organised skills are very difficult to break down.
- Difficult to create kinaesthetic feel/sense of skill.
- Can be **demotivating** for performer.
- Can be **time consuming**.

REVISION SUMMARY CHARTS

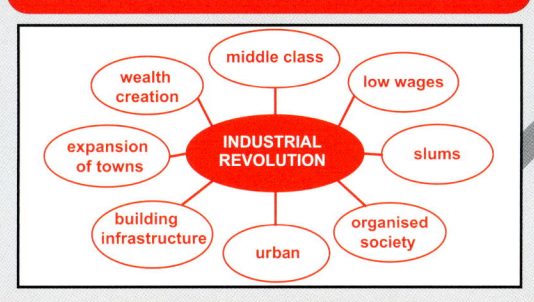

INDUSTRIAL REVOLUTION
- wealth creation
- middle class
- low wages
- expansion of towns
- slums
- building infrastructure
- urban
- organised society

ANSWERS TO QUESTIONS are found on the JRP Website

20) With reference to sporting performance, explain how cognitive and somatic anxiety differ.   5 marks
Answer:
You must use a sporting example in your answer.
- *Cognitive anxiety* is a psychological response consisting of:
- Worry.
- Inability to concentrate.
- Loss of attention.
- Fear of failure.
- For example, worry that a tennis opponent is a much better player than you.

Our Revise Series covers all aspects of the examinable AS and 'A' Level year 1 AQA syllabus which commenced in September 2016. The book consists of student notes, full colour illustrations, photographs and exam questions. Key concepts are clearly defined with examples that can be used in answers to exam questions, enabling the student to self-test. Answers are provided via a link to the JRP Website. This student revision guide supports a comprehensive revision plan and will enhance student grades.

HOW TO ORDER

tel   +44(0)208 644 7788
(open 9am-5.30pm)

fax   +44(0)208 641 3377
(open 24 hours a day)

email orders@heathbooks.co.uk

by post to: Heath Educational Books, Willow House, Willow Walk, Off Whittaker Rd, Sutton, Surrey, SM3 9QQ

For **full listings** see the **JRP Catalogue** or visit www.jroscoe.co.uk

CONTENTS

A2 Revise PE for AQA

Section 1
Applied anatomy and physiology

CHAPTER 1
- 12 ENERGY SYSTEMS PART ONE
- 12 Energy transfer in the body
- 15 Energy continuum of physical activity
- 17 Energy transfer during long duration/lower activity exercise
- 18 Fatigue
- 19 Oxygen consumption during recovery
- 22 OBLA (Onset of Blood Lactate Accumulation)

CHAPTER 2
- 26 ENERGY SYSTEMS PART TWO
- 26 Factors affecting $\dot{V}O_{2max}$/aerobic power
- 27 Measurement of energy expenditure
- 30 Impact of specialised training methods on energy systems

Section 2
Skill acquisition

CHAPTER 3
- 40 MEMORY MODELS
- 40 Information processing
- 40 Input
- 41 Decision making
- 43 The memory system
- 47 Definitions of reaction time, response time and movement time
- 49 Schmidt's schema theory

Section 3
Exercise physiology

CHAPTER 4
- 56 INJURY PREVENTION AND THE REHABILITATION OF INJURY
- 56 Types of injury
- 58 Injury prevention methods
- 62 Injury rehabilitation
- 65 Sleep and nutrition for improved recovery

A2 REVISE PE FOR AQA

Section 4
Biomechanical movement

CHAPTER 5
69   LINEAR MOTION
69   Linear motion
69   Scalars and vectors
76   Graphs and curves of motion
77   Forces in sport
79   Impulse and impact
83   Conservation of momentum in collisions

CHAPTER 6
87   ANGULAR MOTION, PROJECTILE MOTION AND FLUID MECHANICS
87   Angular motion
88   Moment of inertia
91   Projectile motion
93   Fluid mechanics

Section 5
Sport psychology

CHAPTER 7
102   ACHIEVEMENT MOTIVATION, ATTRIBUTION THEORY, SELF-EFFICACY AND CONFIDENCE
102   Achievement motivation
104   Attribution
107   Self-efficacy and confidence

CHAPTER 8
113   LEADERSHIP AND STRESS MANAGEMENT
113   Leadership
114   Theories of leadership
116   Stress management
117   Cognitive relaxation techniques
120   Somatic relaxation techniques

Contents

CONTENTS

Section 6

Sport and society

CHAPTER 9
- 124 **CONCEPTS OF PHYSICAL ACTIVITY AND SPORT**
- 124 Sports development continuum
- 125 Physical recreation
- 126 Sport
- 129 Physical education and school sport
- 131 Outdoor education
- 133 Similarities and differences between these concepts

CHAPTER 10
- 136 **DEVELOPMENT OF ELITE PERFORMERS IN SPORT**
- 139 Organisations providing support and progression from talent identification to elite performance
- 141 National Governing Bodies of Sport
- 142 Talent development and support services
- 144 UK Sport's World Class Performance Programme, Gold Event series and TID

CHAPTER 11
- 148 **ETHICS AND VIOLENCE IN SPORT**
- 148 Ethics in sport
- 151 Positive and negative forms of deviance and the performer
- 152 Violence within sport

CHAPTER 12
- 157 **DRUGS IN SPORT, SPORT AND THE LAW, AND COMMERCIALISATION**
- 157 Drugs in sport
- 162 Arguments for and against drug taking and testing
- 164 Sport and the law
- 167 Impact of commercialisation on physical activity and sport

CHAPTER 13
- 172 **THE ROLE OF TECHNOLOGY IN PHYSICAL ACTIVITY AND SPORT**
- 172 Functions of sports analytics
- 176 The development of equipment and facilities in physical activity and sport
- 172 The role of technology in sport summary tables

- 184 AQA A Level Physical Education Examination Paper
- **186 Index**

SECTION 1
APPLIED ANATOMY AND PHYSIOLOGY

CHAPTER 1
ENERGY SYSTEMS PART ONE

CHAPTER 2
ENERGY SYSTEMS PART TWO

SECTION 1 – CHAPTER 1: ENERGY SYSTEMS PART ONE

CHAPTER 1: Energy systems part one

Energy definitions

Energy is the capacity to do work, and work has a mechanical definition, namely **work = force x distance** moved in the direction of the force. Energy and work are measured in joules (J).

Chemical energy is energy that is produced by a complex series of chemical reactions, which can then be made available as **kinetic energy** (energy due to movement which results from muscular contractions), or **potential energy** which is stored energy due to gravity.

Power is the **rate** at which energy is used, or the energy used per second which is measured in watts (W).
Power can be calculated using the formula:

$$\text{power} = \frac{\text{energy (in joules)}}{\text{time (in seconds)}} \quad \text{(answer in watts)}$$

Energy transfer in the body

We derive our energy from food, namely carbohydrates (CHO), fats, and to a lesser extent proteins.

The energy derived from carbohydrates, fats and proteins is stored in bodily tissues in the form of a high energy compound called **adenosine triphosphate** (ATP), which can be generated via three different processes:
- **ATP-PC** system (also called the alactic anaerobic system).
- **Anaerobic glycolytic** system also known as the **lactic acid** system (which is also anaerobic).
- **Aerobic** system.

ATP - adenosine triphosphate

ATP is the compound which stores energy and is therefore the energy currency linked to **intensity** and **duration** of physical activity. ATP exists in every living tissue and its breakdown gives energy for all life functions - this includes the action of the liver and the brain for example, as well as the contraction of muscle tissue. All muscular activity requires the availability and breakdown of ATP (figure 1.1).

figure 1.1 – all muscle action uses ATP

The energy released during tissue respiration is stored in the chemical bonds in ATP, and this energy is released during the reaction:

$$\text{ATP} \rightarrow \text{ADP} + P_i + \text{energy}$$

Resynthesis of ATP from ADP uses the reaction:

$$\text{energy} + \text{ADP} + P_i \rightarrow \text{ATP}$$

This is an **endothermic** reaction since energy is **given** to the molecule to enable the reaction to happen. This energy will be derived from **food fuels**.

The enzymatic catabolism (breakdown) of fat within the muscle cell mitochondria is termed **beta-oxidation**. Energy derived from the breakdown of **free fatty acids** (FFAs) is the preferred fuel food for long duration, low intensity exercise. The fatty acid molecule transforms into **acetyl-CoA** in the mitochondria. This reaction involves the successive splitting of 2-carbon acyl fragments from the long chain of the fatty acid.

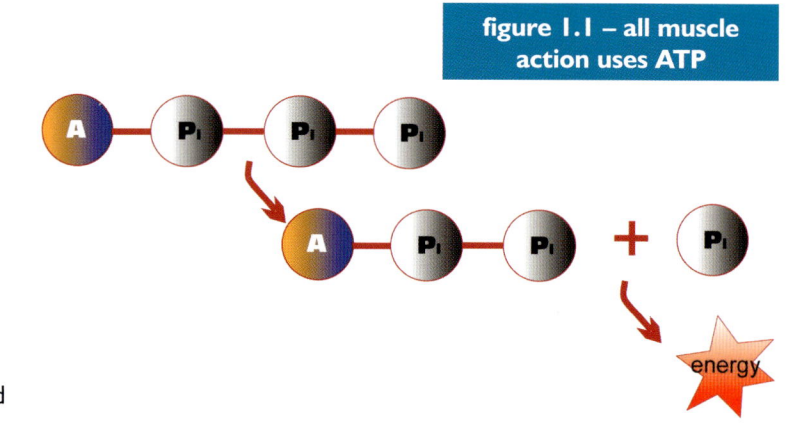

APPLIED ANATOMY AND PHYSIOLOGY

Aerobic energy system

The aerobic energy system releases stored energy from muscle glycogen, fats and proteins.

Figure 1.2 is a graphic of some of the details of the aerobic system showing how between 32 and 34 ATP molecules are resynthesised from one molecule of glucose - which is the food fuel created from the food we eat. This process will continue indefinitely until energy stores run out or the exercise stops.

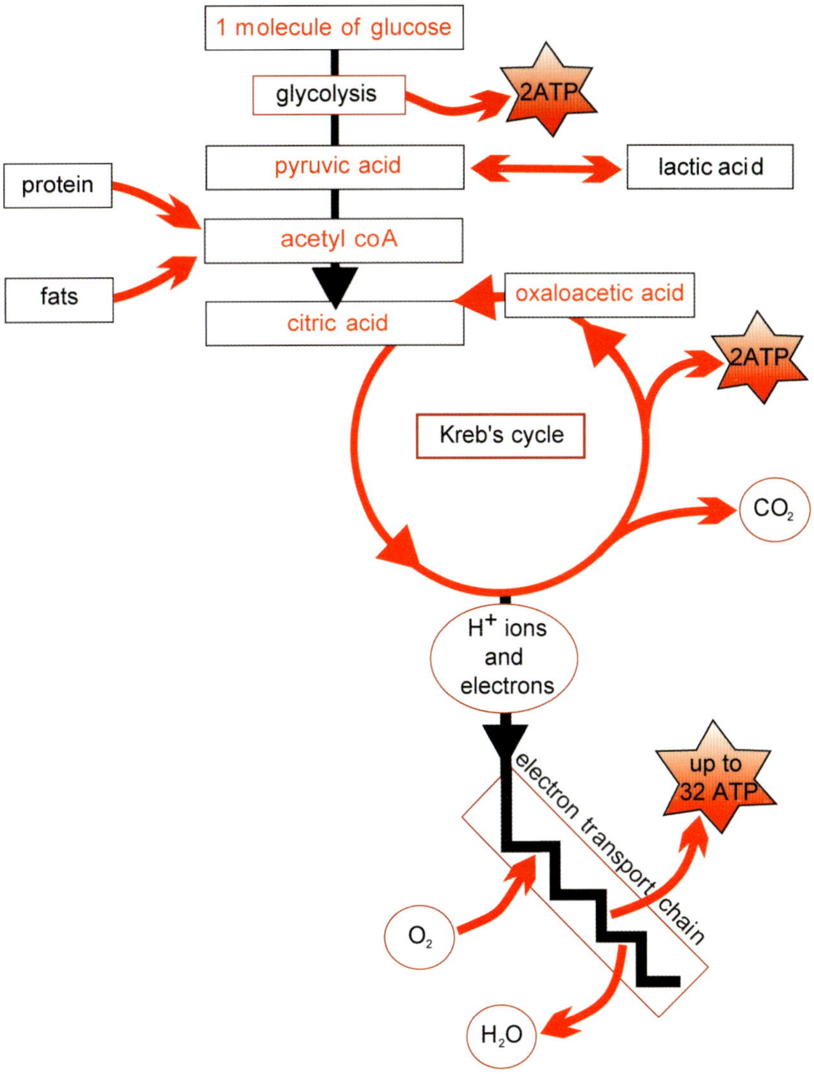

Stage one - glycolysis

Glycolysis takes place in the **muscle cell sarcoplasm**.
- **Carbohydrate** from food you have eaten is stored as **glycogen** (in the muscles and liver).
- Glycogen is converted into **glucose** by the hormone **glucagon** released when blood glucose levels fall (when glucose is used during tissue respiration).
- The breakdown of glucose provides the energy to rebuild ATP from ADP.
- This is facilitated by enzymes such as **glycogen phosphorylase** (GPP) and **phosphofructokinase** (PFK).
- The whole process produces **pyruvic acid**.

ATP regenerated = 2ATP per molecule of glucose.

figure 1.2 – the aerobic system

Stage two - Kreb's cycle (citric acid cycle)

This stage occurs in the **presence of oxygen**, and takes place in the **muscle cell mitochondria** within the inner **fluid filled** matrix. Here, 2 molecules of **pyruvic acid** combine with **oxaloacetic acid** (4 carbons) and **acetyl coA** (2 carbons) to form citric acid (6 carbons). The citric acid is oxidised as hydrogen is removed from this compound to be used in the next stage of energy production, the electron transport chain. Carbon and oxygen are left behind and combine to produce carbon dioxide which is eliminated via the lungs.

In addition, energy sufficient to resynthesise **2 ATPs** is released.

Free fatty acids (FFA) from body fat, facilitated by the enzyme lipoprotein lipase, and protein (keto acids from muscle) can act as fuel foods at this stage, as indicated in figure 1.2. exercise duration increases. Stored fat represents the body's most plentiful energy source.

Protein also serves as a potentially important energy substrate for long duration, endurance-type activities. The protein-to-energy pathways occur at two sites, acetyl-CoA and directly into Kreb's cycle. After nitrogen removal from the amino acid molecule during **deamination**, the remaining carbon skeleton enters the metabolic pathway to produce ATP aerobically or is converted to fat for further future energy needs.

Aerobic energy systems 13

SECTION 1 – CHAPTER 1

ENERGY SYSTEMS PART ONE

Stage three - the electron transport chain

The **electron transport chain** occurs in the presence of oxygen within the **cristae** (inner part of the muscle cell mitochondria). The hydrogen given off at Krebs cycle is carried to the electron transport chain by **hydrogen carriers** (NADs and FADs). The hydrogen is split into hydrogen ions (H^+) and electrons (e^-). During a step-by-step chemical reaction, the hydrogen ions are oxidised to produce water (H_2O) and the electrons provide the energy to resynthesise ATP.

Aerobic respiration

In summary, the total effect of aerobic respiration is that it is an **endothermic** reaction:

glucose + 36ADP + 36P_i + 6O_2 → 6CO_2 + 36ATP + 6H_2O

Fat fuels produce 2 ATPs less per molecule than glucose.

Anaerobic energy systems

The ATP-PC system

This system of replenishing of ATP from ADP is the predominant one for activity which lasts between 3 and 10 seconds, which means for high intensity maximum work, for example, flat out sprinting - the 100 metre sprint.

No oxygen is needed - the process is anaerobic. The chemical reactions within this system are a **coupled reaction** in which ATP is resynthesised via **phosphocreatine** (PC) stored in muscle cell sarcoplasm.

The following reactions take place: PC → P_i + C + energy

energy + ADP + P_i → ATP

The two reactions together are called a **coupled reaction** and are facilitated by the enzyme **creatine kinase** (CK).

The net effect of these two coupled reactions is:

PC + ADP → ATP + C

PC is re-created in muscle cells during the recovery process, which requires energy and is an **endothermic** reaction.

During intense exercise, peak anaerobic power is attained within the first 5 seconds, and depletion of PC occurs between 7 and 9 seconds (figure 1.4).

Look at the graph in figure 1.3 showing changes in muscle ATP and PC. After an initial small fall, the ATP level is maintained, then falls as the PC is used up because the energy from PC is being used to resynthesise ATP.

> **STUDENT NOTE**
>
> This process does not directly require glucose as an energy source - but the re-creation of PC during recovery will do so.

This causes PC levels to fall rapidly to zero after about 10 seconds. The capacity to maintain ATP production at this point depends on the anaerobic glycolytic or lactic acid system.

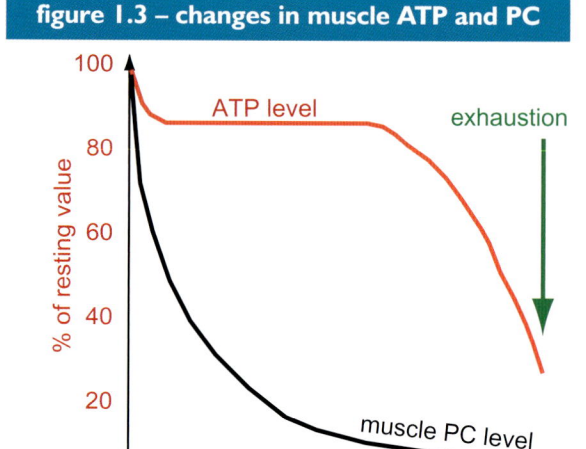

figure 1.3 – changes in muscle ATP and PC

figure 1.4 – triple jump - under 7 seconds to complete

APPLIED ANATOMY AND PHYSIOLOGY

Anaerobic glycolytic system or the lactic acid system

This system depends on a chemical process called **glycolysis** which is the incomplete breakdown of sugar and follows the same pathway as described for stage one of the aerobic energy system on page 13. Figure 1.5 shows the schematic layout of glycolysis.

- **Glycolysis is anaerobic**.
- It takes place in the **sarcoplasm** of the muscle cell.
- No oxygen is needed, and the end product of this reaction (in the absence of oxygen) is lactic acid.
- The enzyme facilitating the conversion from pyruvic acid to lactic acid is **lactate dehydrogenase** (LDH).
- Rapid glycolysis allows ATP to form quickly without oxygen, generating 2 ATPs per molecule of glucose.

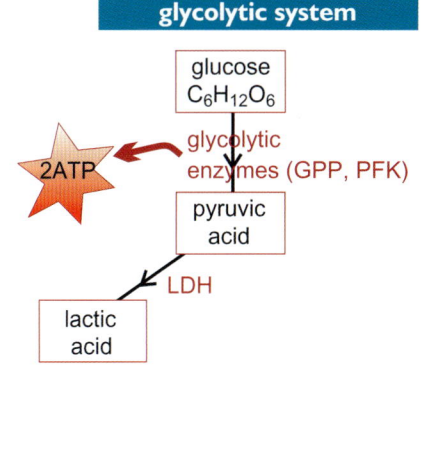

figure 1.5 – anaerobic glycolytic system

glucose $C_6H_{12}O_6$ → glycolytic enzymes (GPP, PFK) → 2ATP → pyruvic acid → LDH → lactic acid

As work intensity increases, lactic acid starts to accumulate above resting values, which produces **muscle fatigue** and pain. The resultant low pH inhibits enzyme action and cross-bridge formation, hence muscle action is inhibited and physical performance deteriorates.

The lactic acid system is the predominant one used to resynthesise ATP in sport or activities in which the flat-out effort lasts up to 30-60 seconds.
For example, a 400m run or a 100m swim.

After exercise stops, extra oxygen is taken up to remove lactic acid by changing it back into pyruvic acid - this is the **EPOC** (**Excess Post-exercise Oxygen Consumption**, sometimes called the oxygen debt), see page 19 for the details of EPOC.

Energy continuum of physical activity

This describes the process by which ATP is regenerated via the different energy systems depending on the **intensity** and **duration** of exercise. Although **all** the systems contribute to ATP regeneration during any activity, one or other of the energy systems usually provides the major contribution for a given activity. Table 1.1 shows approximate proportions of ATP resynthesised via aerobic and anaerobic pathways for some sporting activities.

Table 1.1 – percentage contribution of the aerobic and anaerobic energy systems to different sports

sport or event	aerobic %	anaerobic (all) %
100m sprint	0	100
200m sprint	10	90
100m swim	20	80
boxing	30	70
800m run	40	60
hockey	50	50
2000m rowing	60	40
4000m cycle pursuit	70	30
3000m run	80	20
cross country run	90	10
marathon	100	0

figure 1.6 – variation in contribution of energy systems

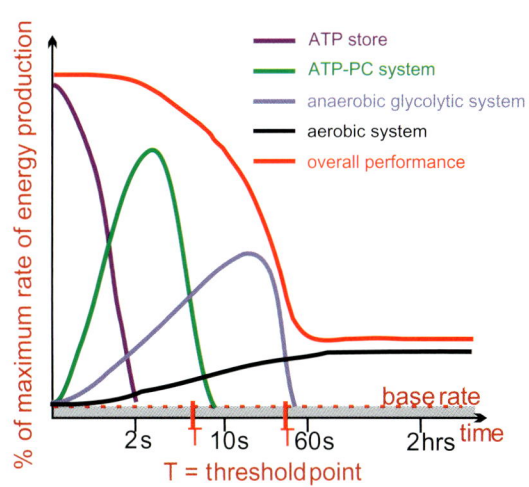

The graph in figure 1.6 shows how the different energy systems contribute resynthesis of ATP during flat-out exercise. Obviously, at reduced intensity of exercise, the contributions will be slightly different. But note that **all systems** are contributing from the start of exercise, only it takes some time for the lactic acid and aerobic systems to get going.

SECTION 1 – CHAPTER 1

ENERGY SYSTEMS PART ONE

Short-term responses - thresholds

The concept of a **threshold** applies to the time at which one particular system of ATP regeneration takes over from another as the major regenerator of ATP during flat out exercise - marked as **T** in figure 1.6 (page 15).

- For example, **ATP muscle stores** are depleted **within 2 seconds**, and towards the end of this period the ATP-PC system has risen enough to be able to provide the ATP necessary for the exercise.
- **Peak anaerobic power** is attained within the first 5 seconds of flat-out exercise, but depletion of PC occurs between 7 and 9 seconds.
- At this point, the lactic acid system has risen enough to be able to provide the ATP required for the next 40 seconds or so.

Hence the **threshold** between **ATP-PC and lactic acid** systems occurs between 7 and 9 seconds after the start of an exercise period. The lactate threshold occurs at the highest oxygen uptake or exercise intensity achieved with less than 1.0 mmol increase in blood lactate level concentration above the pre-exercise level.

Long-term training effects - thresholds

It is found that thresholds are **delayed** by training, so that the trained individual has a greater capacity for ATP-PC, has a greater lactic acid toleration, and more efficient ATP regeneration than the untrained person.

Other factors affecting the proportions of energy systems

- The **level of fitness** (whether adaptations to training have included enhancement of relevant enzymes - which would for example postpone levels of lactate accumulation).
- The **availability of O_2 and food fuels**. For example, a high CHO diet (figure 1.7) would assist replenishment of glycogen stores which would then be available for glycolysis.

figure 1.7 – CHO

Differences in ATP generation between fast and slow twitch muscle fibres

Intensity and **duration** determine the energy system and hence metabolic mixture and muscle fibre type activation.

High powered activities, such as a 60 metre sprint, and other forceful muscular actions and stop and go activities or change of pace in sports such as basketball, netball, soccer and field hockey depend almost entirely on anaerobic metabolism for high energy release needed to activate the **fast twitch fibres**.

STUDENT NOTE

Information on the classification and characteristics of muscle fibres types are located in the AQA AS/A1 Student Revision Guide ISBN 9781901424850, Chapter 3 page 41.

- High energy release is mainly due to **high glycolytic enzyme activity** and **myosin ATPase activity** within the anaerobic glycolytic system.
- Since only **2 ATPs** are produced per molecule of glucose, high powered exercise can only continue for a few seconds before fatigue sets in.
- **Fast twitch muscle fibre type IIb** have a **low aerobic capacity** and therefore quickly **fatigue** during maximal activity.
- **Fast twitch fibres type IIa** possess a relatively **higher aerobic capacity** when compared with type IIb, and so support **increased force** when needed, for example, when running up hills whilst maintaining a constant speed.
- **Slow twitch muscle fibres** generate energy for ATP resynthesis, predominantly by aerobic energy transfer, producing up to **36 ATPs** per molecule of glucose.
- High concentration of **mitochondrial enzymes** and **capillary density** support this fibre's aerobic capacity to **resist fatigue** and power-prolonged aerobic exercise.
- Activities at near maximum aerobic and anaerobic levels, like middle distance running, swimming or multiple sprint sports such as field hockey, soccer basketball and netball, activate both fast twitch and slow muscle fibre types and their relative energy production via both the anaerobic and aerobic pathways.
- Specific exercise training improves the energy-generating capacity of each fibre type.

APPLIED ANATOMY AND PHYSIOLOGY

Energy transfer during long duration/lower activity exercise

The aerobic system requires carbohydrate in the form of **glucose** which is **derived from glycogen** stored in muscle cells (mostly slow twitch - SO type I) or in the liver.

The graph in figure 1.8 shows how the rate of usage of muscle glycogen is high during the first 30 minutes of steady exercise - which has to be replaced if a sportsperson is to continue at the same rate. Hence consumption of energy drinks and bananas during a long tennis match.

After the first 30 minutes of exercise, the body runs out of its glycogen stores and then turns mainly to what is left of the glucose in the blood and then finally to fatty acids and amino acids (derived from muscle protein). By far the largest energy reserve in the human body is adipose tissue **triglycerides**, and these reserves are an important source of fuel during prolonged endurance exercise. As exercise progresses from low to moderate intensity, for example, 25-65% $\dot{V}O_{2max}$, the rate of total fat oxidation increases due to a relatively large use of intramuscular triglycerides.

Endurance athletes can utilise FFAs during prolonged exercise sooner than untrained people. This training adaptation enables the trained athlete to not use glycogen up immediately, but save it for later on in an exercise effort, or when the intensity of exercise increases. This is called **glycogen sparing**.

Oxygen consumption during exercise (maximal and submaximal oxygen deficit)

The amount of oxygen consumed per unit of time (usually 1 minute) is expressed as $\dot{V}O_2$, and the mean value of $\dot{V}O_2$ at rest = 0.2 to 0.3 litres min^{-1}.

> **STUDENT NOTE**
>
> The abbreviation $\dot{V}O_2$ indicates oxygen uptake or consumption where the VO_2 denotes the volume consumed and the dot placed above the V expresses oxygen uptake as per minute.

During exercise, the human body consumes large amounts of oxygen. The characteristics of oxygen uptake ($\dot{V}O_2$) kinetics differ with exercise intensity. When exercise is performed at a given work rate which is below lactate threshold (LT), $\dot{V}O_2$ increases exponentially to a **steady-state level**.

Figure 1.9 illustrates oxygen consumption during a 20 minute slow jog at a steady pace. At rest oxygen consumption is low, followed by a rapid increase during the first minute of the jog, to reach a relative plateau or steady state of aerobic metabolism between 4-6 minutes. This steady state represents a balance between energy required by the body and rate of aerobic ATP production.

$\dot{V}O_2$ increases proportionally to work intensity (figure 1.10) up to a maximum value - called $\dot{V}O_{2max}$.
You can see from figure 1.10 that $\dot{V}O_{2max}$ is bigger for trained athletes. This is an adaptation produced by aerobic training, which means that the athlete can work harder for longer.

$\dot{V}O_{2max}$ is therefore a key component of aerobic endurance and is called **aerobic power** or **maximum oxygen uptake**, and so represents an accurate indicator of an athlete's fitness.

figure 1.8 – change in muscle glycogen during low intensity exercise

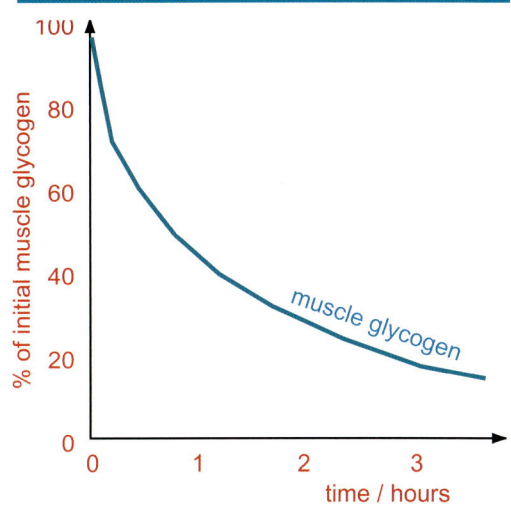

figure 1.9 – oxygen uptake during a slow jog

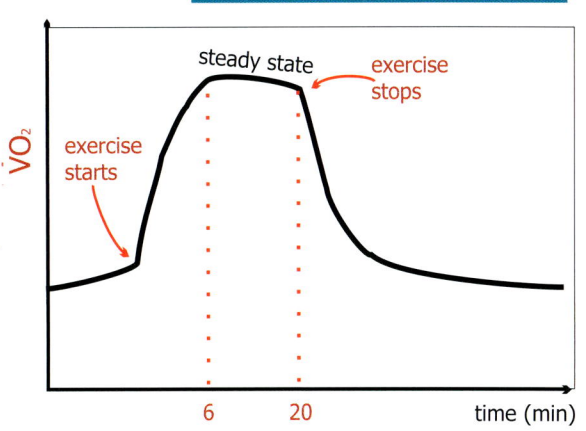

figure 1.10 – oxygen uptake as exercise intensity increases

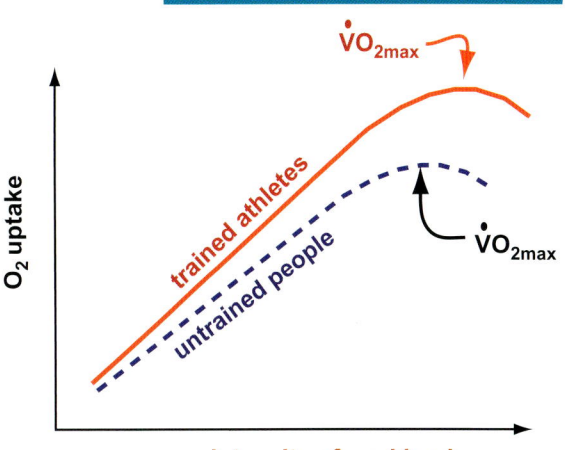

Oxygen consumption during exercise | 17

SECTION 1 – CHAPTER 1

ENERGY SYSTEMS PART ONE

Values for oxygen consumption - $\dot{V}O_2$

To adjust for the effects of body size on oxygen uptake (i.e. bigger people usually consume more oxygen), oxygen uptake is expressed as relative to body mass as millilitres of oxygen per kilogram of body mass per minute (ml kg^{-1} min^{-1}). Absolute $\dot{V}O_{2max}$ does not consider a person's weight and so is a less reliable measure of $\dot{V}O_{2max}$ values.

$\dot{V}O_{2max}$ mean values are:

males (20 yo)	= 3.5 litres min^{-1}
	= 40 ml kg^{-1} min^{-1} (for average male body mass 87.5 kg)
females (20 yo)	= 2.3 litres min^{-1}
	= 35 ml kg^{-1} min^{-1} (for mean female body mass 66 kg)
endurance athletes	= 4 to 6 litres min^{-1}
	= 60 to 90 ml kg^{-1} min^{-1} (for mean body mass 66 kg figure 1.11)

figure 1.11 – world class endurance athletes

Fatigue

Effects of fatigue on performance

Performance can be affected by muscle fatigue, the depletion of energy stores in muscle (and the liver). Various factors contribute to this.

Muscle fatigue

Muscle fatigue can be described as a reduction of muscular performance, and an inability to maintain expected power output. Performance can often be continued at quite a high level in spite of fatigue, but the outcome of 'jelly legs' or 'jelly shoulders' will be well known to all sportspeople after an exhausting performance has been completed.

Depletion of energy stores

- Depletion of **PC** (phosphocreatine) and muscle and liver **glycogen** stores will be the major cause of fatigue.
- Fatigue in marathon runners is due to depletion of **muscle glycogen** in both ST and FT muscle fibres.
- **FT muscle fibres** have low aerobic capacity and therefore **quickly fatigue** during maximal activity. This is because stored ATP and PC are quickly used up (in under 7 seconds) during this sort of activity (weight training, sprinting for example).

Metabolic accumulation

During intense exercise lasting longer than 7 seconds and under 45 seconds, **accumulation of lactic acid** and **CO_2** in muscle cells causes extreme fatigue and complete loss of muscle function. This is because increase in H$^+$ ions (decrease in pH due to the lactic acid acidity) inhibits both aerobic and anaerobic enzyme activity required for ATP regeneration.

Body fluid balance and dehydration

- Fluid loss **decreases plasma volume** which reduces blood pressure and hence produces a reduction in blood flow to skin and muscles.
- This means that the heart has to work harder, body temperature rises, and **fatigue** occurs.
- Hence **fluid intake is important** during endurance activities (figure 1.13).

figure 1.12 – fatigued athlete

figure 1.13 – taking in water throughout a marathon

The first two of these factors require oxygen in substantial quantities, hence the need for rapid breathing and a high pulse rate to carry oxygen to the muscle cells.

APPLIED ANATOMY AND PHYSIOLOGY

Oxygen consumption during recovery

Bodily processes do not immediately return to resting levels after exercise ceases. The time taken for this to occur is called the **recovery period**. The recovery period is dependent on the intensity and duration of the exercise.

Excess post-exercise oxygen consumption (EPOC)

After every strenuous exercise (figure 1.14), there are **four** tasks that need to be completed before the exhausted muscle can operate at full efficiency again.

- **Replacement of ATP and phosphocreatine** (fast replenishment component).
- **Removal of lactic acid** (slow replenishment component).
- **Replenishment of myoglobin** with oxygen.
- **Replacement of glycogen**.

figure 1.14 – factors contributing to EPOC

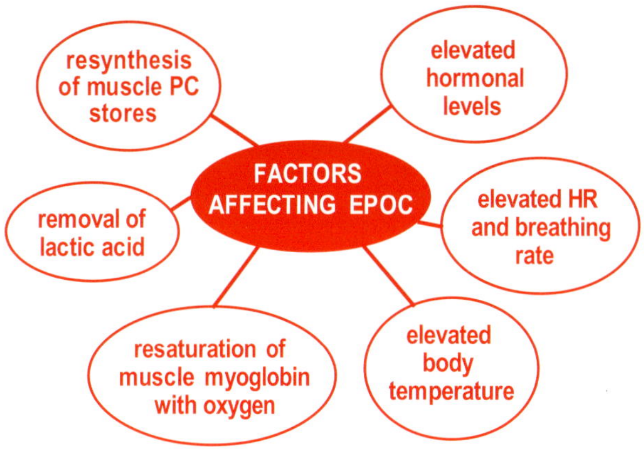

FACTORS AFFECTING EPOC:
- resynthesis of muscle PC stores
- elevated hormonal levels
- elevated HR and breathing rate
- elevated body temperature
- resaturation of muscle myoglobin with oxygen
- removal of lactic acid

The need for oxygen

The need for oxygen to rapidly replace ATP and remove lactic acid is known as the oxygen debt. The more modern term for oxygen debt is **excess post-exercise oxygen consumption** (EPOC) or oxygen recovery. This represents the elevation of the metabolic rate above resting values which occurs after exercise during the recovery period.

EPOC is the excess O_2 consumed following exercise needed to provide the energy required to resynthesise ATP used and remove lactic acid created during previous exercise. EPOC has **two** components (figure 1.15):

- **Alactic or alactacid**.
- **Lactic or lactacid**.

The **oxygen deficit** is the difference between the oxygen required during exercise and the oxygen actually consumed during the activity. The graph in figure 1.15 shows the relationship between oxygen consumption and the time before, during and after exercise.

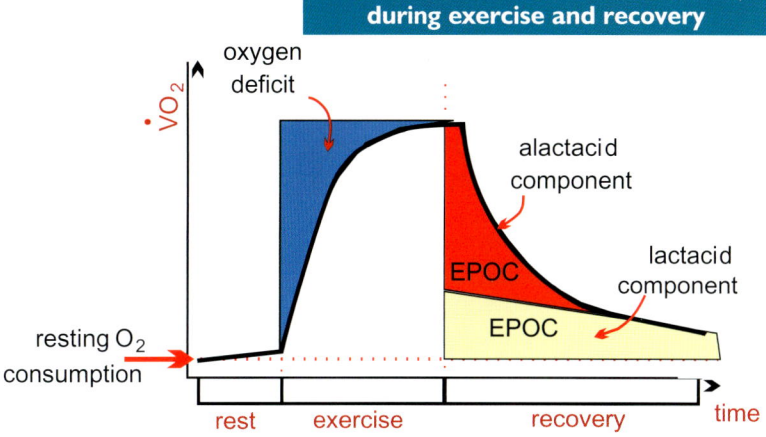

The alactacid component

Figure 1.15 follows a single-component exponential curve termed the fast component of recovery oxygen uptake. This component involves the **conversion of ADP back into PC and ATP**, and is known as **restoration of muscle phosphagen**. This is a very rapid process (120 seconds to full restoration) (figure 1.16) and is of size 2 to 3.5 litres of O_2.

figure 1.15 – oxygen consumption during exercise and recovery

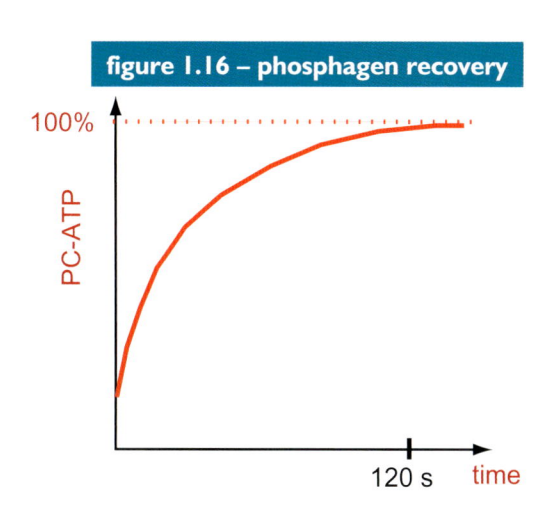

Phosphagen Recovery

Phosphagen recovery (figure 1.16) is achieved via **three** mechanisms:
- There is **aerobic** conversion of carbohydrates into CO_2 and H_2O to resynthesise ATP from ADP and P_i.
- Some of the ATP is immediately utilised **to create PC** using the coupled reaction: **ATP + C → ADP + PC**.
- A small amount of ATP is **resynthesised via glycogen,** producing small amounts of lactic acid.

figure 1.16 – phosphagen recovery

Oxygen consumption during recovery 19

SECTION 1 – CHAPTER 1
ENERGY SYSTEMS PART ONE

Continuous oxygen recovery

During the **post-exercise period**, oxygen recovery is continuous.

This is because:
- Muscle myoglobin recovers.
- Temperature falls.
- Hormone levels fall.

During the **recovery period**, temperature and hormone levels are higher than normal (although falling), which:
- Keeps metabolic rate high.
- Keeps respiratory rate high.
- Keeps heart rate high.
- Requires more oxygen than normal.

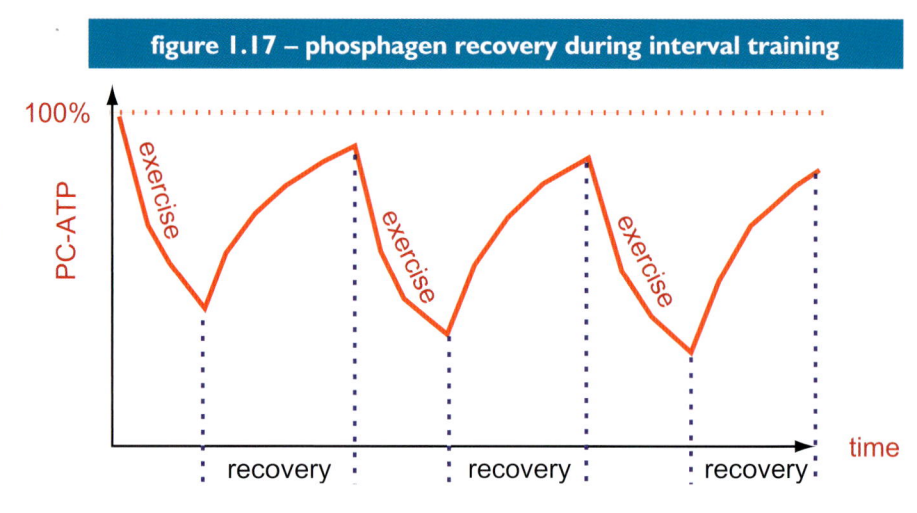

Hence **EPOC** increases.

figure 1.17 – phosphagen recovery during interval training

The implications for interval training

- If there is only a short interval between bouts of exercise, the level of phosphagen stores gradually reduces (see figure 1.17) thereby reducing the energy available for the later bouts.
- This stresses the ATP and PC storage and forces the muscle cells to adapt by storing more of these quantities.
- Also, cells will adapt by improving their ability to provide O_2, and hence increase the possible size of the alactic component.
- Anaerobic interval training studies have shown that 30 second bouts of exercise increase the activities of **glycolytic enzymes**, such as phosphorylase, phosphofructokinase and lactate dehydrogenase, from around 10% to 25%.
- This increase in **glycolytic capacity** will allow the muscle to develop greater tension for a longer period of time as the muscle tissue increases its **tolerance to lactate**.

Lactacid oxygen recovery

High intensity exercise up to about 60 seconds creates **lactic acid**, and **oxygen is needed** to remove this lactic acid. This process begins to restore muscle and liver glycogen, and is relatively slow with **full recovery** taking up to 1 hour (figure 1.18).

Relatively large amounts of lactic acid (15 to 20 times the resting value of 1 to 2 mmol litre^{-1}) are produced during high intensity exercise, which is removed according to the proportions listed in table 1.2, page 21.

A small proportion of EPOC resynthesises lactate to glycogen (table 1.2 page 21). This **gluconeogenic** mechanism would probably progress faster during activity in trained individuals, for example an elite 400 m athlete.

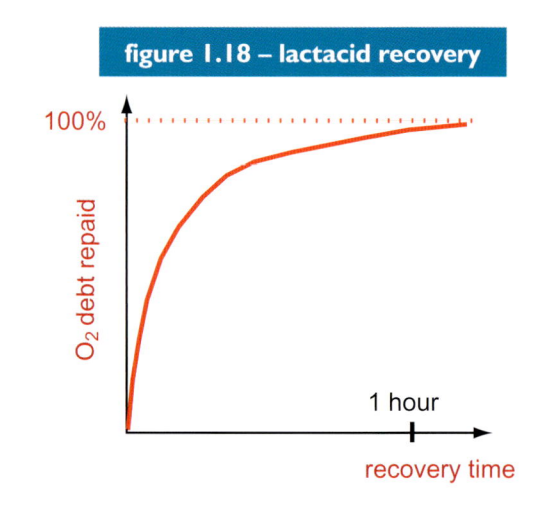

figure 1.18 – lactacid recovery

Removal of the lactic acid

Table 1.2 – removal of the lactic acid

oxidation into CO_2 + H_2O	65%
conversion into glycogen then stored in muscle and liver (Cori cycle)	20%
conversion into protein	10%
conversion into glucose	5%

The lactate shuttle

During the recovery process after intense exercise, a small proportion of the lactic acid produced is recycled back into glucose in the muscle cell. This is the reverse process to glycolysis and requires energy from ATP breakdown.

Buffering

A **blood buffer** is a chemical substance which resists abrupt changes in hydrogen ion (H^+) concentration. For example, when H^+ concentration increases as a result of intense exercise, H^+ reacts with oxyhaemoglobin (buffer) to form haemoglobinic acid. These ions are released when H^+ concentration falls. So this is a temporary solution to rapid changes in acidity or alkalinity which would otherwise cause rapid fatigue symptoms.

Cool-down following exercise

Cool-down (the process of continuing low level exercise immediately after the end of a high intensity exercise bout) **continues to provide oxygen** to skeletal muscle. This therefore **enhances oxidation of lactic acid** and ensures that less lactic acid remains in tissue. Hence there is less muscle soreness (**less DOMS**).

Figure 1.19 shows how **blood lactate** falls after exercise, and that when an active cool-down is undertaken less lactate remains in muscle tissue.

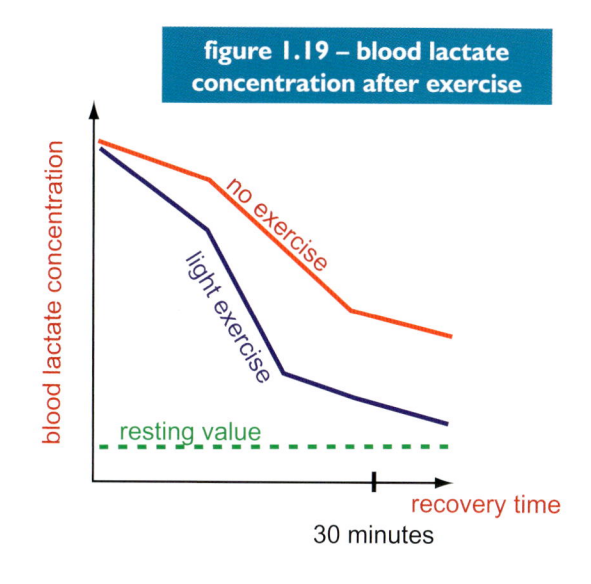

figure 1.19 – blood lactate concentration after exercise

Restoration of muscle glycogen stores

- During short duration high intensity exercise, restoration of glycogen takes up to 2 hours, and after prolonged low intensity aerobic exercise, restoration can take days.
- A **high carbohydrate diet** speeds up the glycogen recovery process, and there is a need for the athlete to restore stores as soon as possible after activity, with for example, a high CHO loaded drink immediately following exercise.

Restoration of myoglobin

Muscle myoglobin (an iron protein molecule located in skeletal muscle similar to haemoglobin) serves as a storage site for O_2, and has a temporary but greater affinity for O_2 than haemoglobin. Hence it acts as a **carrier of O_2** from HbO_2 (in blood) to mitochondria (in a muscle cell). Myoglobin is reoxygenated within 2 minutes.

Restoration of muscle myoglobin is important for recovery from high intensity exercise.

During high intensity exercise an increase in the recruitment of low-efficiency type IIb fibres (the fibres involved in the slow component) can cause an increase in the oxygen cost of exercise. A change in the pattern of motor unit recruitment, and thus less activation of type IIb fibres, may also account for a large part of the reduction in the slow component of $\dot{V}O_2$ observed after physical training.

SECTION 1 – CHAPTER 1   ENERGY SYSTEMS PART ONE

Recovery

There is improved oxygen recovery as a result of long-term aerobic training because of **better muscle capillarisation**. If an efficient cool-down is used, **lactic acid removal** is improved, hence there is a reduction in **DOMS** (delayed onset muscle soreness).

OBLA (Onset of Blood Lactate Accumulation)

As discussed on page 14 onwards, the anaerobic energy systems have a limited capacity of ATP production. As **work intensity** increases, **lactic acid** starts to **accumulate** above resting values. At a certain point (called the OBLA point) this produces muscle fatigue and pain, since the resultant low pH (high acidity) inhibits enzyme action and cross-bridge formation during muscle contraction. This means in turn that muscle action is inhibited and **physical performance deteriorates**.

The exact cause of OBLA remains controversial:
- It could be due to the point of **muscle hypoxia** or inadequate oxygen.
- It could be due to **muscle lactate accumulation** even in the presence of adequate muscle oxygenation.
- It could be due to **decreased total lactate clearance** or increased lactate production only in specific muscle fibres.

OBLA can be expressed as a percentage of $\dot{V}O_{2max}$ as shown in figure 1.20.

This point governs the **lactic aerobic threshold**.
- In the graph (figure 1.20), as exercise intensity increases and $\dot{V}O_2$ increases, untrained people have blood lactate which increases sharply at about 50% of $\dot{V}O_{2max}$.
- But trained athletes can exercise up to 70% of $\dot{V}O_{2max}$ before lactate concentration in the blood increases markedly.
- Hence **trained athletes** begin **OBLA at higher work intensities** - especially since trained athletes have higher values of $\dot{V}O_{2max}$ than untrained people in the first place.
- All this means that the **lactic aerobic threshold** moves to **higher values of $\dot{V}O_{2max}$**.

figure 1.20 – onset of blood lactate

Hence OBLA effectively predicts endurance performance.

Summary of factors affecting OBLA

- **Rate of blood lactate removal**: when removal and production are roughly equal, then blood lactate concentrations should stay constant. Only when production exceeds removal will lactic acid levels rise.
- **Exercise intensity**: as a performer works towards a higher intensity workload it is less likely to be performed aerobically and more likely to be performed **anaerobically** thereby producing lactic acid. Regular anaerobic physical activity increases the ability of the performer to tolerate higher levels of lactate and is able to remove lactic acid more quickly through a process called buffering (a chemical process that converts a strong acid to a weaker acid).
- **Muscle fibre type recruited**: slow twitch muscle fibres produce less lactic acid at the same intensity as fast twitch fibres due to increased mitochondria density.
- **Type of fuel being used**: RER (page 29) the closer the value is to 1, the more glycogen is being used and the more likely lactic acid is to be produced.
- **Training status of muscles**: trained muscles will have adaptive responses including more mitochondria, greater capillary density, improved used of FFAs as fuel, and higher myoglobin content, increasing aerobic capacity of muscle and reducing lactic acid production.

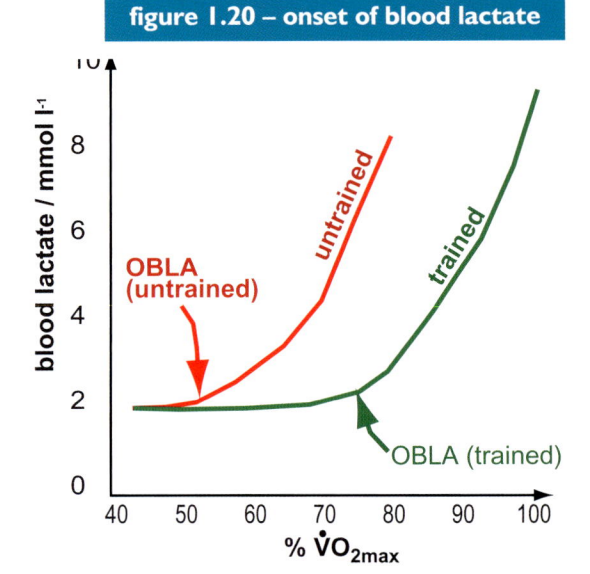

APPLIED ANATOMY AND PHYSIOLOGY

Practice questions

1) Which of the following reactions would liberate the most energy?
   a. complete oxidation of a molecule of glucose to carbon dioxide and water.
   b. conversion of a molecule of ADP to ATP.
   c. respiration of molecule of glucose to lactic acid.
   d. conversion of a molecule of glucose to carbon dioxide and water.

2) Which activity below is fuelled primarily by the anaerobic energy system?
   a. walking for 30 minutes.
   b. jogging for 50 minutes.
   c. taking part in an 400 m race.
   d. playing football.

3) Mary runs up a hill for as hard as she can. After two minutes she is so tired she cannot continue to run. Physiologically what is happening?
   a. Mary's aerobic system has been her predominant energy pathway during this bout of physical exertion.
   b. ATP was produced to fuel muscle contraction using an anaerobic energy pathway and lactic acid has now accumulated as a result of this process and is causing her to stop exercising at such a high intensity.
   c. ATP is being produced by the breakdown of fats and protein and her aerobic conditioning is inadequate to meet the demands of this exercise.
   d. Mary's blood pressure has decreased to the point where she has to stop and this has allowed lactic acid to build up in her system.

4) Which one of the following would result in the greatest decrease in muscle glycogen concentration?
   a. four 30 second print intervals (total time = 2 minutes).
   b. six 30 second endurance intervals at 100% $\dot{V}O_{2max}$.
   c. 4 minutes of continuous exercise at 100% $\dot{V}O_{2max}$.
   d. 60 minutes of continuous exercise at 75% $\dot{V}O_{2max}$.

5) Which one of the following would have least effect on the maximal anaerobic capacity of a muscle?
   a. an increase in muscle glycogen concentration.
   b. an increase in phosphocreatine (PC) concentration.
   c. an increase in muscle $Na+/K+$ pump capacity.
   d. an increase in muscle buffering capacity.

6) For which of the following sports would a training programme for increasing phosphocreatine (PC) stores be least important?
   a. basketball.
   b. 100 metres track event.
   c. high jump.
   d. javelin throw.

7) a) Define energy, and briefly describe how energy is released from food in the body. 5 marks

   b) Identify the only form of usable energy in the body. 1 mark

   c) What is meant by an exothermic reaction? Illustrate this definition with an example. 2 marks

   d) What is meant by an endothermic reaction? Illustrate this definition with an example. 2 marks

8) Explain the specialist role of mitochondria in energy production. 4 marks

SECTION 1 – CHAPTER 1

ENERGY SYSTEMS PART ONE

Practice questions

9) An elite swimmer performs a flat-out 100 metre freestyle swim in 50 seconds. Describe how most of the ATP is regenerated during the swim. Sketch a graph which shows the use of the appropriate energy systems against time during the swim. **8 marks**

10) a) Taking part in a triathlon involved swimming, cycling and running. Briefly describe how the aerobic energy system within the cell mitochondria supports this endurance event. **6 marks**

   b) Construct a graph which illustrates the food fuel usage against time during a triathlon race lasting 2 hours. **3 marks**

11) Compare the relative efficiency of ATP production via the aerobic and anaerobic routes. Explain your answer. **3 marks**

12) Identify the predominant energy system being used in the following activities: shot put, 200 metres breaststroke, a game of hockey, 100 metres hurdles race, gymnastics vault and modern pentathlon. **6 marks**

13) Figure 1.21 illustrates the contribution of the anaerobic and aerobic energy systems to the total energy requirements for four different track events: 200 m, 400 m, 800 m and 1500 m.
   a) Which column, grey or pink, represents the contribution from the anaerobic system? **1 mark**
   b) With reference to the data provided, justify your answer. **3 marks**
   c) What is the role of the anaerobic systems in the 1500 m event? In your response, refer to the data provided. **2 marks**

14) Elite games players require high levels of fitness and psychological preparation, therefore regular fitness testing and after-match performance analysis are common.
Using your knowledge of energy systems, outline and explain the relationship between energy sources and intensity of exercise. **15 marks**

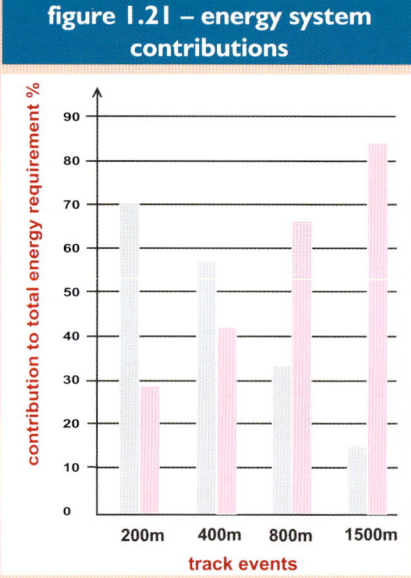

figure 1.21 – energy system contributions

15) Figure 1.22 illustrates the relationship between blood lactate and % $\dot{V}O_{2max}$.
   a) What do you understand by the term lactate threshold? **2 marks**
   b) Mark on the graph in figure 1.22 the point at the point at which the onset of blood lactate accumulation (OBLA) occurs. **1 mark**
   c) Explain why lactic acid tends to be produced when a player is exercising. **3 marks**

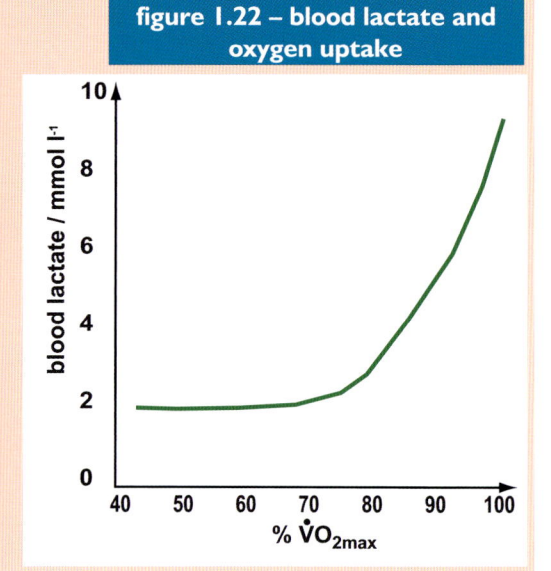

figure 1.22 – blood lactate and oxygen uptake

APPLIED ANATOMY AND PHYSIOLOGY

Practice questions

16) Figure 1.23 shows oxygen uptake of an elite games player undertaking exercise followed by a recovery period.

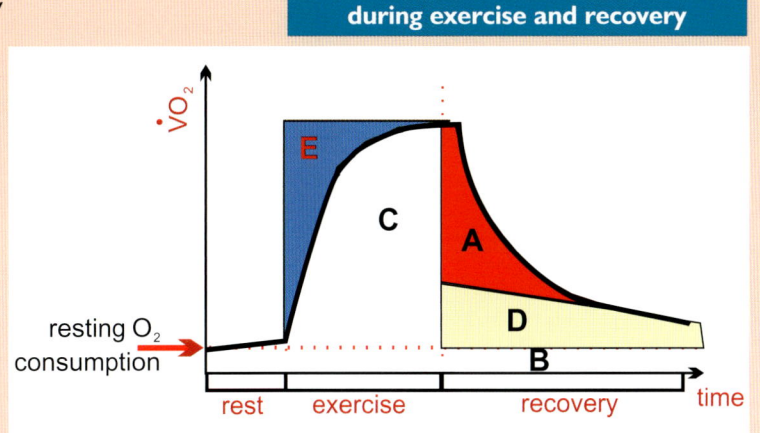

   a) Using the appropriate letters, identify the oxygen deficit and Excess Post Oxygen Consumption (EPOC). 3 marks

   b) Why does the elite player incur an oxygen deficit during exercise? 2 marks

   c) Excess Post Oxygen Consumption (EPOC) is considered to have two components. State two aims of the first component and explain how this component is achieved. 4 marks

   d) Describe the process of ATP production that restores the oxygen debt or EPOC. 6 marks

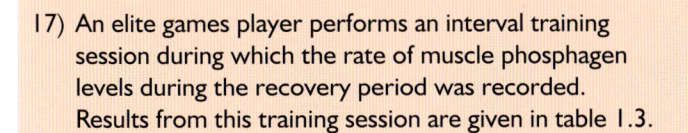

figure 1.23 – oxygen consumption during exercise and recovery

17) An elite games player performs an interval training session during which the rate of muscle phosphagen levels during the recovery period was recorded. Results from this training session are given in table 1.3.

   a) Using the results in table 1.3, plot a graph of recovery time against the percentage of muscle phosphagen restored. 3 marks

   b) What resting value would you recommend for a full recovery, and what would be the effect of restarting the exercise after 30 seconds? 2 marks

   c) Part of the recovery mechanism after anaerobic exercise involves myoglobin. Explain the function of myoglobin during the recovery process. 3 marks

Table 1.3 – muscle phosphagen during recovery

recovery time / s	muscle phosphagen restored / %
10	10
30	50
60	75
90	87
120	93
150	97
180	99
210	101
240	102

18) How could information on oxygen debt recovery be of use to an athlete and coach in designing training sessions? 5 marks

19) Competitive swimmers will often compete in several events and suffer from fatigue due to limited recovery time. Explain the possible causes of fatigue during a race. 3 marks

Answers link: http://www.jroscoe.co.uk/downloads/a2_revise_pe_aqa/AQAA2_ch1_answers.pdf

SECTION 1 – CHAPTER 2   ENERGY SYSTEMS PART TWO

CHAPTER 2: Energy systems part two

> **STUDENT NOTE**
>
> Cardio-respiratory endurance is the component of fitness which is a contributory factor to many sporting situations. As discussed in Chapter 1 from page 17 the major influencing factor of cardio-respiratory performance is the maximum volume of oxygen an individual can consume ($\dot{V}O_{2max}$).

Factors affecting $\dot{V}O_{2max}$ /aerobic power (figure 2.1)

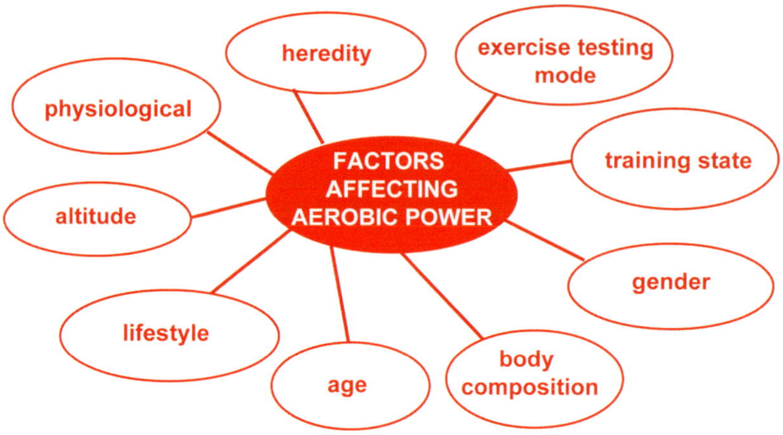

Physiological

The availability of O_2 in the tissue depends upon:
- Whether **haemoglobin** arriving at tissue is fully saturated with O_2.
- The limitations of the **cardiovascular** and **pulmonary** systems which varies from individual to individual.
- Whether the **myglobin** in muscle cells is fully saturated with O_2 and sufficient recovery time has elapsed.

Heredity

- Current estimates of the **genetic effect** ascribe about 20-30% role of $\dot{V}O_{2max}$, 50% for maximum heart rate and 70% for physical working capacity.

figure 2.1 – aerobic power

(Diagram: FACTORS AFFECTING AEROBIC POWER — heredity, exercise testing mode, training state, gender, body composition, age, lifestyle, altitude, physiological)

Exercise testing mode

- Variations in $\dot{V}O_{2max}$ during different test modes reflect the **quantity** of activated muscle mass.
- For example, bench stepping generates $\dot{V}O_{2max}$ scores nearly identical to treadmill values, but higher than an arm-crank test.

Training state

- $\dot{V}O_{2max}$ must be evaluated relative to a person's training status at the **time of measurement**.
- Following a **period of aerobic training**, such as regular continuous, aerobic interval and fartlek training, aerobic capacity improves between 6% and 20%.
- Larger $\dot{V}O_{2max}$ improvements occur among the most sedentary individuals.

Gender

- $\dot{V}O_{2max}$ expressed in ml kg^{-1} min^{-1} for women typically average 15% to 30% below values for men.
- Even among **trained endurance athletes**, the disparity ranges between 10% and 20%.
- Apparent gender differences in $\dot{V}O_{2max}$ have been attributed to differences in **body composition** and **blood haemoglobin** concentration.
- Untrained young adult women possess about **26% body fat**, while the corresponding value for men averages around 15%.
- Trained athletes have a lower body fat percentage, yet trained women possess significantly more body fat than their male counterparts.
- Consequently, males generate more total aerobic energy simply because of their **larger muscle mass** and **lower total fat** than females.
- Men have 10% to 14% greater concentration of **haemoglobin** than women.
- This difference in the **blood oxygen carrying capacity** enables men to circulate more oxygen during physical activity and gives them the edge in aerobic capacity.
- Despite these limitations, the aerobic capacity of **physically active women** exceeds that of sedentary men.

APPLIED ANATOMY AND PHYSIOLOGY

Body composition

- Differences in body composition explain roughly 70% of the differences in $\dot{V}O_{2max}$ expressed as ml kg^{-1} min^{-1}. This is per kilogramme of body mass, so different sizes of people can be compared.
- Although there are other biological differences between the sexes, research suggests $\dot{V}O_{2max}$ decreases as body fat percent increases.
- Adjusting the arm-crank $\dot{V}O_{2max}$ test (figure 2.2) for variations in arm and shoulder size equalises values between men and women, suggesting gender differences in aerobic capacity largely reflect the **size of the active muscle mass**.
- This research implies that **no true gender difference** exist in active muscle mass capacity to generate ATP aerobically.

figure 2.2 – arm crank

Age

- Changes in $\dot{V}O_{2max}$ relate to **chronological age**.
- After the age of 25, $\dot{V}O_{2max}$ decreases by 1% per year.
- However, available data indicates that regular physical activity throughout life can offset much of the decline as illustrated in figure 2.3.

figure 2.3 – $\dot{V}O_{2max}$ changes with age

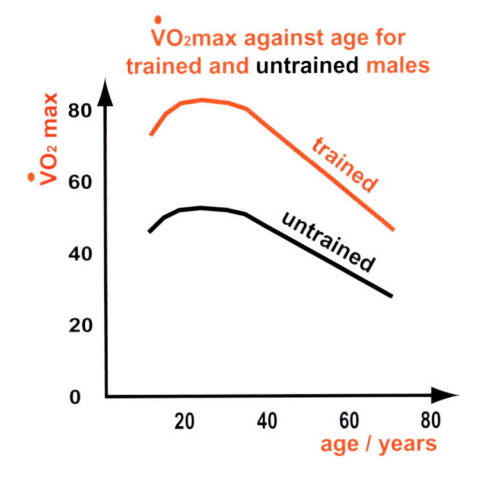

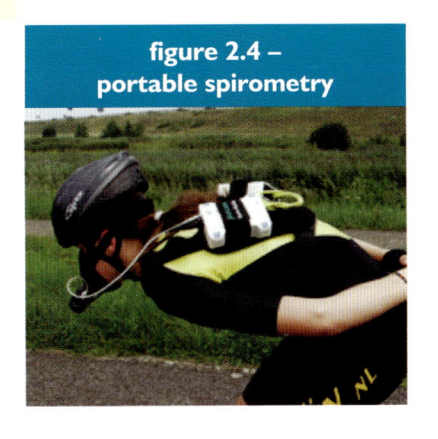

$\dot{V}O_2$max against age for **trained** and **untrained** males

Lifestyle

- A **sedentary** lifestyle, **smoking** and a poor **diet** all reduce $\dot{V}O_{2max}$ values.

Altitude

- $\dot{V}O_{2max}$ decreases proportionally to the atmospheric pressure. Refer to page 30 for further details.

Measurement of energy expenditure

Methods for measurement of the various components of daily energy expenditure can be assessed using a variety of techniques. In this section your syllabus indentifies four popular techniques namely indirect calorimetry, lactate sampling, $\dot{V}O_{2max}$ testing and the respiratory exchange ratio (RER).

Indirect calorimetry

> **STUDENT NOTE**
>
> Indirect calorimetry is discussed in relation to the metabolic cart in AS/A1 Revise PE for AQA ISBN 9781901424850, Chapter 15, page 200 onwards.

Indirect calorimetry determines the body's rate of energy expenditure from oxygen consumption or uptake and carbon dioxide production and a measure of substrate utilization as reflected in the Respiratory Quotient (RQ).

There are three common indirect calorimetry procedures that measure oxygen consumption during physical activity:

Portable spirometry
Is discussed in the AS/A1 text, as illustrated in figure 2.4.

figure 2.4 – portable spirometry

SECTION 1 – CHAPTER 2
ENERGY SYSTEMS PART TWO

Bag technique
Whereby expired air passes into a large Douglas bag for subsequent analysis of O_2 and CO_2 composition.

Computerised laboratory instrumentation
In which a subject's expired air performs metabolic calculations based on electronic signals it receives from the instruments, giving reliable and valid measurements including $\dot{V}O_{2max}$ results.

$\dot{V}O_{2max}$ tests

Tests for $\dot{V}O_{2max}$ rely on activities with sufficient **intensity** and **duration** to activate large muscle groups to properly engage maximum aerobic energy transfer. Considerable research effort has been directed toward the development and standardisation of $\dot{V}O_{2max}$ tests and norms that consider age, gender, state of training, body mass and body composition. Hence, there are many different standardised tests that assess actual and predicted $\dot{V}O_{2max}$.

figure 2.5 – a gas analyser worn during a lab test

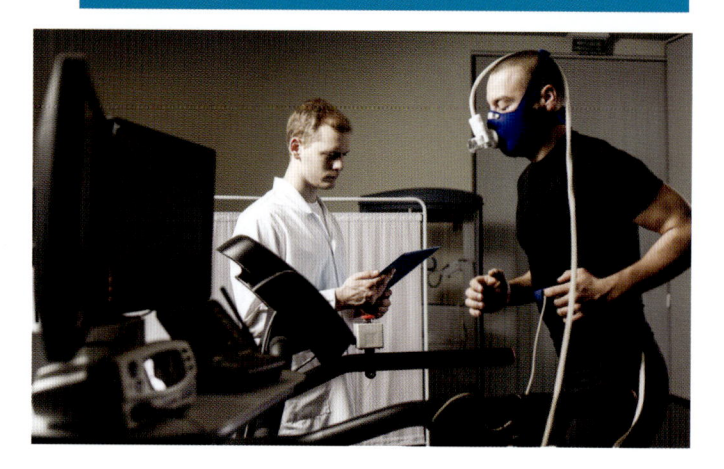

Within the Sports Science laboratory a **treadmill** protocol is an example of a progressive test of $\dot{V}O_{2max}$ to exhaustion as the treadmill gets **steeper** and moves **faster** with each stage of the test. This indirect calorimetry test lasts between 8 and 10 minutes depending on the fitness of the performer (figure 2.5).

$\dot{V}O_{2max}$ is obtained by measuring exhaled air oxygen consumption using a gas analyser. The $\dot{V}O_{2max}$ criteria, when using direct gas analysis, must show a levelling off or **peaking-over** in oxygen consumption/uptake during increasing exercise intensity as illustrated in figures 2.6.

The region where oxygen consumption fails to increase the expected amount or even decreases slightly with increasing intensity represents the $\dot{V}O_{2max}$.

This type of progressive test to **exhaustion** is not recommended for the untrained individual who may not have the fitness level to cope with a progressive maximal test.

figure 2.6 – results from treadmill test

speed km h^{-1}	4.8	8.0	11.2	11.2	11.2	11.2	11.2
time min	0-2	2-4	4-6	6-8	8-10	10-12	12-14
treadmill grade %	0	5.5	7.5	9.5	11.5	13.5	15.5

Predicted $\dot{V}O_{2max}$ tests

These may require 3-5 minutes of **submaximal** or **maximal** effort and are used as an indicator of aerobic fitness or stamina. Reliable and valid tests include the Physical Work Capacity test (PWC170), the Cooper's run/walk test, the Queen's College step test and the Multi-stage shuttle run test.

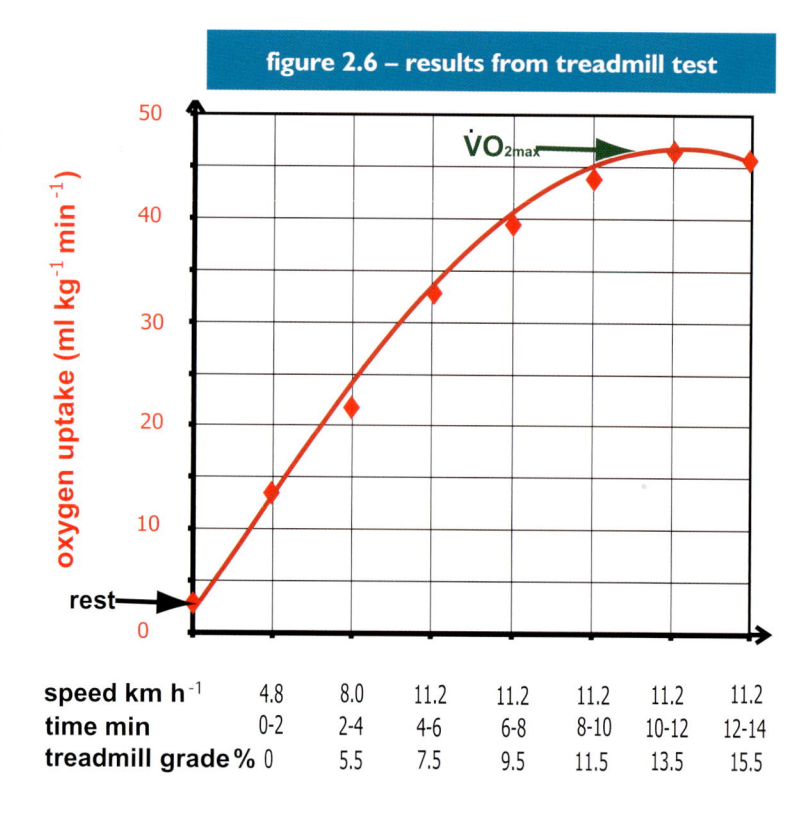

For example, the **Queen's College Step test** is a **submaximal** predicted $\dot{V}O_{2max}$ test that requires the subject to step up and down on a 41.3 cm step bench at a rate of 22 steps per minute for females and at 24 steps per minute for male using a four-step cadence, 'up-up-down-down' for 3 minutes. The subject stops immediately on completion of the test, and the heart beats are counted for 15 seconds from 5-20 seconds of recovery. This heart rate reading is multiplied by 4 to give the beats per minute (bpm) value, which is then converted by referring to a percentile ranking table for a predicted $\dot{V}O_{2max}$ value.

APPLIED ANATOMY AND PHYSIOLOGY

Predicted $\dot{V}O_{2max}$ tests

For example, the **NCF multi-stage shuttle run test** (the bleep test, figure 2.7) is a **maximal** 20 metre shuttle run test whereby the subject runs progressively quicker shuttle runs to a point when he or she can no longer keep up with the set pace. Each level in the progression is numbered and the level reached by the subject is correlated to the standard $\dot{V}O_{2max}$ results table. Unlike the step test described on page 28, this test requires the subject to be highly motivated to push him or herself to a maximal limit of aerobic endurance.

Lactate sampling

A **lactate sampler** is a small hand-held device (figure 2.8) that can be taken into the training environment, with which top athletes take pin prick blood samples and test for lactate concentration (immediate read-out from the device). This enables them to work out the maximum possible exercise intensity within which they must work to avoid **Onset of Blood Lactate Accumulation** (OBLA).

One of the **advantages** of lactate testing is that it may be more sensitive to changes in **fitness** than a $\dot{V}O_{2max}$ test. An athlete may have a stable $\dot{V}O_{2max}$ through a hard training period, yet the fitness of that athlete may be increased significantly, and this change in fitness is usually reflected in the lactate response to exercise rather than the $\dot{V}O_{2max}$ measurement.

Lactate sampling can be taken at fixed times during an interval training session, such as a set time at the completion of each repetition of 6x300 metre paced sprints. The readings measure lactate threshold and OBLA which occurs at around 4 mmols of lactic acid.

Lactate sampling can be used as accurate and objective **guide** to recovery between repetitions. Readings from lactate sampling can be used by the coach to determine **training intensity**. Different athletes will produce higher or lower amounts of lactate, depending upon factors, such as muscle fibre composition. The athlete should be treated as an **individual**, and so a lactate profile for that athlete should be recorded and the training programme evolved from such an individual profile.

figure 2.7 – results from shuttle run test

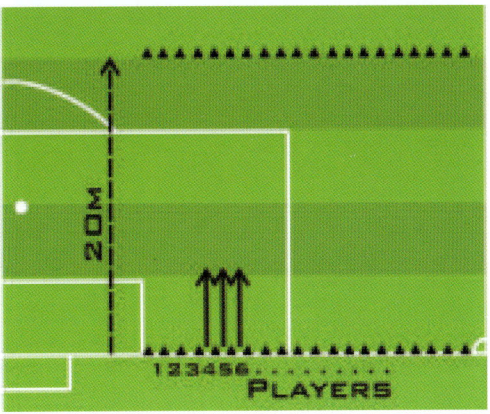

figure 2.8 – lactate sampler

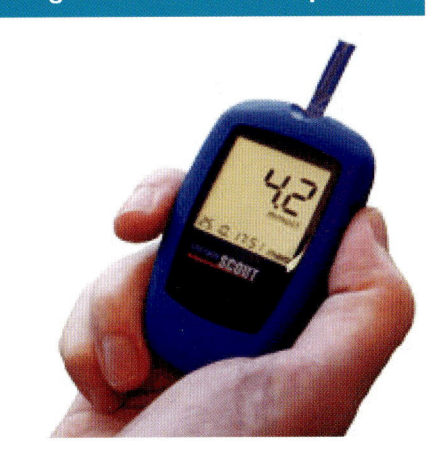

Respiratory exchange ratio (RER)

RER is an indicator which is a way of estimating which fuel type (CHO, fat or protein) is being used within a given activity. It can be estimated by measuring oxygen taken in and carbon dioxide expired during the activity, using a portable or laboratory based gas analyser. Estimation of RER for a person can also tell you whether or not the sportsperson is operating anaerobically (without sufficient oxygen for aerobic effort) or not.

Energy released by a given volume of oxygen

- This energy depends on whether the fuel is carbohydrate, fat or protein.
- Different amounts of energy are released by combination with oxygen because of the different chemical formulae of CHO, fat or protein.
- Complete combination with oxygen will produce CO_2 and water.
- The amount of O_2 needed to completely oxidise a molecule of CHO, fat or protein is proportional to the amount of carbon in the fuel.

Respiratory exchange ratio

SECTION 1 – CHAPTER 2

ENERGY SYSTEMS PART TWO

RER

RER is the ratio: $\dfrac{\text{volume of CO}_2 \text{ produced}}{\text{volume of O}_2 \text{ consumed}}$

For **glucose**: $\quad 6O_2 + C_6H_{12}O_6 \rightarrow 6CO_2 + 6H_2O +$ energy to resynthesise 36ATP

Therefore for **glucose**: $\quad RER = \dfrac{6CO_2}{6O_2} = 1.00$

For **fat**: $\quad 23O_2 + C_{16}H_{32}O_2 \rightarrow 16CO_2 + 16H_2O +$ energy to resynthesise 129ATP

Therefore for **fat**: $\quad RER = \dfrac{16CO_2}{23O_2} = 0.70$

For **protein**: $\quad C_{72}H_{112}N_2O_{22}S + 77O_2 \rightarrow 63CO_2 + 38H_2O + SO_3 + 9CO(NH_2)_2$ (for example)

Therefore for **protein**: $\quad RER = \dfrac{63CO_2}{77O_2} = 0.82$

Protein is rarely utilised as an energy source except in extreme conditions.

Measuring RER

RER is estimated for a sportsperson by measuring CO_2 output and O_2 input while exercising either on a treadmill or a cycle ergometer, or while out running with a portable spirometer device (figure 2.9). During this process, the sportsperson breathes in and out of a tube connected to a gas analyser.

A value of RER near 1.0 means that the sportsperson is deriving most of his or her energy from CHO aerobically.

A value of RER over 1.0 means that less O_2 is being used than is required to produce the CO_2 from aerobic respiration which means that anaerobic respiration and lactate production are occurring.

So measurement of RER can tell a sportsperson whether he or she is reaching his or her aerobic limit or not, and whether the training intensity is too high for aerobic work. The average value for RER for a mixed diet and for mild aerobic exercise is 0.82, showing a mixed uptake of carbohydrate and fats.

figure 2.9 – measuring RER while in action

Impact of specialised training methods on energy systems

Altitude training

Partial pressure (**p**) is defined as '**the pressure a gas exerts within a mixture of gases**'.

At sea level, the **partial pressure** of oxygen is 160 mm/Hg, which is 21% of the total atmospheric pressure of 760 mm/Hg. As the atmospheric pressure decreases with an increase in altitude, the partial pressure of oxygen will also decrease, even though it will still remain 21% of the total air mass.

The effects of altitude on body systems are summarised in figure 2.10.

figure 2.10 – effects of altitude

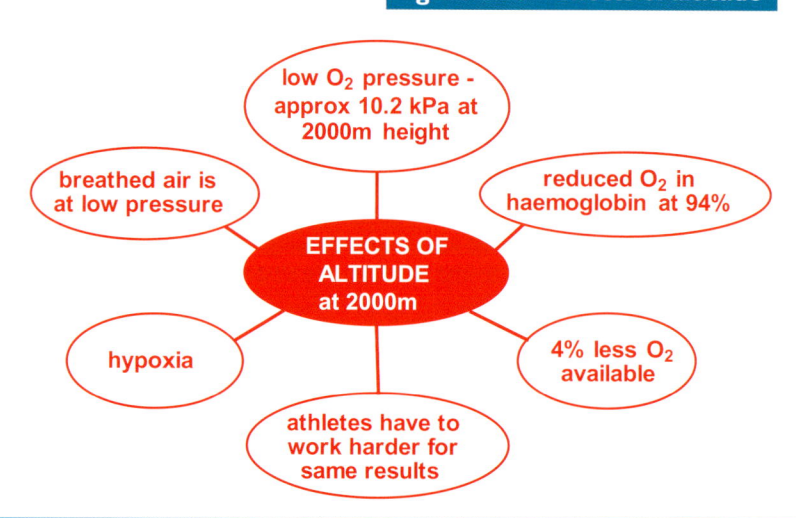

EFFECTS OF ALTITUDE at 2000m
- low O_2 pressure - approx 10.2 kPa at 2000m height
- reduced O_2 in haemoglobin at 94%
- 4% less O_2 available
- athletes have to work harder for same results
- hypoxia
- breathed air is at low pressure

APPLIED ANATOMY AND PHYSIOLOGY

Altitude training

Athletes who travel to altitude for training purposes are at risk of suffering the detrimental effects of altitude. In addition to altitude illness (hypoxia), weight loss, immune suppression and sleep disturbance may serve to limit athletic performance.

Sea level residents who train at altitude are found to adapt by producing more haemoglobin at a rate of 1% and 2% per week.

This is done by increased manufacture of red blood cells (**erythropoietin - EPO**) production and an associated reduction in plasma volume, a slower long-term adaptation to living at altitude.

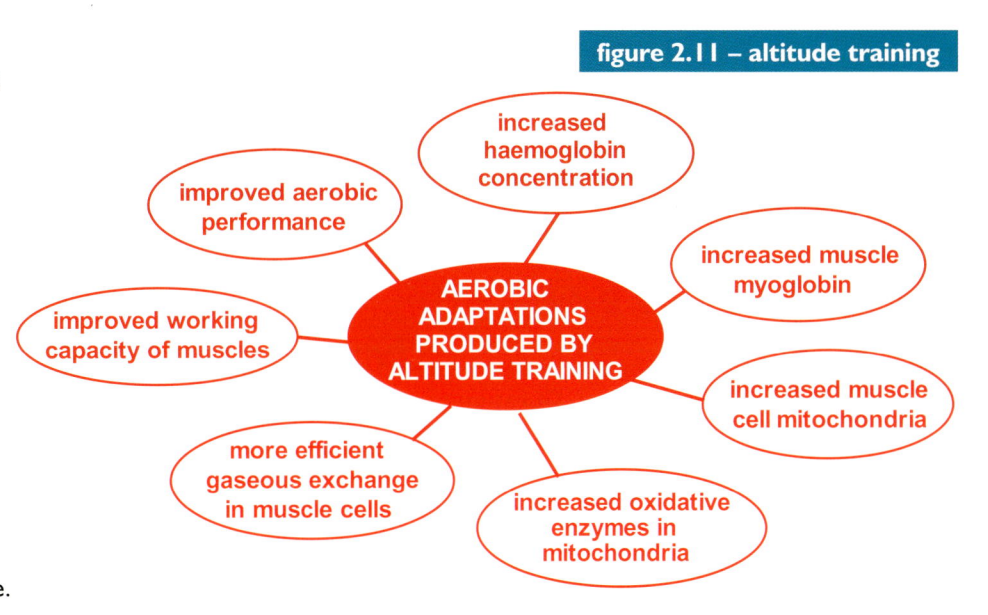

figure 2.11 – altitude training

AEROBIC ADAPTATIONS PRODUCED BY ALTITUDE TRAINING
- increased haemoglobin concentration
- improved aerobic performance
- increased muscle myoglobin
- improved working capacity of muscles
- increased muscle cell mitochondria
- more efficient gaseous exchange in muscle cells
- increased oxidative enzymes in mitochondria

The effect of these two factors is to increase haemoglobin concentration in the blood flowing to active tissue, and hence an increase in the oxygen-carrying capacity of the blood.

Aerobic physiological adaptations produced by altitude training, are summarised in figure 2.11.

- High altitude training is regarded as an integral component of modern athletic preparation, especially for a range of endurance sports such as middle/long distance running and triathlon.
- Most elite athletes have a minimum of 2 training blocks or visits per year, one long training block of between 4-6 weeks during the preparation training phase, and then a shorter block of between 2-3 weeks just prior to a major competition. During a second visit the body adapts more quickly.
- Some elite athletes spend several weeks training at altitude. For example, Sir Mo Farah spends up to three months at a time training at altitude in Kenya's Rift Valley (2400 metres) and in Bekele's training camp in Ethopia (2,566 metres) preparing for key sea level events such as the London Marathon figure 2.12.
- **Short-term symptoms** to altitude exposure include headaches and dizziness and increased breathing and heart rates. The key is to adjust gradually (**acclimatise**) to higher altitude.
- During the first week of altitude training an elite athlete would normally work at between 60-70% of sea level intensity thus avoiding very hard lactate sessions.
- During the second week, the training would increase to full intensity (within days 10-14) and continue until returning to sea level. This would include 'tapering' or reducing the workload during the final couple of days just prior to a major competition. Paula Radcliffe chose to compete 2 days after returning to sea level.
- The process of altitude training will stimulate production of more **haemoglobin** and bigger increases in **myoglobin**, **mitochondria** and **oxidative enzymes** than at sea level in the way outlined above and in figure 2.11.
- Hence on return to sea level the sportsperson would have **increased $\dot{V}O_{2max}$** and tissue cell respiration, leading to enhanced aerobic performance.
- The optimum time to compete is within 2 to 14 days of return to sea-level. After this, the adaptations gradually return to sea-level norms over a period of weeks, depending on the time spent at altitude and the individual's basic physiological state.

figure 2.12 – Sir Mo Farah

Altitude training | 31

SECTION 1 – CHAPTER 2

ENERGY SYSTEMS PART TWO

Altitude training and the energy systems
As explained on page 31, altitude training, for sea level endurance athletes, stresses the aerobic energy system, however, the physiological aerobic adaptations are temporary.

While **endurance performance** generally **declines at altitude** in running events longer than 400 metres, explosive **anaerobic events** such as sprinting, jumping and throwing, **benefit** from the rarefied air as exemplified by the world records achieved in the Mexico Olympic Games in 1968. Note that all track events in excess of 400 metres were won by African athletes who lived at altitude.

High Intensity Interval Training (HIIT)

This is a type of interval training that involves repeated bouts of **high intensity training** followed by a varied **recovery** time. **Duration** of work periods may range from 5 seconds to 8 minutes long and are performed at an **intensity** of between **80% to 95% of HRmax**.

Repetitions and **sets** are created depending on the intensity and duration of the exercise period.
Recovery periods are performed at an intensity of between **40% to 50% of HRmax**. Exercise continues with alternating work and a **1:1 rest relief ratio**.

HIIT benefits both aerobic and anaerobic fitness, blood pressure, cholesterol profiles and body fat whilst increasing muscle mass. The completion of Physical Activity Readiness Questionnaire (**PAR-Q**) is a sensible first step for participants who are planning to increase their levels of physical activity.

HIIT workouts can be created for every exercise preference which could take as little as 10 minutes for the novice performer. For example, following a warm-up, 30 seconds brisk walk, 30 seconds sprint x 10 repetitions, followed by a cool down. The specific sprint part of the session is anaerobic stressing both **ATP-PC** and **anaerobic glycolytic** energy systems. During the recovery the **aerobic** energy system is stressed.

A more general session (figure 2.13) could involve one minute activity bouts at about 90% of HR_{max}, followed by one minute of easy recovery with 10 total intervals and recovery, for a total workout time lasting 20 minutes. Note that in this type of session the exercise has alternating **work and recovery at a 1:1 rest relief ratio**.

figure 2.13 – TRX HIIT training

An increase in skeletal muscle buffering capacity may be one mechanism responsible for an improvement in HITT training.

HIIT has demonstrated that **improved insulin action** stimulates glycogen synthesis, thereby improving glycaemic control (the maintenance of glucose levels) in healthy middle aged individuals at risk of developing type 2 diabetes.

HIIT and energy systems
The HIIT training method stresses all three energy systems when the high intensity part of the session utilises the both ATP-PC and anaerobic glycolytic energy systems for explosive energy and the aerobic energy system is fully utilised during the recovery part of the session.

APPLIED ANATOMY AND PHYSIOLOGY

Plyometric training

A type of power training **involving eccentric-to-concentric actions at 100% effort** designed to improve elastic strength and power.

Plyometric leg training occurs when, on landing, the muscle performs an eccentric contraction (lengthens under tension) performed quickly so that the loaded agonist muscle stretches slightly prior to concentric action. This stimulates adaptation within the neuromuscular system as muscle spindles cause a **stretch reflex** to produce a more powerful concentric muscle contraction. The throwing and catching of medicine balls is a way of developing elastic shoulder strength.

In figure 2.14, two athletes are throwing a medicine ball back and forth. The catch phase of this movement is eccentric for the trunk musculature and the shoulders, with the throw movement being concentric in the same muscle groups.

Normally this exercise is done too slowly to activate the stretch reflex, but a rapid rebound movement could have the desired effect.

figure 2.14 – catch and throw as eccentric then concentric exercise – similar to plyometrics

In figure 2.15, the athlete is performing two-footed jumping (bunny jumps), which would have to be performed quickly to activate the stretch reflex in time with the concentric phase of the jump.

figure 2.15 – bounding and jumping can be plyometric

Further examples of plyometric training sessions:
- Depth jumping from a box and rebounding quickly from impact point.
- Two foot bounds over a flight of hurdles.
- 3-5 sets of 3-10 repetitions with medium recovery of 1-3 minutes.

Plyometric training and the energy systems
Plyometric drills predominantly stress **anaerobic** energy systems namely the ATP-PC system and the anaerobic glycolytic system (lactic acid system).

The **ATP-PC system** depends on energy stores that already exist in skeletal muscle tissue. **Plyometric drills**, such as repeated depth jumping of a series of boxes lasting 4 to 8 seconds, deplete this energy source very quickly. The **lactic acid threshold** is reached when the muscles' energy stores have exhausted the ATP-PC stores.

SECTION 1 – CHAPTER 2

ENERGY SYSTEMS PART TWO

Plyometric training and the energy systems

After this **threshold** point, energy is supplied predominantly by the **anaerobic glycolytic system**, for example, multiple bounding drills that take between 10-20 seconds duration to complete.

A short recovery period or rest relief should be allotted between high quality plyometric drills.

Speed agility and quickness training (SAQ)

Speed represents the maximum velocity an athlete can achieve and maintain.
Agility is the ability to change direction quickly without losing speed or balance.
Quickness involves rapid and energetic movements.

SAQ combines speed, agility and quickness over **short distance**s using a variety of drills and agility as the main motor fitness component, with emphasis on **precision** and **speed of foot placement**. The drills vary from using equipment such as foot ladders (placed on the floor), low hurdles and cones in a variety of foot placement patterns, forcing rapid changes of direction that can replicate specific movement patterns required by the athlete in his or her specific sport.

figure 2.16 – low hurdle agility drill

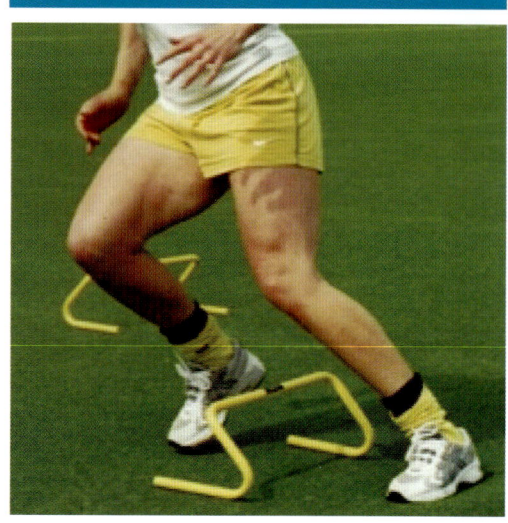

Examples of SAQ training drills

Example 1: low hurdle agility drill
Ten low hurdles are set out in a set spaced formation. The athlete moves over the hurdles as fast as possible (figure 2.16). This drill is intended to replicate specific movement patterns needed in games such as soccer and rugby.

Example 2: foot ladder agility drills
Foot ladder agility drills are an excellent way to improve foot speed, agility, coordination and overall quickness. In figure 2.17, the athlete is sprinting between each rung of the ladder. In figure 2.18, the athlete is taking alternating single step in, single step out into and out of the ladder. There are many possible foot combinations for ladder agility drills.

SAQ training and the energy systems

SAQ drills are performed at **maximum effort**, predominantly utilising the ATP-PC system and activating fast twitch muscle fibres for short duration. This training method enhances the practical athletic abilities in a wide variety of sports.

figure 2.17 – footladder agility drill

figure 2.18 – foot ladder agility drill

APPLIED ANATOMY AND PHYSIOLOGY

Practice questions

1) Which one of the following is defined as the greatest amount of oxygen the body can take in and utilise during exercise?
   a. $\dot{V}O_2$.
   b. cardiovascular endurance.
   c. $\dot{V}O_{2max}$.
   d. ppO_2.

2) The respiratory exchange ratio is a measurement of:
   a. lactic acid accumulation.
   b. lack of oxygen (hypoxia).
   c. the ratio between the amount of hydrogen produced in metabolism and oxygen used.
   d. the ratio between the amount of carbon dioxide produced in metabolism and oxygen used.

3) Which one of the following is not an aerobic adaptive response to altitude training?
   a. improved working capacity of muscles.
   b. increased muscle myoglobin.
   c. increased utilisation of fast twitch motor units.
   d. increased haemoglobin concentration.

4) Which one of the following best describes the plyometric training method?
   a. involves mainly stretching.
   b. involves continuous running.
   c. involves interval training.
   d. involves mainly bounding/hopping.

5) Which one of the following is not a maximal predicted $\dot{V}O_{2max}$ test?
   a. Multi-stage shuttle run test.
   b. 1-mile jog test
   c. Cooper's run/walk test
   d. 1.5 mile run test

6) a) Define the term $\dot{V}O_{2max}$ and describe two main factors which limit $\dot{V}O_{2max}$. 3 marks

   b) Describe a field test used to estimate a person's $\dot{V}O_{2max}$. 3 marks

7) a) Figure 2.19 shows variation in $\dot{V}O_{2max}$ between three different sports. Suggest reasons for variations in $\dot{V}O_{2max}$ between these three sports. 3 marks

   b) Explain the potential physiological advantages for endurance athletes having a high $\dot{V}O_{2max}$. 2 marks

8) Discuss the factors that affect maximal oxygen consumption ($\dot{V}O_{2max}$) and the accuracy of $\dot{V}O_{2max}$ prediction from submaximal exercise heart rate. 15 marks

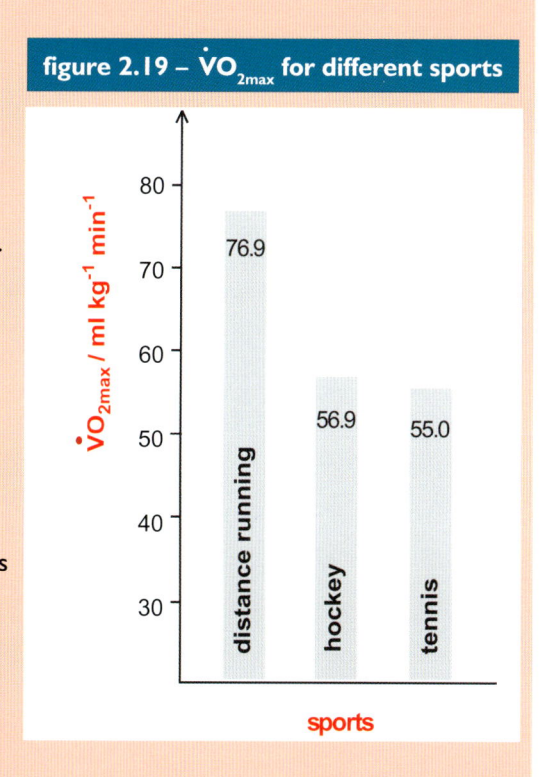

figure 2.19 – $\dot{V}O_{2max}$ for different sports

$\dot{V}O_{2max}$ / ml kg^{-1} min^{-1}

distance running: 76.9
hockey: 56.9
tennis: 55.0

SECTION 1 – CHAPTER 2

ENERGY SYSTEMS PART TWO

Practice questions

9) Two female athletes, one trained runner and the other untrained runner, performed a $\dot{V}O_{2max}$ test on a cycle ergometer. The results of the test are shown in the graph in figure 2.20.

	female 1	female 2
body mass	75 kg	65 kg
height	174 cm	176 cm

figure 2.20 – cycle ergometer test

(Graph: oxygen uptake $\dot{V}O_2$ L min⁻¹ vs time (minutes), showing female 1 and female 2 data)

a) Use the information in the graph and table to determine if the values given are absolute or relative measures. Explain which measure (absolute or relative) is more useful when comparing the oxygen uptake for the two runners.　　3 marks

b) Using the data in figure 2.20, explain which female is the trained runner.　　2 marks

c) Identify one chronic adaptation to the cardiovascular system and explain how it has resulted in the trained runner achieving a greater result.　　2 marks

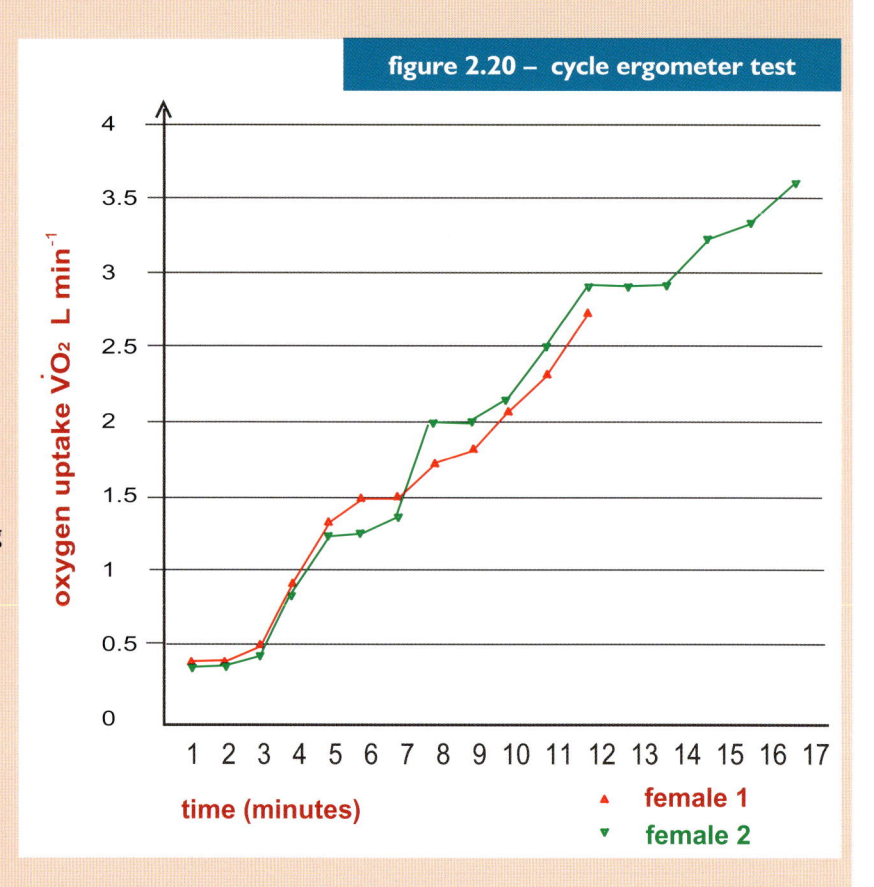

d) For female 2, explain what occurs physiologically between 12 and 14 minutes, and then what happens between 14 and 15 minutes.　　4 marks

e) The cycle ergometer test is not specific to running. Name a recognised field test that could be used to determine a runner's $\dot{V}O_{2max}$.　　1 mark

10) Volleyball is a team sport and a match generally takes between 30 and 60 minutes. Players are involved in high intensity, short duration play, such as serving, passing, spiking and blocking. The game is explosive in nature with rest periods between points.

a) Using the information provided, describe the interplay of the three energy systems in a volleyball match.　　6 marks

b) Plyometric training can improve muscular power and is a suitable training method for volleyball players. Outline two principles needed to create a plyometric training session supporting your answer with a practical example.　　3 marks

c) Why does muscle soreness (DOMS) often occur following a plyometric training session and how could muscle soreness be reduced?　　4 marks

APPLIED ANATOMY AND PHYSIOLOGY

Practice questions

11) Many elite swimmers use blood lactate sampling during training as a means of establishing their training load.
    a) What do you understand by the term lactate threshold? 2 marks

    b) How is lactate threshold related to $\dot{V}O_{2max}$? 2 marks

    c) How might knowledge of blood lactate levels taken during a swimming session assist both coach and elite swimmer? 2 marks

12) a) Show how the data in the following equation can be used to calculate the respiratory exchange ratio (RER) and identify which fuel food is being used.
    Show your workings. $6O_2 + C_6H_{12}O_6 \rightarrow 6CO_2 + 6H_2O +$ energy. 3 marks

    b) How can this information be of value to an elite sports performer? 2 marks

13) Altitude training is used by some marathon runners as part of their physiological preparation for sea level racing. Discuss whether altitude training is always beneficial to marathon runners. 8 marks

14) a) Describe the conditions at altitude that could limit performance. 3 marks

    b) An elite group of endurance athletes spend three weeks training at 2400 metres. What major physiological responses and adaptations would they expect during this period of acclimatisation? 8 marks

15) Elite athletes must develop and maintain extremely high levels of fitness to maximise their chances of winning, and may use the results from lactate sampling and the respiratory exchange ratio (RER) to ensure that their training is effective.
Explain the terms lactate sampling and respiratory exchange ratio and how elite athletes benefit from these two measurements of energy expenditure. 4 marks

16) Discuss the impact of specialist training methods on energy systems. 15 marks

Answers link: http://www.jroscoe.co.uk/downloads/a2_revise_pe_aqa/AQAA2_ch2_answers.pdf

SECTION 1 – CHAPTER 1 & 2

STUDENT'S NOTES

SECTION 2
SKILL ACQUISITION

CHAPTER 3
MEMORY MODELS

SECTION 2 CHAPTER 3 — MEMORY MODELS

CHAPTER 3: Memory models

Information processing

The information-processing approach is a set of **theories** which seek to explain human action by showing how we take information from our surroundings and make decisions about what to do next on the basis of our **interpretation** of that information.

For example, the badminnton player in figure 3.1 has to take in the surroundings of the court, the positions and actions of his opponent in sending the shuttle over the net, and then decide what to do in returning the shot. He then has to activate his relevant muscles to perform this task, and perceive the outcome, where the shuttle has travelled to, and how the opponent has moved in reponse. This acts as feedback to inform the player what to do next as part of the subsequent phase of the game.

The **simplest model** of information processing is that shown in figure 3.2

figure 3.1 – decisions?

Input

Input is the **information from the environment** received via the senses which the player uses to decide on a response to the situation.

Decision making

Decision making refers to the combination of recognition, perception and memory processes used to **select an appropriate response** to the demands of the situation.

Output

Output is the **response** which the player makes. In sport this is usually in the form of a movement of some kind. Output becomes a form of input or feedback.

figure 3.2 – simplest information processing model

Feedback

Feedback occurs because the player **perceives the outcome** of his or her response and this in turn becomes part of the input for the basis for further decision making.

Input

Almost any aspect of the immediate environment can act as input and is called a **display** from which the performer can select using his or her senses that which is relevant to his or her game or activity.

Senses

The senses used to collect information are collectively known as the **receptor systems**. When we are doing any physical activity we are aware of our surroundings. We use all our senses to locate ourselves in space and decide on the requirements of the task, whether it is to pass a ball or perform a gymnastic or dance movement. Taste and smell are not used to any great extent in physical activity but vision, hearing and proprioception are (figure 3.3, page 41).

Information is passed **to and from the brain** by the nervous system. This consists of two elements, namely the **brain and the spinal cord** which together form the **central nervous system** (CNS), and the **peripheral nervous system**, which comprises the nerves that connect the spinal cord with **all parts of the body**, radiating from (the **efferent** system) and returning to (the **afferent** system) the CNS.

SKILL ACQUISITION

Senses

The **afferent** system transmits information to the CNS about events and processes that are happening both inside and outside the body. For example, if you are running a marathon on a warm day, you can both see the sunlight and feel yourself getting hot. The **efferent** system transmits information from the CNS to the muscles which are then activated to perform a skill or execute a movement.

Vision and hearing (audition)

Vision and hearing (**audition**) deal with information from the **external** environment. As light falls upon the retina at the back of the eye, it is converted into electrical impulses and so transmitted to the brain, which allows us to see the image through visual perception.

Hearing works in a similar way; in this case, sound waves cause the eardrum to vibrate and this is converted into electrical impulses and transmitted in a similar way to visual images, though dealt with in a different part of the brain.

figure 3.3 – sensory input

Proprioception

Proprioception is the means by which we know how our body is **oriented in space** and the extent to which muscles are contracted or joints extended; proprioception allows us to feel the racket or ball. The three components of proprioception are touch, equilibrium and kinaesthesis, and these are known as **internal** input.

Touch
Touch (or the tactile sense) enables us to feel **pain**, **pressure** and **temperature**. In sports and dance we are mostly concerned with the pressure sense to tell us how firmly we are gripping a racket, for example, or whether our climbing partner is on a tight rope or whether we struck the ball hard or 'stroked' it. If we are sensible we take heed of any pain warnings we receive.

figure 3.4 – a sprint swim start, an example of balance

Equilibrium or balance
Equilibrium is the sense that tells you when your body is balanced (figure 3.4) and when it is tipping, turning or inverting. It is important for divers, gymnasts and trampolinists, as well as dancers, to be able to orientate themselves in space. This is done by means of the sense organs in the vestibular apparatus of the **middle ea**r.

Kinaesthesis
Kinaesthesis is the sense that **informs the brain of the movement or state of contraction of the muscles, tendons and joints**. A skilled performer knows whether a movement has been performed correctly or not not only from seeing its effect but also from sensing how the movement felt to perform.

This is known as **intrinsic feedback**. You may have experienced a foot or a limb 'going to sleep' and you will know how difficult it is not only to move the limb but also to know what is happening to it. The messages to and from the muscles have been interrupted and kinaesthetic sense impaired.

Decision making

Following the input, a performer must make decisions based on all the information available, but there usually will be so much of this that he or she must select that which is relevant.

This is done by a process called **selective attention**.

Senses

SECTION 2 CHAPTER 3 — MEMORY MODELS

Perception (figure 3.5)

Perception is described as **stimulus identification**.
As information is received from the environment, the performer needs to **make sense** of it, to **interpret** it and to **identify** the elements which are **relevant** and **important**.
Perception consists of three elements:

- **Detection** - the performer needs to be aware that something notable is going on around him or her. In a field game situation, this could be where the ball is, where the other players from both sides are in relation to the pitch dimensions, and what the goalkeeper is doing.
- **Comparison** - in which the performer will compare what is happening with his or her past experiences of similar situations, where are the players in comparison with set plays rehearsed in a training situation?
- **Recognition** - in which the performer realises that what is happening requires an activity in response, for example, what is the response to the rehearsed set play in the field game?

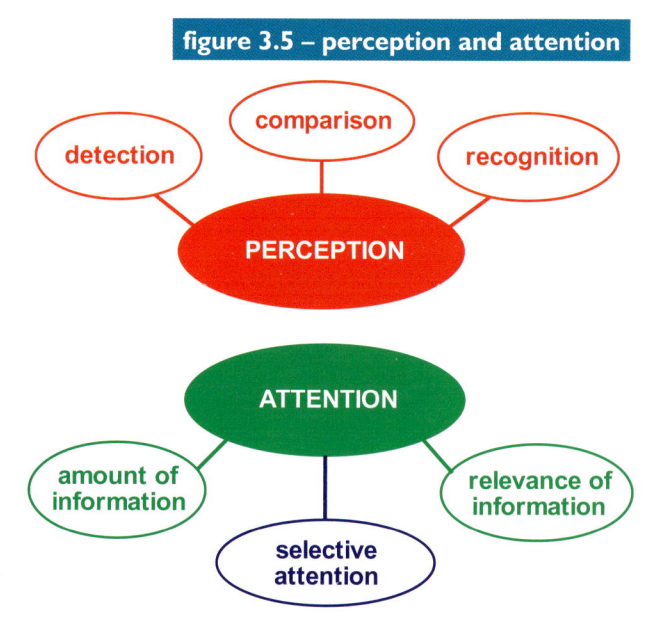

Attention (figure 3.5)

Attention relates to:

- **Amount of information** we can cope with, since the amount of information we can attend to **is limited**, and therefore we have limited **attentional capacity**.
- **Relevance of the information**. The performer must therefore attend to only **relevant information**, and **disregard irrelevant** information. This is called **selective attention**.

Selective attention

This is the process of sorting out **relevant** bits of information from the many which are received. Attention passes the information to the **short-term memory** which gives time for **conscious analysis**. A good performer can **focus totally** on an important aspect of his or her skill which **can exclude other elements** which may also be desirable. Sometimes a performer may desire to concentrate on several different things at once.

When some parts of a performance become **automatic**, the information relevant to those parts does not require attention, and this gives the performer **spare attentional capacity**.

This allows the performer to attend to new elements of a skill such as tactics or anticipating the moves of an opponent (figure 3.6). The coach will therefore need to help the performer to make best use of spare attentional capacity, and will also need to **direct the attention** of the performer to enable him or her to **concentrate** and reduce the chance of **attentional switching** to irrelevant information or distractions.

Developing selective attention

- Lots of **relevant** practice.
- Increase the **intensity** of the stimulus.
- Use **verbal** or **kinaesthetic** cues to focus on important information.
- For example, 'keep your eye on the ball' or a swimmer might selectively attend on the feel of the hand pulling through the water.
- Use **visualisation** or mental rehearsal techniques without movement.
- Watch performer's **video replays** to refine technique.
- **Observe and copy** the behaviour of a player who plays in the same position as the subject.

figure 3.5 – perception and attention

figure 3.6 – selective attention

SKILL ACQUISITION

Developing selective attention

- Coach needs to direct attention and give appropriate **feedback** to improve performer's motivation and alertness.
- Use **concentration** exercises, such as players scanning the field of play, followed by correct pass, alongside distracting background sounds or different instructions that may simulate the presence of noisy spectators that could distract players (figure 3.7).
- Develop **performance rituals** that automatically trigger focused attention that leads to good performance. Continue to **evaluate** and **reappraise** methods to ensure refinement and adjustments to selective attention techniques are an ongoing process.

Benefits of selective attention

- Directs performer's attention on particular aspects of performance thereby **avoiding distractions**.
- Gives performer a better chance of making the correct **decision**.
- Improves performer's **reaction time** significantly.
- Hence helps performer to make **quicker** decisions.
- Helps **regulate** performer's **arousal** and **anxiety** levels.
- Reduces performer's potential **memory overload**.

figure 3.7 – distraction?

The memory system

All the senses feed a vast amount of information into the CNS. Think for a moment of all the aspects of your surroundings and your body on which you can focus your attention if you choose.

The games player can **switch attention** from the opponent to the ball to the grip on the bat very quickly (figure 3.8). He is able to do this because all the information that enters the sensory system is held for a **very short time** in a section of the memory known as the **short-term sensory stores** (figure 3.9 page 44).

Evidence suggests that there is a **separate store** for each sense. In these stores, the coded message for each stimulus is compared with all the information held in the long-term memory to allow it to be identified/recognised. This has to be done very quickly because the short-term stores have a **large capacity** but retain each stimulus for **less than a second**.

If the **perceptual mechanism** decides that the stimulus is not **relevant** or important, the sensory memory held in the short-term sensory store fades and is lost. All this happens before we are conscious of it.

The short-term sensory store has a very large capacity for information but a minimal storage time; its purpose is to **filter out irrelevant information** so the system is **not overloaded**.

figure 3.8 – switching of attention

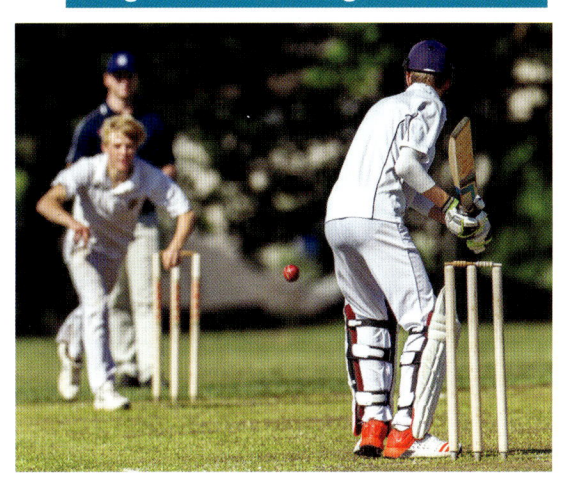

Selective attention and processing capacity

If we are looking out for some particular stimulus (**intentional attention**) or if a particular happening catches our attention (**involuntary attention**), then we focus on that by the process of selective attention. This focusing of attention passes the selected information into the short-term memory and allows more detailed processing. The short-term memory holds the information for up to 30 seconds and allows it to be consciously analysed.

The memory system 43

SECTION 2 CHAPTER 3 — MEMORY MODELS

Memory model (figure 3.9)

- **Short-term sensory storage (STSS)** is the **area of the brain** which receives information and holds it for a **short time** (less than 1 second) **prior to processing**. Information deemed unimportant is lost and forgotten and replaced by new information.
- **Selective attention** is used to sort out **relevant bits of information** from the many which are received.
- **Short-term memory (STM)** is the **part of the brain** which keeps information for a short period (20 - 30 seconds) after it has been deemed **worthy of attention**. The STM can carry between 5 and 9 separate items of information which can be improved by **chunking** (page 51).
- The information can be used for problem solving (**decision making** in which it is decided what to do) or passed on to the long-term memory for permanent storage.
- **Long-term memory** is the **part of the brain** which retains information for **long periods of time** - up to the lifetime of the performer. Very **well-learned information** is stored, and LTM is **limitless** and not forgotten but may require a code for the information to be recalled.

figure 3.9 – memory

Baddeley and Hitch working memory model (figure 3.10)

Baddeley and Hitch proposed a basic version of **Working Memory**, which can be defined as '**a temporary storage system under attentional control that underpins our capacity for complex thought**'. This therefore replaces the short term memory in the memory systems theory so far dealt with.

Within Working Memory, one memory system handles sound (the **Phonological Loop** or 'inner ear') and another handles vision (the **Visuospatial Sketchpad** or 'inner eye').

These two slave systems are managed by the **Central Executive** (CE) which organises memories.

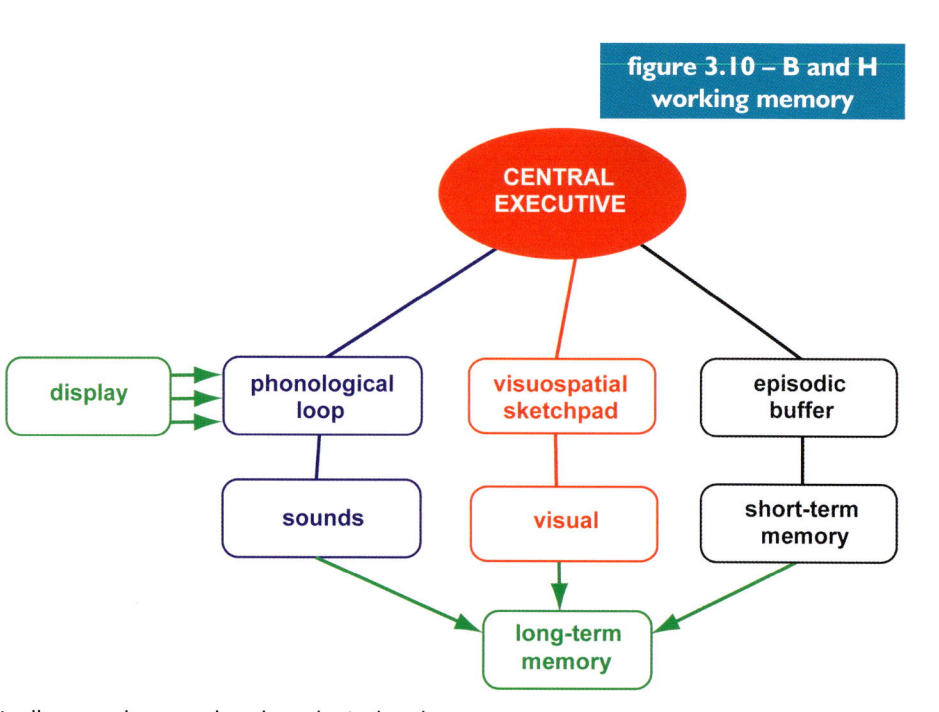

figure 3.10 – B and H working memory

Central Executive

The CE itself doesn't handle memories but it allocates them to the phonological and visuospatial (VSSP) systems.

It retrieves information from the **5 senses** (the display) or from long-term memory (LTM) and assigns it to the loop or the sketchpad for processing. It is **non-specific** – it can process sight, sound or any of the 5 senses.

SKILL ACQUISITION

Visuospatial Sketchpad
The VSSP system receives and sorts out visual information (figure 3.11) ready for processing in the long-term memory. Note that this information is integrated with other inputs to form the totality of the memory.

Phonological Loop
The Phonological Loop seems to be split into two sub-systems:
- An **Articulatory Loop** (inner voice) which voices information you are rehearsing.
- A **Primary Acoustic Store** which just holds on to the memory of sounds.

The Articulatory Loop engages in something called **subvocalising** which is that mental 'talking to yourself' that goes on in your head.

Episodic Buffer
The third slave system, the **Episodic Buffer** works between the Loop and the VSSP and brings elements of information together into patterns or stories into the long-term memory (LTM). It is **a temporary storage system that is able to combine information from the loop, the sketchpad, long-term memory, or indeed from perceptual input, into a coherent episode**.

Such a buffer is a linking element between what your brain sorts out, and a summary or rational chunk of data stored for long-term access and use in the LTM.

The Episodic Buffer is **multi-modal** which means that it is not limited to one sense only, like the other two input systems. Its job seems to be to 'bind' memories together, weaving visual memories and phonological memories into single episodes, which then get stored in Episodic LTM.

The **Central Executive** picks and chooses the information from the Phonological Loop and the VSSP that go into the Episodic Buffer to form an episode of memory. The Episodic Buffer also seems to 'download' episodes from LTM, sending them on to the Central Executive to be analysed and maybe recalled to conscious memory.

figure 3.11 – visuospatial input will be very important

Summary of characteristics and actions of the working memory
- Working memory makes sense of a **range of tasks** - verbal reasoning, comprehension, reading, problem solving and visual and spatial processing.
- Working memory is characterised by a **limited capacity**. It is thought to hold four to five elements of new information at one time.
- The capacity of working memory depends on the **category** of the elements or chunks as well as their features.
- Working memory has a **limited time scale** – up to 30 seconds.
- It is next either encoded into **long-term memory** or it is forgotten or replaced.
- Information is **retrieved** from long-term memory into working memory in order to make sense out of new information.

This more **complicated model** of memory perhaps best describes what happens in the brain when a very complicated field of inputs is digested by a performer as he or she attempts to decide what to do next.

Baddeley and Hitch working memory model

SECTION 2 CHAPTER 3 — MEMORY MODELS

Sporting example of working memory

In the case of a basketballer taking a shot at the basket (figure 3.12), the predominant display element will provide the visuospatial sketchpad of the basketball court, other players (on own side) and opponents. The phonological loop receives sound from feet movements on the court floor, and the roar from the spectator group which informs the player about player positions and the adulation of the crowd toward a pending score.

The noise of the crowd (adulation or booing) can provide **motivation** in terms of the **social facilitation** or **evaluation apprehension** about the crowd. All this noise will occupy the primary acoustic store.

Also, his team colleagues will be shouting about availabilty for a pass, and encouragement to success of the shot, and this will occupy the articulatory loop which will provide inner voices which attempt to guide the player toward success.

During this process, the **central executive** has made its selection of relevant inputs and then the episodic buffer will begin to assimilate and sort out these inputs into a 'success or fail' scenario, and link this into the recall of previous successful shots from the **long-term memory**.

Most of this activity is temporary and is within the short-term memory, with elements (namely the success or failure and the circumstances of the shot) only retained in the long-term memory.

figure 3.12 – working memory enables this shot

Whiting's model of information processing

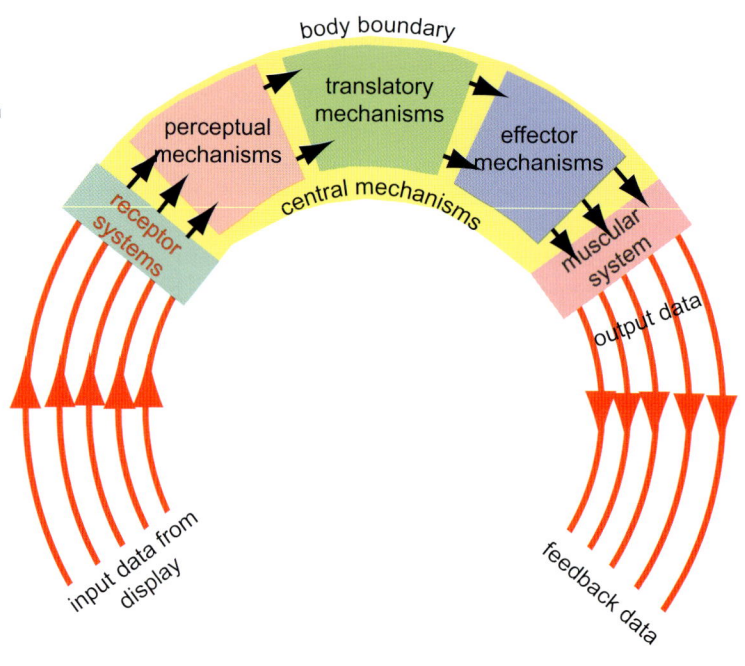

This model (figure 3.13) describes in more detail how informartion is processed duning a physical activity.

- The model applies itself to an **environment** in which a stimulus towards a sporting action occurs.

- **Input data from display** involves information from the **environment** which enters the brain via the **sensory organs**. For example, before catching a ball, the catcher sees the ball and is aware of the thrower's movement.

- The **sensory organs** which receive information are referred to as **receptor systems** in the model.

- **Perceptual mechanism** is the part of the brain which perceives the surroundings and gives them meaning.

- The **translatory mechanism** consists of the part of the brain which makes decisions and sorts out and processes the few relevant bits of information from the many inputs from the surroundings.

- The **effector mechanism** is the part of the brain which carries out the decisions and sends messages to the limbs and parts of the body via the nervous system.

- **Output** involves the effector mechanism and the **muscular system**. The nerves send messages to the muscles which move in order for the ball to be caught.

- **Feedback data** is **information** which is used **during and after** an action or movement which enables a performer to adjust or change performance according to this new information.

figure 3.13 – Whiting's model of information processing

SKILL ACQUISITION

Definitions of reaction time, response time and movement time

Reaction time
Reaction time (RT) is the time between the **onset** of a stimulus and the **start** of the response. This is an **inherent ability** or trait. The stimulus could be kinaesthesia, hearing, touch, vision, pain, or smell. From this list, the fastest reaction times occur to stimuli at the front of the list, the slowest to those at the end of the list. This is also known as **simple reaction time**.

Response time
Response time is the time it takes to **process information** and then to **make a response. Response time = reaction time + movement time.**

Movement time
Movement time is the time it takes to **complete the onset** of a movement.

Choice reaction time

If **several stimuli** are given but only one must be selected for response, then a choice must be made of which stimulus to respond to. The **more choices** a person has, the **more information** needs processing, and the **longer it takes** to process the information, the **slower** the reaction time. This is **Hick's Law** (figure 3.14).

figure 3.14 – Hick's Law
showing increase in reaction time as number of stimuli increases

y-axis: reaction time; x-axis: number of possible alternative stimuli

Factors affecting reaction time (figure 3.15)

- **Age**, the older we get, the slower our reaction times.
- **Gender**, males have quicker reaction times than females, but reaction times reduce less with age for females.
- Increase in **stimulus intensity** will improve reaction time, a louder bang will initiate the go more quickly than a less loud bang.
- **Tall people** will have slower reactions than short people because of the greater distance the information has to travel from the performer's brain to the active muscles, short sprinters tend to win 60m races.
- **Arousal levels** affect reaction times. Arousal levels are best when the performer is alert but not over aroused.
- The performer must attend to the most **important cues** (which act as a stimulus).
- Factors like body language or position might give a cue which enables the performer to **anticipate** a stimulus by for example, identifying favourite strokes or positions, particularly if the play involves an attempted dummy or fake.

figure 3.15 – factors affecting reaction time

REACTION TIME: age, gender, stimulus intensity, height, arousal levels, importance of cues, anticipation

Psychological refractory period

The **psychological refractory period (PRP)** is about what happens when following an initial stimulus (which may cause a reaction) there is a presentation of a **second stimulus**. The PRP is the time lag that occurs in responding to the second of two stimuli which occur close together, because a response to the first stimulus is still being processed.

Hence the **slowing down** of the processing of information between the relevant stimulus and an appropriate response. For example, defending a dummy in rugby (figure 3.16).

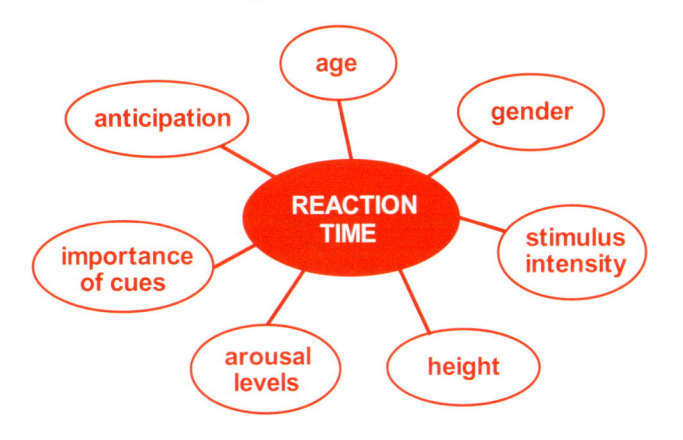

figure 3.16 – side step left then right

Psychological refractory period 47

SECTION 2 CHAPTER 3 — MEMORY MODELS

Psychological refractory period - example

Looking at figure 3.17, **S1** (1st stimulus) would be the dummy. **S2** (2nd stimulus) would be the definite move. If the dummy (**S1**) had been the only stimulus then the reaction would have been at time **R1**. In the meantime, **S2** has happened, but the performer cannot begin his or her response to this until the full reaction **R1** has been processed by the brain, so there is therefore a period of time (the **PRP**) after **S2** but before the time break to **R2** can begin. A person who can do a multiple dummy (figure 3.17), can leave the opposition with no time to react and hence miss a tackle.

figure 3.17 – psychological refractory period

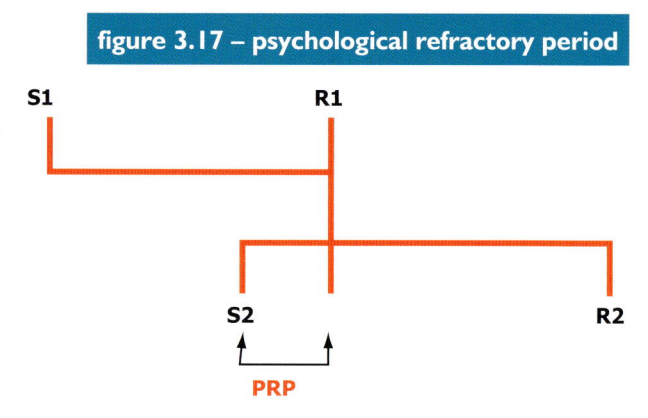

Single channel theory

This theory says that a performer can only attend to **one thing at a time**, so information is processed **sequentially**, that is one after another. Attentional switching would occur by **transferring attention** from one situation to another, so although attention would be **shared** between situations, only one situation would be attended to at a time (one then two then one then two). Therefore this can only be done if each situation requires **small** attentional capacity.

Anticipation

This is the ability to **predict** future events **from** early signals or **past events**.

Temporal anticipation is pre-judging **when** the future event will occur.
Spatial anticipation is pre-judging **where** and **what** the future event will be.

Reaction time can be **speeded up** if the performer learns to anticipate certain actions.

Good performers **start** running motor programmes **before the stimulus is fully recognised**, they anticipate the strength, speed and direction of a stimulus, which would enable a performer to partially eliminate the **PRP** (psychological refractory period).

However, **opponents** will also be trying to anticipate the performer's own actions, and a good performer will attempt to **increase** opponents' reaction times by increasing the number of choices of stimulus they have (this uses the choice reaction time theory, Hick's law - figure 3.14, page 47). For example, increasing the number of fakes or dummies.

Strategies to improve response times

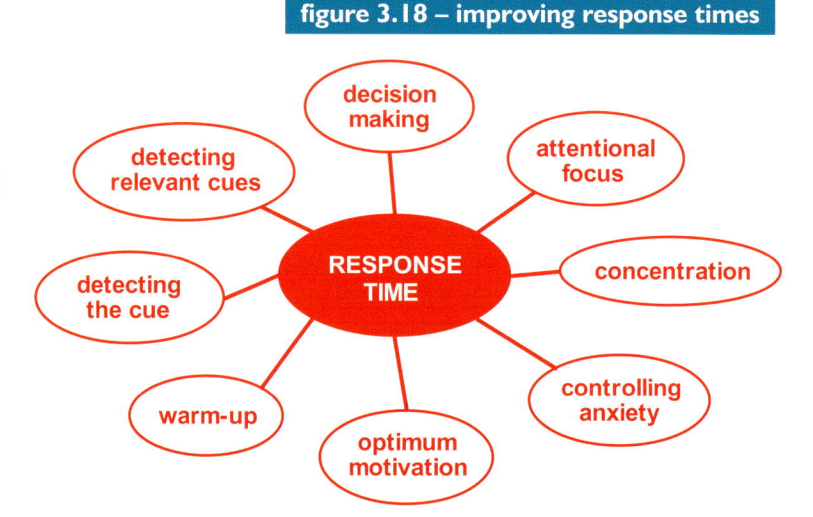

Response times can be improved using the following tactics (figure 3.18):

- **Detecting the cue**: in which the **stimulus** (starter's gun) is sorted out from the **background** (spectator noise).
- **Detecting relevant cues**: in which the relevant stimulus is picked out from other possible ones, and **choice reaction time is reduced** by eliminating alternative choices.
- **Decision making**: in which performers work on **set pieces** in open skill situations so that an **'automatic'** complex response can be made to a simple open stimulus.
- **Concentration**: in which there is a **change in attentional focus**, in which the performer practices **switches of concentration** quickly from one situation (for example, opponents in defence) to another (for example, field of play in attack).
- **Controlling anxiety**: Here, we know that anxiety would increase response times, so the performer would reduce anxiety by using **calming** strategies.
- **Creating optimum motivation**: in which the performer or team uses **psyching-up** strategies.
- **Warm-up**: which ensures that sense organs and nervous system are in their **optimum state** to transmit information and that the muscles are in an optimum state to act on it.

figure 3.18 – improving response times

SKILL ACQUISITION

Schmidt's schema theory

Schema theory

Schema theory (figure 3.19) explains how sports performers can undertake so many actions with very **little conscious control**.

The long-term memory **isn't big enough** to store all the motor programmes required. **Schema** theory says that **generalised motor programmes** exist which can be modified by taking in information while a skill is being performed. Hence the LTM has to store **far fewer** motor programmes, since any **new movement** can be performed by running a schema which **closely matches** the needs of the new movement. The **bigger** the schema the more **efficient** the movement, and large amounts of **varied practice** are needed to improve a schema.

Feedback is very important to **correct** and **update** a schema. A schema is made up of two elements (figure 3.20).

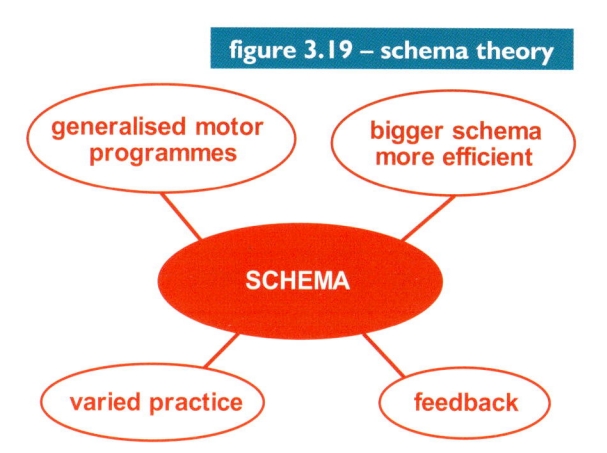

figure 3.19 – schema theory

- generalised motor programmes
- bigger schema more efficient
- SCHEMA
- varied practice
- feedback

Recall schema

The first element of a schema is the **recall schema** which consists of all the information needed to **start** a relevant movement.

This includes the **knowledge of the environment** (initial conditions):
- Playing conditions (pitch, playing surface, weather).
- Positions of team mates and opposition.
- Condition of equipment (kit, bike, car).

The recall schema also includes the **response specifications** (the correct technical model):
- Speed and force required.
- Size and shape of movement required.
- Techniques and styles used.

The recall schema is used for quick ballistic movements when there **isn't enough time** to process feedback.

Recognition schema

The second schema element is called a **recognition schema** which contains:

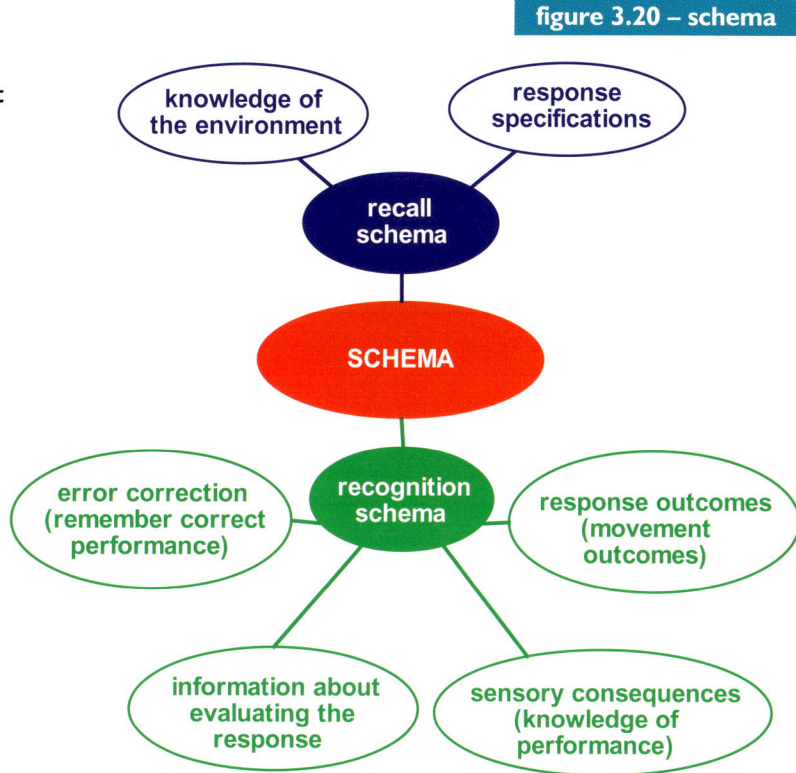

- Information needed to **correct errors** and remember **correct performance**.
- **Information** about evaluating the response.
- **Sensory consequences** (knowledge of performance) which would be the feeling and look of the performance.
- **Response outcomes** (movement outcomes) which would be the results of performance and the knowledge of results (how far, fast or many).

The recognition schema would be important when there is **enough time** to process feedback or for evaluating performance.

figure 3.20 – schema

- knowledge of the environment
- response specifications
- recall schema
- SCHEMA
- recognition schema
- error correction (remember correct performance)
- response outcomes (movement outcomes)
- information about evaluating the response
- sensory consequences (knowledge of performance)

Schmidt's schema theory 49

SECTION 2 CHAPTER 3 — MEMORY MODELS

> **STUDENT NOTE - SUMMARY OF SCHMIDT'S SCHEMA THEORY**
>
> 1. **Knowledge of environment (initial conditions)**, for example, a basketballer who is aware of how far he or she is away from the basket.
> 2. **Response specifications**, for example, the basketballer recognising that he or she must carry out a jump shot because of an opponent.
> 3. **Sensory consequences**, for example, the basketballer is intrinsically aware of his or her body movements as the jump shot is being performed.
> 4. **Movement** or **response outcomes**, for example, the basketballer being aware of whether or not the shot has succeeded.

Sporting application of schema theory

In the case of a tennis first serve (Andy Murray, figure 3.21), a single schema could perform most of the movement required and the content in Andy's brain would click onto this single item rather than the thousands of tiny elements which make up the serve.

The **recall schema** includes knowledge of the court, the playing surface, and the position of the opponent. Further inputs would be the speed of the serve required, and the precise direction (wide or narrow down the T). This would be performed without feedback (during the actual movement which is so quick that there would not be time for feedback to reach Andy's brain),

The **recognition schema** would provide the elements of the sensory consequences (the knowledge of where the serve actually ended up - was it returned? Was it in the required direction (the response outcome or knowledge of results)? Did it enable Andy to recover and begin a response to the return if made?

At this point feedback would inform Andy of the next movement in the game.

There would be a different schema for the second serve, which although it looks similar to the first serve (and technically it would be similar - the movements, rhythms and timing would appear similar to the first serve), it would feel completely different.

This must be true, since if the schema for the second serve were too similar to that for the first serve, the performer might mistakenly use the wrong serve at the wrong time in the game.

Top players like Andy are able to switch between these schema, and use the first serve when normally the second serve would be played.

Also, this schema could be used for an overhead smash, given that this is in a more open skilled situation.

figure 3.21 – schema for a tennis serve

SKILL ACQUISITION

Strategies to improve information processing

Retention of information and facts in the memory (figure 3.22) can be improved by:

Input:
- **Educate** the performer about the details of a skill.
- **Explain** what to do and how to do it.
- Ensure that input is **clear** and **uncluttered**.
- Keep advice or instruction **simple** and **clear.**
- **KISS** - keep it simple stupid.
- Carefully **separate** similar skills to enable the performer to distinguish between them
- Organise the process of skill learning to ensure the information is **meaningful**.
- Be **brief** and do **not overload** the short-term memory which can only hold small amounts of data.

Chunking:
- More information can be held in STM if information is **lumped together**.
- This is called chunking.

Chaining or association:
- **Link new** information **with old** already learnt information.
- Multiple links can form a chain.

Schema:
- **Practice makes perfect**.
- The more **practice** that can be done to a **correct technical model,** the better the **schema** will be formed and the better the immediate performance.
- Perfect practice makes a skill perfect.
- **Repetition** of any information or skill will enable it to be remembered better.

Response time:
- See page 47 for details of how to improve response time in the context of sporting activities.

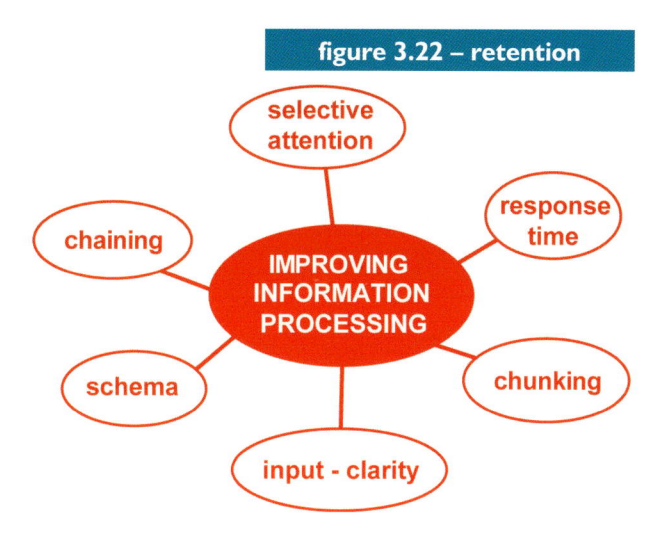

figure 3.22 – retention

Strategies to improve information processing

SECTION 2 CHAPTER 3
MEMORY MODELS

Practice questions

1) Which of the following best describes the sequence of activity in information processing?
   a. input data from display followed by action of the effector mechanism.
   b. input data received by receptor systems then analysed by peceptual mechanisms.
   c. input data received by the translatory mechanisms then feedback to input.
   d. input data analysed by receptor systems then effector mechanisms, then the musculsr system.

2) A signal carried from the brain to the muscular system which initiates movement is best described by which of the following processes?
   a. translatory mechanism.
   b. detection comparison recognition (DCR).
   c. selective attention.
   d. effector mechanism.

3) Selective attention is best described as:
   a. many bits of information are received.
   b. focusing on at least five bits of information.
   c. focus on the relevant bits of information from the many which are received.
   d. disregarding undesirable bits of information.

4) Which one of the following does not help in retaining memories?
   a. chunking.
   b. chaining.
   c. practice.
   d. overload.

5) A schema consists of recall and recognition elements, which one of the following best describes the features of recognition schema?
   a. response outcomes.
   b. sensory consequences followed by error correction.
   c. knowledge of performance followed by correct performance.
   d. information about evaluating a response before the correction of performance.

6) Which of the following best describes the meaning of reaction time?
   a. the time between the onset of a stimulus and the start of a response.
   b. the time it takes to complete the onset of a movement.
   c. the time it takes to process information then to make a response.
   d. the time taken to repond to multiple stimuli.

7) What is the predominant feature of anticipation?
   a. reaction time can be speeded up.
   b. a perfomer is delayed beginning the next motor programme.
   c. the ability to peridct future events from past events.
   d. a performer will attempt to reduce an opponents reaction times.

SKILL ACQUISITION

Practice questions

8) Identify the three main receptor systems used by a performer in sport.
   Where is the filtering mechanism found in an information processing model? Explain what happens with information as it passes through this mechanism. **8 marks**

9) Identify and describe the three elements of perception. **3 marks**

10) Improvement in performance of a skill can be better understood by reference to the processes involved. Figure 3.23 shows Whiting's information processing model.

   a) Explain the meanings of the terms: perceptual mechanism, translatory mechanisms, and effector mechanisms, and relate these terms to stages in the Whiting model. **5 marks**

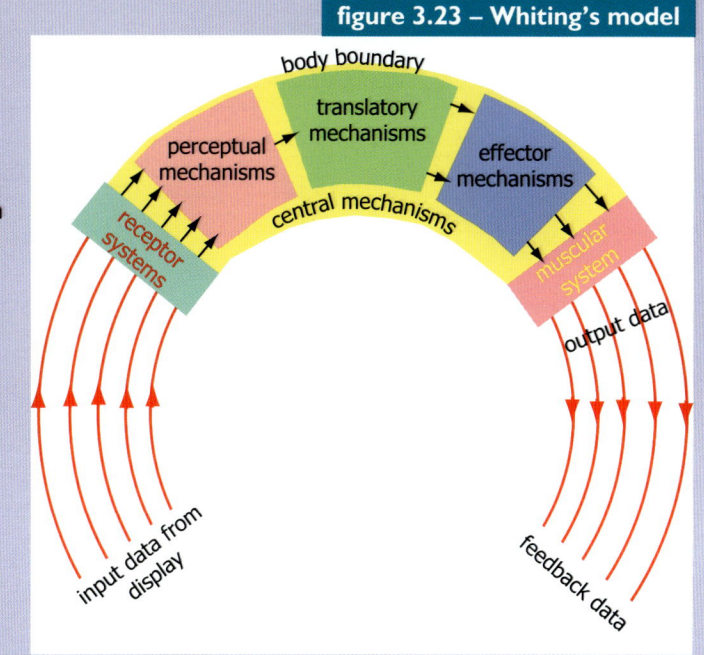

figure 3.23 – Whiting's model

   b) The diagram also shows five arrows entering the perceptual mechanism and only one leaving. What is the name given to this process and why is it necessary? **4 marks**

   c) Identify three factors which might help a performer with his or her perceptual mechanisms. **3 marks**

11) a) Using figure 3.24 representing the human motor control mechanism, explain what is meant by short-term memory and long-term memory. **2 marks**

figure 3.24 – human motor control mechanism

   b) How can information be retained in the long-term memory? **4 marks**

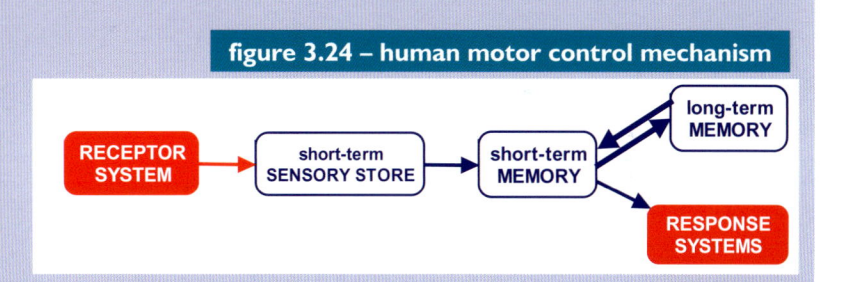

12) a) Using the example of a table tennis player receiving a serve, what information would be held in the short-term sensory store and for how long? **4 marks**

   b) Name and describe the purpose of the process by which information is transferred from the short-term sensory store to the short-term memory. **4 marks**

13) a) Explain the difference between reaction time, movement time and response time? What advice would you give to a sprinter to cut down on reaction time at the start of a race? **4 marks**

   b) Sketch and label a graph to illustrate Hick's Law.
   How does the number of choices available to a performer affect his or her performance? **4 marks**

   c) When taking part in a badminton game, the shuttle occasionally hits the netcord during a rally, and the receiver has to adjust his or her return shot. This causes a delay before the final response can be made. What is this delay called and explain why it occurs? **4 marks**

   d) What factors could affect response time in any game or sport? **4 marks**

Practice questions 53

SECTION 2 CHAPTER 3

PRINCIPLES AND THEORIES OF LEARNING, GUIDANCE AND FEEDBACK

Practice questions

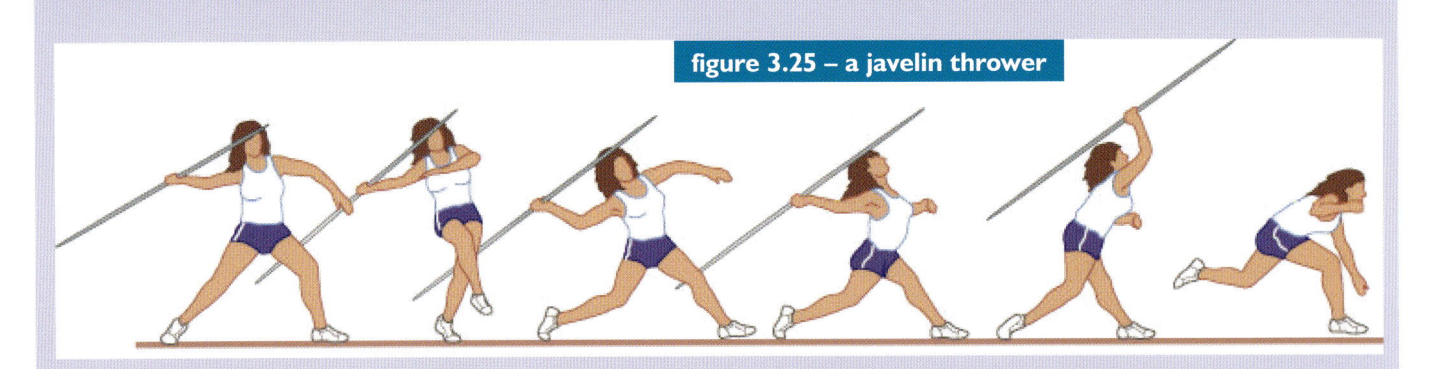

figure 3.25 – a javelin thrower

14) a) Looking at figure 3.25, using examples from javelin throwing, identify four items of information stored as schema. **4 marks**

b) Comparing the skills of throwing the javelin and taking a free throw at basketball, explain how the skills are related using schema theory. **4 marks**

c) Briefly explain how the analysis of skills will influence a coach in organising training for javelin throwing as compared with a basketball free throw. **4 marks**

15) a) Explain, using a sporting example, how the use of selective attention depends on an athletes' level of ability. **3 marks**

b) How can a coach improve an athlete's selective attention. **3 marks**

16) What is meant by Hick's Law? Illustrate your answer by plotting a graph which represents this theory. **7 marks**

17) During sporting situations it may be necessary to process information using memory systems.

What are the features and functions of the working memory?

Using figure 3.26 how can a single recall schema assist the attacking player to decide on his next move?

What strategies could the player use to improve his memory system? **15 marks**

figure 3.26 – soccer player's attack

Answers link: http://www.jroscoe.co.uk/downloads/a2_revise_pe_aqa/AQAA2_ch3_answers.pdf

SECTION 3

EXERCISE PHYSIOLOGY

CHAPTER 4
INJURY PREVENTION AND THE REHABILITATION OF INJURY

> **SECTION 3**
> **CHAPTER 4**

INJURY PREVENTION AND THE REHABILITATION OF INJURY

CHAPTER 4: Injury prevention and the rehabilitation of injury

Types of injury

figure 4.1 – sports injuries

A **sports injury** is any kind of injury, pain or physical damage that occurs as a result of sport, exercise or physical activity.

Sports injuries are unfortunately inevitable, and are dependent on a performer's intensity of training, the preparation he or she makes to avoid injury, and the ways in which rest and recovery are planned into a training and competitive programme. Figure 4.1 outlines the factors influencing how injuries are caused and can be dealt with.

Sports injuries are:
- Most commonly associated with the musculo-skeletal system, which includes muscles, joints and their associated tissues such as ligaments and tendons.
- Commonly classified as **acute** or **chronic**.
- Mild, moderate or severe.
- Characterised by pain, swelling, tenderness, weakness and the inability to use or place weight on the injured area.
- **Acute** injuries refer to sports injuries that happen in a moment.
- **Chronic** injuries are characterised by a slow, sustained development of symptoms, that culminate in a painful inflammatory condition.

Acute injuries

Common symptoms associated with acute sports injuries:
- Sudden severe **pain**.
- **Stretching painful** in the case of a muscle strain.
- Swelling, **inflammation**, bruising or tenderness over injured area.
- **Restricted mobility** above and below injured area.
- Loss of **stability** in the case of leg injuries.
- Loss of **function** in the injured area.
- **Protruding bone** from the skin in the case of a compound fracture.
- **Deformity** around injured area.
- Cold **purple colouration** of skin indicating a lack of proper blood circulation in that injured part.

Fractures
A bone fracture is a break in the bone and is caused by excessive external forces and so is classified as traumatic fracture. There are two major classes:
- **Simple fractures** (figure 4.2) are broken bones that remain within the body and do not penetrate the skin.
- **Compound fractures** are broken bones that penetrate through the skin and expose the bone and deep tissues to the exterior environment, creating an open wound with a risk of infection.

Dislocations
A dislocation occurs when the **bones which meet at a joint, are separated by a violent action so that the joint no longer functions**.
- For example, a shoulder dislocation occurs when a player's arm is forced outwards and upwards by a tackle or heavy landing and the shoulder joint pops out.
- Injuries can occur quite **easily** because the shoulder joint is a shallow ball and socket when compared to the hip joint.
- A dislocation is usually accompanied by a **sprain** (page 57).
- **Repeat dislocations** of the same joint are common because the initial dislocation stretches the joint capsule and ligaments, and results in joint hypermobility.

figure 4.2 – simple fracture

EXERCISE PHYSIOLOGY

Strains
- Muscles can be damaged both by **direct** trauma (impact) or **indirect** trauma (overloading).
- A strain (pull or tear) refers to **damage to muscle fibres** or its attaching tendons caused by a sudden stretching force or a very forceful contraction of the muscle.
- The tearing of the muscle can also damage small blood vessels, causing local bleeding, or **bruising** (known as a **haematoma**), and pain caused by **irritation of the nerve endings** in the area.
- The most common muscle injuries occur in **high speed activities** such as sprinting and weight lifting, which load muscles such as the hamstrings, quadriceps, calf, back and biceps.
- Muscle tears range from a mild to moderate to severe strains or complete rupture.

Sprains
- A ligament is an extension of a joint capsule consisting of tough, fibrous connective tissue that provides stability by joining bone to bone positioned inside a joint (intrascapular) and outside of a joint (extracapsular).
- In a sprain, **ligaments** reinforcing a joint are **stretched** or torn.
- When a ligament is torn completely, it can be replaced with a **graft**, for example, the anterior cruciate ligament of the knee joint can be replaced using a hamstring tendon graft.
- Common sites of sprains are the ankle, knee and thumb joints.
- Sprains happen most often in the **ankle** (figure 4.3) in sports that involve twisting and turning movements, such as in netball.
- Knee sprains are common football injuries.
- Thumb sprains are common in skiing and contact sports such as judo.

figure 4.3 – a sprained ankle

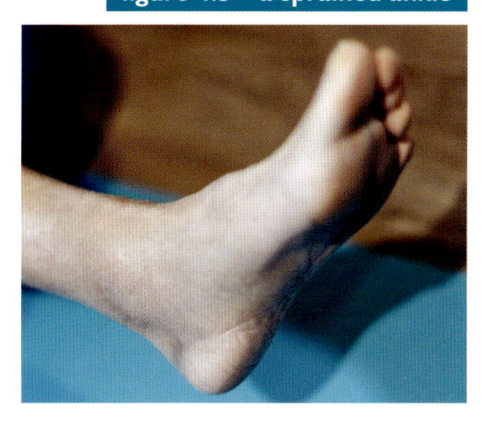

Ice therapy is a method used for acute joint and muscle injuries and is part of the traditional **RICE** First Aid procedure as follows:
- **Rest** - stop the activity as soon as the injury occurs to prevent making it any worse.
- **Ice** - apply to injured area for 10-15 minutes then remove for 20 minutes (and repeat) to reduce internal bleeding and swelling.
- **Compression** - reduces swelling, supports soft tissues, minimising further damage, and so speeds recovery.
- **Elevation** - elevating the injured area above the heart aids the drainage of any liquid/leakage caused by the injury thereby reducing swelling and inflammation.

Chronic injuries

Common symptoms associated with chronic overuse sports injuries:
- Chronic injuries start off with **mild symptoms** that enable performer to ignore the injury and carry on with his or her activities.
- Followed by a gradual **increase of pain** and inflammation over a period of time resulting from continued **overuse**.
- Increase in pain during sporting activity.
- Mild swelling after completion of sporting activity.
- Constant **aching** at rest.

Achilles tendon injuries
A **tendon** is a tough cord or band of dense white fibrous connective tissue which connects a muscle to a bone and transmits the force which the muscle exerts.
- Tendonitis is **inflammation** of tendon sheaths, caused by excessive stress being transmitted through the tendon.
- Achilles tendonitis occurs when the tendon that attaches the calf muscles to the heel becomes painful and inflamed.
- Weak calf muscles, poor ankle range of motion, and excessive pronation have all been connected with the development of Achilles problems.
- Achilles tendon injuries account for 5-12% of all running injuries.

Chronic injuries 57

SECTION 3 CHAPTER 4 — *INJURY PREVENTION AND THE REHABILITATION OF INJURY*

Stress fractures

A stress fracture is an **overuse** injury.
- It occurs when muscles become **fatigued** and are unable to absorb added shock.
- Eventually, the fatigued muscle transfers the overload of **stress to the bone** causing a tiny crack called a stress fracture.
- More than 50 percent of all stress fractures occur in the **weight-bearing bones** of the foot and lower leg because of the **repetitive** forces they must absorb.
- Stress fractures affect people of all ages who participate in repetitive sporting activities and are especially common in tennis players, runners, gymnasts, and basketball players.

Tennis elbow

The elbow joint is surrounded by muscles that move the elbow, wrist and fingers.
- The tendons in the elbow join the bones and muscles together, and control the muscles of the forearm.
- Caused by **overusing** muscles attached to the elbow and used to **straighten** the wrist.
- If the muscles and tendons are strained, tiny tears and inflammation can develop near the bony lump (the lateral epicondyle) on the outside of the elbow joint.
- Tennis elbow is a common injury associated with racket sports such as tennis, badminton and squash.

Recovery from chronic injuries takes time and needs careful programming to restore the individual back to pre-injury activity levels using many of the rehabilitation methods discussed on page 62 onwards.

Injury prevention methods (figure 4.4)

There is a growing body of evidence to support the use of scientifically tested exercise and training methods that help prevent certain injuries in certain sports.

Screening

Screening is a search for a **specific** condition and plays a key part of the professional sportspersons daily life. **Regular** screening identifies past and current injuries, which can lead to specific exercise prescriptions aimed at managing the condition and preventing further injury.

Screening can help to detect health risk factors. For example, British Athletics has worked with **Cardiac Risk in the Young** (CRY) for several years, providing a screening service to athletes on the World Class Performance Programme. Sport itself does not lead to cardiac arrest, but can trigger a sudden death by aggravating an undetected cardiac abnormality. CRY can prevent such fatalities.

Physiotherapy screening services are designed for sports persons of all ability. Standard tests are used to assess strengths and weaknesses in key areas, such as strength, flexibility (figure 4.5), core control and balance. This information can be used for **exercise prescription** for musculoskeletal conditioning thereby decreasing the risk of getting injured.

Screening can highlight **differences** between athletes. This can then direct conditioning training programmes to be set for various levels of fitness, to encourage the lower level athlete to strive to be able to compete with their teammates in training and games.

Regular screening provides information about **physical changes over time**, which is particularly important in the growing athlete and for an athlete following long hours of training or competition.

On the other hand, poor test selection and inaccurate readings may lead to a wrong diagnosis, greater susceptibility to injury and increases in a performer's anxiety levels.

figure 4.4 – injury prevention

- warm-up
- mobility training
- fitness training
- screening
- cool-down
- clothing

INJURY PREVENTION

figure 4.5 – sit and reach test

EXERCISE PHYSIOLOGY

Protective equipment and clothing

Many sports require specialist protective clothing (examples in figure 4.6), with well known examples from fencing, ice hockey, field hockey, cricket, baseball, American football and equestrianism.

Boxing and other martial arts require helmets (with or without face guards), padding, boxes, strapping, gloves, mouth guards and so on, depending on the rules of the sport, and the damage allowed to be
inflicted within the rules of the sport. All these pieces of equipment are designed to prevent injury to vulnerable parts of the body.

Specialist clothing is also required for low and high temperatures to maintain body temperature within a safe range.

Compression sportswear is thought to reduce the risk of muscle injury and speed up muscle recovery after injury.

Footwear are key items of an athlete's sports equipment. When choosing sports footwear, the sport involved and the playing surface must be considered.
Anyone participating in sports that require a lot of jumping and running such as jogging, tennis, basketball and football are more susceptible to repetitive strain injury.

figure 4.6 – specialist equipment for injury prevention

It is important therefore to wear **proper fitting** footwear that is **activity-specific**, to avoid putting him or herself at risk of injury to the soft tissues, bones or joints of the lower limb.

Warm-up

A warm-up is a session which takes place prior to doing physical activity, and warm-up activities are a crucial part of any exercise regime or sports training.

The importance of a **structured warm up** routine should not be underestimated when it comes to the prevention of sports injury. An effective warm up has a number of very important key elements that work together to minimize the likelihood of sports injury from physical activity:

- General **cardiovascular aerobic exercise**, such as jogging or stationary biking involving gross motor activity and major muscle groups.
- Mainly **active stretching** or flexibility of relevant joints and muscles. .
- **Sports specific activity** that includes specific dynamic flexibility exercises and strength or skill drills of increasing intensity up to the moment of the game or competition beginning.

Most warm-up sessions will last between 20 minutes and half an hour. This gives the body plenty of time to **gradually get ready** for physical activity.

The cardiovascular exercises are designed to **increase circulation**, increase **body temperature** and bring the **heart rate** up. By working at maximal steady state, energy is predominantly being supplied via the **aerobic** energy system without the athlete experiencing fatigue. Stretching warms the muscles and prepares them for the **movements** they will be required to carry out during the activity.

> **STUDENT NOTE**
>
> For full details of warm-up and flexibility training, refer to AS/A1 Revise PE for AQA, ISBN 9781901424850, Section 4, page 148 onwards.

SECTION 3 CHAPTER 4 — INJURY PREVENTION AND THE REHABILITATION OF INJURY

Warm-up

Explosive strength exercises, which may include sprint drills or jumps, gently increase the level of **intensity** and prepare the body for sudden movements in the game or activity which will follow. These exercises should only be done once the muscles are warm, thus reducing the risk of potential injuries.

A warm-up session can also be used to practice skills and team drills.
The aim of the **sports specific** part of the warm-up is to get the sportsperson into the rhythm and flow of their forthcoming activity, practice skills and movements expected later, and build up confidence before the event starts.

For example, a high hurdler will incorporate lead and side leg drills and practice starts to the first hurdle as final preparation for a race.

The most important reason for doing a warm-up is to prevent injury during exercise. Keeping the muscle tissue warm will reduce the risk of hamstring strains and will stave off **overuse** injuries by allowing the body to prepare steadily and safely.

In more static sports, such as cricket, it is a good idea to stretch **throughout** the game as this will keep the muscles warm and allow them to function effectively. Substitutes should also continue to run and stretch while they are waiting to join a game; this is commonly seen in football or rugby matches where the substitutes jog and stretch along the sidelines.

Types of stretching or flexibility exercises

Flexibility refers to '**the range of motion (ROM) that you can achieve at any joint through any particular movement**' and is joint specific. In simple language this can be expressed as how far you can reach, bend and turn.

Joint flexibility depends on the distensibility of the joint capsule, adequate warm-up, muscle viscosity and the compliance of ligaments and tendons. Flexibility is improved by stressing all these components.

There are two main types of stretching (figure 4.7):
- **Static**.
- **Dynamic**.

figure 4.7 – flexibility or stretching

STATIC STRETCHING: active, passive, static, PNF

DYNAMIC STRETCHING: dynamic, ballistic

Static stretching
Static stretching refers to **stretching exercises that are performed without movement**. In other words, the individual gets into a stretch position and holds the stretch for a specific amount of time.
Mostly used during a cool-down

Active stretching
Active stretching is **slow stretching in which flexibility is achieved without assistance**. This form of stretching involves using only the strength of the opposing muscles (antagonist) to generate a held stretch (held for 10-15 seconds) within the agonist. The contraction of the opposing muscles helps to relax the stretched muscles.

Passive stretching
Passive stretching is similar to static stretching, however a **partner or apparatus** can be used to help further stretch the muscles and joints. This is used by gymnasts working on ROM.

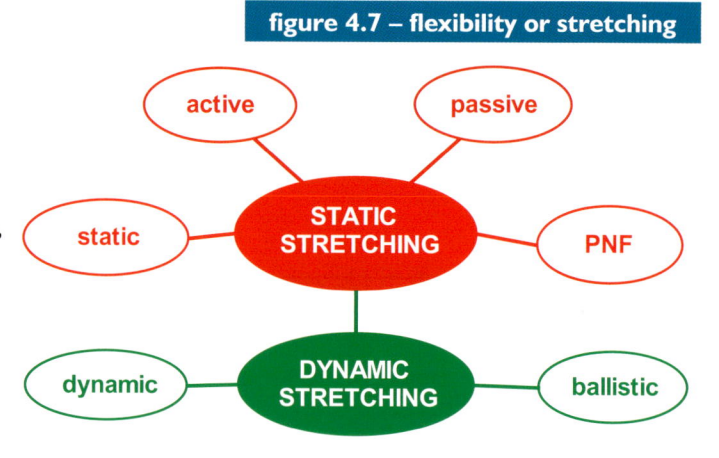

> **STUDENT NOTE**
>
> For details of PNF (proprioceptive neuromuscular facilitation) and dynamic stretching, refer to AS/A1 Revise PE for AQA, ISBN 9781901424850, pages 46 and 149 respectively.

EXERCISE PHYSIOLOGY

Ballistic stretching

This type of stretching **involves aggressive, dynamic, rapid, bouncing or swinging movements** during which the contraction of the agonist forces the antagonist to relax.

Ballistic stretching fails to allow the stretched muscle time to adapt to the stretched position and instead may cause the muscle to tighten up by repeatedly triggering the stretch reflex.

Ballistic stretching should be **used towards the end of a warm-up** because the muscle temperatures are slightly higher than at the start of the warm-up phase.

Taping and bracing

Taping

This is the process of applying tape to the skin.

- **Taping** has many roles including **supporting** and **compressing** ligaments and capsules of unstable joints by limiting excessive or abnormal anatomical movement. Taping also enhances proprioceptive feedback from the limb or joint.
- **Elastic adhesive bandage** is a lightweight strapping fabric that can be used for ankle taping, knee taping, hand taping and wrist taping, used by sports physiotherapists in the prevention and treatment of injuries such as sprained ankles.
- Tape can help relieve muscle pain, promote the healing process, prevent injuries, increase blood flow to muscles and joints, and strengthen weak or fatigued muscles.
- Many therapeutic tapes are highly elastic and adhesive, thus enabling the athlete to continue training and competing, whist offering protection and support to vulnerable body parts (figure 4.8).
- **Strapping** is often used in training, for example, strapping a shot putter's hand or gymnasts wrists.

figure 4.8 – therapeutic taping

Braces

- The risk of a sprained ankle and other similar injuries has been shown to significantly be reduced by wearing braces such as ankle supports (as worn by tennis star Andy Murray figure 4.9).

- Braces can offer hinged support providing greater stability to muscles and joints and are extensively used following major joint surgery (figure 4.10).

figure 4.9 – ankle bracing

figure 4.10 – hinged knee bracing

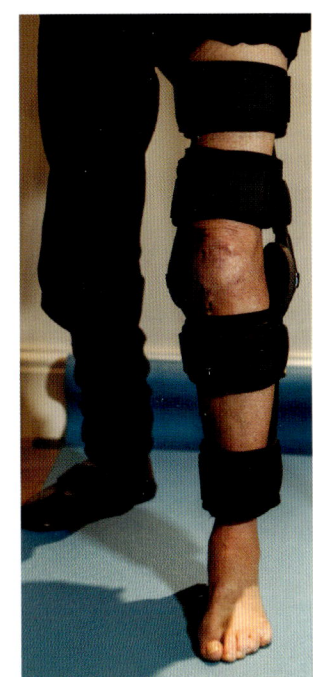

Cool-down following exercise

- **Cool-down** (the process of continuing low level exercise immediately after the end of a high intensity exercise bout) **continues to provide oxygen** to skeletal muscle.
- Using activities sych as light jogging and static and passive stretching.
- This therefore **enhances oxidation of lactic acid** and ensures that less lactic acid remains in tissue. Hence there is less muscle soreness (**less DOMS**).

Taping and bracing **61**

SECTION 3 CHAPTER 4
INJURY PREVENTION AND THE REHABILITATION OF INJURY

Injury rehabilitation

As well as reducing injury potential from acute and chronic injuries, it is the role of the medical team to use rehabilitation methods as a way of enhancing an athlete's recovery to full fitness. Figure 4.11 summarises the methods surrounding rehabilitation used after injury.

Rehabilitation is the process of restoring full physical function after injury.

Proprioceptive training

Proprioception is subconscious system that refers to the body's ability to sense movement within joints and joint position, enabling us to know where our limbs are in space without having to look.

It is made up of **receptor** nerves such as muscle spindles and golgi tendon organs that are positioned in the muscles, joints and ligaments around joints. These receptors can sense tension and stretch and pass this information to the brain where it is processed. The brain then responds by signalling to muscles to contract or relax in order to produce the desired movement.

Following injury to joints and ligaments the receptors are also damaged, which means the **information** that is usually sent to the brain is **impaired**. As a consequence the joint feels odd or just doesn't feel right.

Once a joint has been damaged, or a ligament has been torn or partially torn, there will be a **deficit** in the **proprioceptive ability** of the individual. This can leave the person prone to re-injury, or decrease his or her coordination during sport.

figure 4.11 – injury rehabilitation

- cryotherapy
- hyperbaric chambers
- proprioceptive training
- strength training
- hydrotherapy

REHABILITATION AFTER INJURY

STUDENT NOTE

For full details of proprioceptors in muscles, joints and tendons, refer to AS/A1 Revise PE for AQA, ISBN 9781901424850, Section 1, page 45 onwards.

Proprioceptive ability can be trained through **specific exercises**. For example, the use of a **wobble board** (figure 4.12) which is commonly used in the rehabilitation of **ankle injuries**, such as ankle sprains and other lower leg and **knee injuries**. In the case of the injured athlete, the improvement can compensate for the loss caused by injury.
This has the effect of decreasing the chances of re-injury.
Proprioceptive training also helps **speed** an athlete's **return to competition** following injury. The exercises should be initiated as soon as possible following injury.

figure 4.12 – wobble board exercise

Strength training

One of the major detraining effects that occur during long-term injuries is **muscular atrophy** of the unused limb. It is therefore essential that these particular muscles increase their size back to normal. Within the early stages of muscle rehabilitation, muscular size can be increased by effective electrical stimulation to the muscle (page 174).

Core stability exercises should not be neglected and can be combined with the start of performing some more traditional weight training exercises. The **plank** (figure 4.13) is one of the best body weight training exercises for improving core conditioning (which is often compromised following injury) but it also works gluteal and hamstring muscle groups, supports proper posture and improves balance.

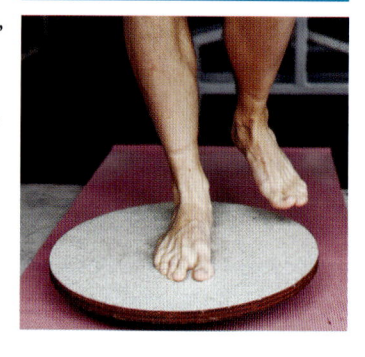

figure 4.13 – the plank

As soon as the injured athlete can tolerate increased loading her or she can progress through their rehab process back into more traditional strength and conditioning training programmes.

For example, free squats can progress to single leg squats.
Strengthening the quadriceps and hamstrings will directly result in increased stability of the knee joint and in turn further reduce the reoccurrence of hamstring injuries such as tears. The injured athlete will start to benefit from anatomical adaptations, such as **muscular hypertrophy** as he or she gradually progresses to pre-injury strength levels.

EXERCISE PHYSIOLOGY

Elastic band training and tubing

Elastic resistance is a unique type of resistance training that can be safely used in injury rehabilitation. The resistance provided by the latex **elastic band** or **tubing** is based on the amount that the band or tubing is stretched. Thera Band (a brand name for a type of elastic band of varying strength) elastic resistance training increases strength, mobility and muscle function, as well as reducing joint pain.

For example, following a shoulder injury, the main focus is to increase the **range of movement** and **muscle strength**, especially the rotator cuff which is a group of muscles that rotate the arm (figure 4.14).

figure 4.14 – Thera Band exercise

Hyperbaric chambers

Research has found that healing is promoted by increasing the oxygen partial pressure surrounding affected areas. The various techniques employed to promote this are:
- Oxygen tents.
- Sleeping in a greater than normal proportion of oxygen in breathed air.
- Hyperbaric (meaning high pressure) chambers (figure 4.15), in which an injured athlete will spend periods of time in a zone in which the air pressure is above normal.
- Therefore forcing oxygen above normal pressure into the body. This is called **hyperbaric oxygen therapy** (**HBOT**).

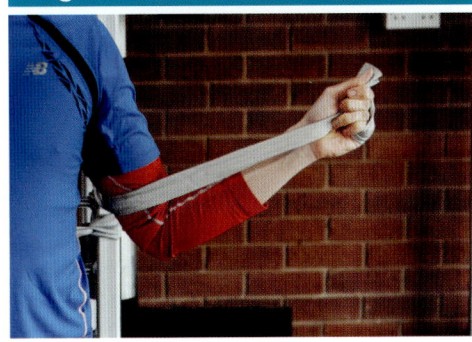

figure 4.15 – hyperbaric chamber

HBOT is a treatment which enhances the body's natural healing process by inhalation of 100% oxygen in a **total body chamber**, where atmospheric pressure is increased and controlled. Initially HBOT served to provide a means of therapy to facilitate a speedier resumption to pre-injury activity levels as well as improve the short and long-term prognosis of the injury.

HBOT sessions can commence as soon as the injured athlete has recovered from the initial treatment phase.

However, HBOT is now commonly used as a regular therapy within professional sports such as rugby, soccer and cricket, with its known benefits listed below. Such benefits allow athletes of every level to recover faster, perform sharper, and train longer.

HBOT benefits
- Delivers up to 25 times normal levels of oxygen to body tissues.
- Stimulates the **growth of new blood vessels**, thus improving blood flow to areas with an arterial blockage that may have resulted from an impact injury.
- Reduces **fatigue** from inadequate oxygen supply to body tissues.
- Speeds up **recovery** from fatigue such as DOMS.
- Boosts **immune** system function by stimulating white blood cell activity, thereby controlling infection.
- Decreases swelling and **inflammation**.
- Promotes **regeneration** of injured tissues.
- Decreases ligament and tissue **healing time**.
- Aids the **repair** of stress fractures and breaks.

Cryotheraphy

Cryotherapy is the treatment by means of applications of **cold temperatures**, and can be used as soon as the wound has healed. Cryotherapy treatment decreases skin, subcutaneous and muscle temperature, causing narrowing of the blood vessels (**vasoconstriction**). Its goal is to decrease cellular metabolism, decrease **inflammation**, pain and muscle spasm. A variety of cold applications can be used to treat sports injuries.

SECTION 3 CHAPTER 4 — INJURY PREVENTION AND THE REHABILITATION OF INJURY

Whole body cryotherapy (WBC)
WBC involves exposing individuals to extremely cold dry air (below -100°C) for two to four minutes in a **cryogenic chamber**.
Reduction in skin and muscle tissue temperatures reduces blood flow to the arms and legs (**vasoconstriction**) and divert blood flow to the body's central core.

On leaving the chamber, blood flow returns to the arms and legs (**vasodilation**) reinstating normal oxygen levels, thus aiding the healing process.
WBC relieves muscle soreness and **inflammation** following high intensity training, as a result of reduced muscle metabolism.
WBC is a much quicker alternative to ice baths, but does require specialist expensive equipment.

Alternative cold therapy methods
Various alternative and cheaper cooling therapies are used in acute sports injuries as well as rehabilitation of the injured athlete, injury prevention and recovery from training and competitions. For example, ice packs, ice towels, ice massage and frozen gel packs.

Ice baths
Ice baths (figure 4.16) use the fact that **chilling** the affected area can **reduce local inflammation**. The ice bath is thought to constrict blood vessels, flush waste products such as lactic acid and reduce swelling and tissue breakdown.

Total cold water immersion
Studies have shown that total cold water **upright immersion** (at an optimal temperature of 10 degrees and up to 10 minutes immersion) **decreases inflammation** following injury and aids recovery from training. The effect is best when the water pressure is greatest. In addition, it gives the athlete a feeling of perceived freshness.

Precautions should be taken because prolonged application of very low temperatures could have detrimental effects.

Hydrotherapy

Hydrotherapy is a therapeutic whole-body treatment that involves moving and exercising in a warm water pool. The temperature, pressure and movement of water are controlled and changed according to who's using the pool.

For example, **aquajogging** (figure 4.17) has proven to be a very good form of injury rehabilitation. This is because of its **low impact** on the muscles and the use of water resistance as an effective way of applying force to the lower limbs.

This combination avoids muscle soreness, stress fractures and aching joints and enables an injured athlete to **maintain fitness** during a rehabilitation programme. This method of hydrotherapy can be used as an alternative option to training on hard running surfaces, in addition to supporting recovery from hard impact training.

figure 4.16 – ice bath

figure 4.17 – aquajogging

EXERCISE PHYSIOLOGY

Recovery from exercise

Compression clothing

figure 4.18 – compression clothing

Compression clothing (figure 4.18) increases **venous return** and $\dot{V}O_{2max}$ during high intensity exercise. Recovery is improved and DOMS reduced. Products include socks, short and long tights and short-sleeve and long-sleeve tops. It is important that the compression garments fit well to get most benefit from wearing them.

Compression stockings are tight at the feet with a gradually looser fit on the leg (graduated compression). Compression stockings are known to decrease post-exercise soreness, by increasing circulation and reducing the lactic acid build-up during the exercise period, thereby reducing **DOMS**. Compression stockings are used to prevent medical conditions such as **deep vein thrombosis** (DVT).

Rest and active rest

- Modern rehab includes **rest** as essential recovery time after trauma. **Active rest** means that low level exercises are undertaken in order to improve the blood flow through affected areas without physical stress, and therefore to promote healing via blood carried nutrients, particularly oxygen.
- This also has the effect of preventing a muscle or other soft tissue from healing at a shorter length than it was before the injury. This is because post-trauma muscle length is unpredictable depending on joint flexibility and nutrition.
- Low level activity also has the effect of keeping muscle fit enough to exert force once an injury is healed.

Massage

figure 4.19 – roller massage

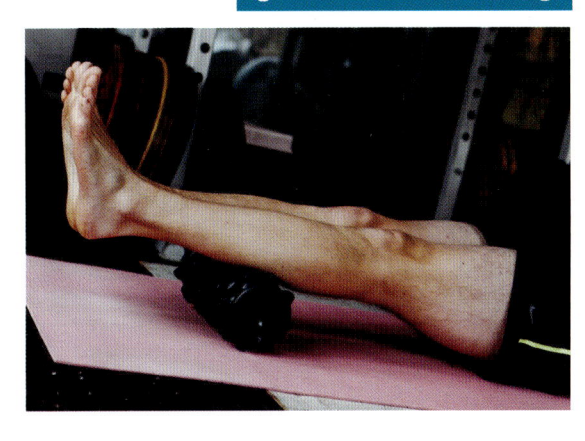

During **massage** (also used in rehab from injury), joints and associated muscles can be passively moved to full range. Massage helps reduce DOMS symptoms. Care must be taken that excessive forces are not applied to traumatised tissue.

Regularly using a **foam roller** offers a much cheaper way and has many of the same benefits as a sports massage, including reduced inflammation, scar tissue and joint stress, as well as improved circulation and improved flexibility (figure 4.19).

Rolling breaks down knots that limit range of motion, it preps muscles for stretching and so is a valuable part of a healthy runner's warm-up and cool-down.

Sleep and nutrition for improved recovery

Whilst training and diet play an important part in improving recovery, getting a **good night's sleep** is just as important.

The two main types of sleep are rapid-eye-movement (**REM**) sleep and non-rapid-eye-movement (**NREM**) sleep.

REM consolidates learning, and learned muscle movements are moved into the **long-term memory** (discovered in extensive experiments with sleeping people).

NREM consists of stages of sleep which get progressively **deeper** and during which most of the recovery from the day's activities takes place. During NREM brain waves are at their slowest and heart rate, body temperature and blood pressure all decline. **Blood flow** is redirected towards muscles and organs, and carries nutrients such as oxygen, amino acids and glucose that support substantial **tissue repair** and muscle and liver **glycogen** restoration.

SECTION 3 CHAPTER 4

INJURY PREVENTION AND THE REHABILITATION OF INJURY

Sleep for improved recovery

During sleep the body produces extra **protein** molecules that help strengthen the body's immune system.

Sleep requirements vary depending on age and activity level of the individual. Most elite athletes will train twice a day and have an afternoon nap, aimed at giving the body short-term recovery before the start of the second training session of the day. This is in addition to 8-9 hours sleep each night.

Post-competition or training nutrition for improved recovery

When an athlete completes a hard training session, **glycogen depletion** will have taken place.
It is essential that a **restoration** of energy stores is completed for recovery of the athlete prior to the next session or competition.

Post-competition or **training nutrition** should consist of:
- A **hypertonic** sports drink (figure 4.20) immediately after exercise has finished.
- This begins **replenishment of blood glucose** and **glycogen** stores.
- A **high CHO** meal within 15 minutes of exercise ending (or as soon as possible) continues glycogen replenishment.

- For optimal recovery, carbohydrate mixed with protein enhances all-round recovery due to an increase in **protein synthesis** post-exercise.
- Many athletes regularly consume sports drinks (figure 4.20) that are designed to supplement the **energy**, **fluid** and **protein** needs of the athlete.

- **Protein supplements**, such as whey protein, enable muscle hypertrophy and muscle repair following hard training.
- This particularly applies to sports requiring large muscle mass, as in weight lifting and gymnastics.

- During a hard training session **micro muscle tears** occur and can cause **local inflammation**.
- Some foods contain **anti-inflammatory** agents as found in avocados, fish (mackerel and salmon), mixed nuts, seeds and garlic.
- **Avoid** pro-inflammatory foods, such as **processed foods** high in saturated fats, and foods containing trans fats found in cakes, pies and cookies.
- Eat foods that are rich in **vitamins** and **minerals**.
- For example, vitamin D is found in fatty fish, eggs and dairy produce, aids the absorption of calcium and phosphorus needed for skeletal recovery and repair.

- **Iron**, found in dark green vegetables such as spinach, is a **constituent of haemoglobin**.
- Iron therefore helps the transfer of oxygen in red blood cells.

Most elite athletes are advised by nutritionists who can assess the requirements of the individual's needs based on the training or competition demands and the **severity** of the training phase.

figure 4.20 – sports drinks

EXERCISE PHYSIOLOGY

Practice questions

1) Elevation of an injured body part helps reduce injury by:
   a. helping support the weight of the limb.
   b. allowing white bold cells to be released to fight infection.
   c. reducing blood flow to the area.
   d. increasing blood flow to the area.

2) Overuse of tendons in physical activity can cause problems. Which one of the following symptoms is associated with tendon overuse?
   a. inflammation.
   b. arthritis.
   c. hypertrophy.
   d. bruising.

3) Which one of the following is not a method of reducing risks of injury when participating in physical activities?
   a. wearing shin pads when playing hockey or football.
   b. making sure you warm up before participating in an exercise class.
   c. playing with others of similar ability in a rugby match.
   d. wearing fashionable sports equipment when going to the gym.

4) A sprain during a sport activity is to be immediately attended to by:
   a. application of ointment.
   b. elevation of affected body part.
   c. cold compression.
   d. massage.

5) Which one of the following would you recommend to prevent inflammation of the joints during or after physical activity?
   a. rub massage oil into your joints before and after exercise.
   b. use carbo-loading to increase energy levels.
   c. stretch your muscles thoroughly before exercising.
   d. do not do too much activity at any one time.

6) Why are joint sprains a particular problem? — 2 marks

7) Sports injuries can be broadly classified as either acute or chronic injuries. Explain what is meant by these two classifications, using examples where appropriate. — 4 marks

8) Playing kit and equipment are major factors that an athlete needs to consider in injury prevention. Identify the key factors that affect the selection of their use. — 4 marks

9) Discuss the principles and guidelines for injury prevention. — 5 marks

10) Why should stretching be part of an injury preventative training programme? — 2 marks

11) Hyperbaric oxygen chambers and ice baths are aids to rehabilitation for elite performers. Briefly describe how each of these therapies assist in this process. — 6 marks

SECTION 3 CHAPTER 4
INJURY PREVENTION AND THE REHABILITATION OF INJURY

Practice questions

12) Warm-up and cool-down are useful in preventing injury and in aiding the recovery process after intense exercise.
    a) What activities would you include in the warm-up and why?   3 marks

    b) What would you include in the cool-down and why?   3 marks

13) Screening is a key part of the professional sportspersons daily life. How can it be used in injury prevention?   4 marks

14) Rapid recovery from injury is vital for elite performers and they now use a wide range of injury recovery techniques.
    For each of the following methods describe the treatment and its purpose.
    a) Cryotherapy.   3 marks

    b) Proprioceptive retraining.   3 marks

    c) Therapeutic massage.   3 marks

15) Explain how the use of an ice bath can help to reduce the delayed onset of muscle soreness (DOMS).   4 marks

16) Discuss the importance of sleep and nutrition for improved recovery after training and competitions.   15 marks

Answers link: http://www.jroscoe.co.uk/downloads/a2_revise_pe_aqa/AQAA2_ch4_answers.pdf

SECTION 4

BIOMECHANICAL MOVEMENT

CHAPTER 5
LINEAR MOTION

CHAPTER 6
ANGULAR MOTION, PROJECTILE MOTION AND FLUID MECHANICS

SECTION 4 CHAPTER 5

LINEAR MOTION

CHAPTER 5: Linear motion

Linear motion

Linear means in a straight line. Chapter 5 attempts to put into perspective concepts involving movement in a single direction such as speed, velocity, acceleration and force (through Newton's Second Law of Motion).

> **STUDENT NOTE**
>
> Newton's first, second and third laws of motion are discussed in detail in AS/A1 Revise PE for AQA, ISBN 9781901424850, Section 5 page 162 onwards.

Scalars and vectors

The ideas behind **scalars** and **vectors** are used extensively in maths and physics.

Scalar

A **scalar** is a quantity which has size or value only. Quantities like mass, speed, energy, power, and length have a value only. For example, a person could have a mass of 60 kg, or 1000 joules of energy are used up when performing an exercise.

No directional angle is required when talking about these quantities.

Energy is a scalar which has a value only, and the value of energy consumed daily by a Tour de France cyclist is 6,000 kilocalories - which has no direction.

Speed (measured in metres per second - ms^{-1}), distance and time are scalars which are linked by a simple equation.

Speed = distance travelled per second (ms^{-1})

Speed = $\dfrac{\text{distance travelled in metres (m)}}{\text{time taken to travel in seconds (s)}}$

Vector

A **vector** is a quantity which has **size** (called magnitude) and **direction**. By quantity we mean something like weight, displacement, velocity, acceleration, force, and momentum, all of which are vectors, and therefore have to have a direction connected to them as well as value or size. For example, a force could be 100 newtons downward (the downward specifies the direction), an acceleration could be 10 metres per second squared forwards (the forwards specifies the direction).

Usually in maths, the direction is specified by the angle θ (measured in an anticlockwise direction to the x-axis) in a graph of an arrow drawn on the graph, with the size (magnitude) represented by the length of the arrow (figure 5.1).

figure 5.1 – direction of a vector

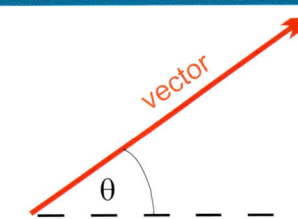

Force as a vector

Force is a vector and therefore has a direction (shown as angle θ to the horizontal in figure 5.1) as well as a size or value. This point is very important to anyone thinking about what happens when forces are applied, because it enables a force in one direction to cancel out completely an equal force in the opposite direction so that, in spite of very large forces being involved in a given situation, forces cancel out to give a **zero** (or very small) net or **resultant force**.

BIOMECHANICAL MOVEMENT

Force as a vector

A **resultant vector** is **two or more vectors added together**, taking into account their directions.

For example, consider the weight lifter in figure 5.2. As he pulls upwards on the bar, he exerts a force of 1000 newtons (N) upwards on the bar and gravity exerts a force of 980 newtons downwards on the bar.

The resultant or net force acting on the actual bar is therefore only about 20 N upwards, just enough to accelerate the bar off the floor.

The idea that net force causes acceleration is linked with **Newton's First** and **Second Laws** of Motion and is a fundamental property of force.

Also, it is possible for many forces acting in all sorts of different directions to cancel one another out. When this happens, from Newton's First Law we know that the object (or sportsperson) on which the forces act will either be stationary or moving at constant velocity (in a straight line). This situation is called **equilibrium**: where the object is stationary this is static equilibrium and where it is moving at constant velocity this is dynamic equilibrium.

Net Force

The point of this is that when more than one vector has to be taken into account, then they must be added together taking note of the direction of each vector.

In figure 5.3 for example, two forces of 500 newtons are acting, the green force acts upwards, and the red force acts downwards. Because they are acting in opposite directions, they add up to nil, in other words they exactly cancel out to give zero net force. Note that this gymnast is also in unstable equilibrium.

- In figure 5.4, the **vertical forces** acting on the sprinter are the weight (W = force due to gravity) acting downwards, and the ground reaction force (R) acting upwards. These two forces are identical in value but opposite in direction and therefore cancel out exactly to give zero net force vertically.
- The **horizontal forces** are the friction force (F) acting forwards, and the **air resistance** or **drag** (A) acting backwards. These two forces are equal in value but opposite in direction, and hence cancel out to give zero net force acting horizontally.
- Hence relatively large forces can act, but they can cancel out because of their direction. Note that zero net force does not mean that the sprinter is stationary, (from Newton's first law of motion).
- Equally, when the forces are added up and there is an unbalanced **resultant** (the forces **do not cancel out**), then there is a **net force** acting. The body on which this force is acting will then accelerate in the **direction** of this net force as specified by Newton's second law.

figure 5.2 – forces acting on a bar

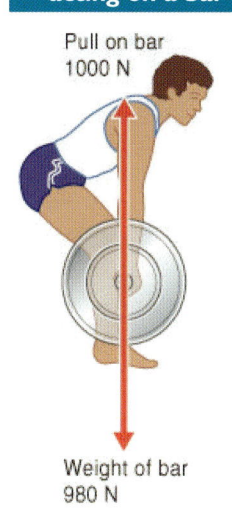

figure 5.3 – vectors cancel out

figure 5.4 – forces cancel out

SECTION 4
CHAPTER 5
LINEAR MOTION

Further notes on vectors

There are specific mathematical rules that enable you to add together vectors that are not in the same direction. You may notice from figures 5.5 and 5.6 that the resultant of two forces at an angle has been drawn by completing a **parallelogram** (in figure 5.5) or a **rectangle** (in figure 5.6, where the forces are at right angles). The resultant then lies along the diagonal of the parallelogram.

In figure 5.5, the resultant of the forces in the wires (T_1 and T_2) supporting the gymnast upwards **cancels out** exactly his/her weight (W) downwards (static equilibrium).

figure 5.5 – forces balance

figure 5.6 – forces balance

In figure 5.6, again, the **resultant** of the normal reaction force (R) and the combined friction forces (air resistance and friction with the ground) exactly cancels out the weight of the skier – note the geometric vector diagram (dynamic equilibrium).

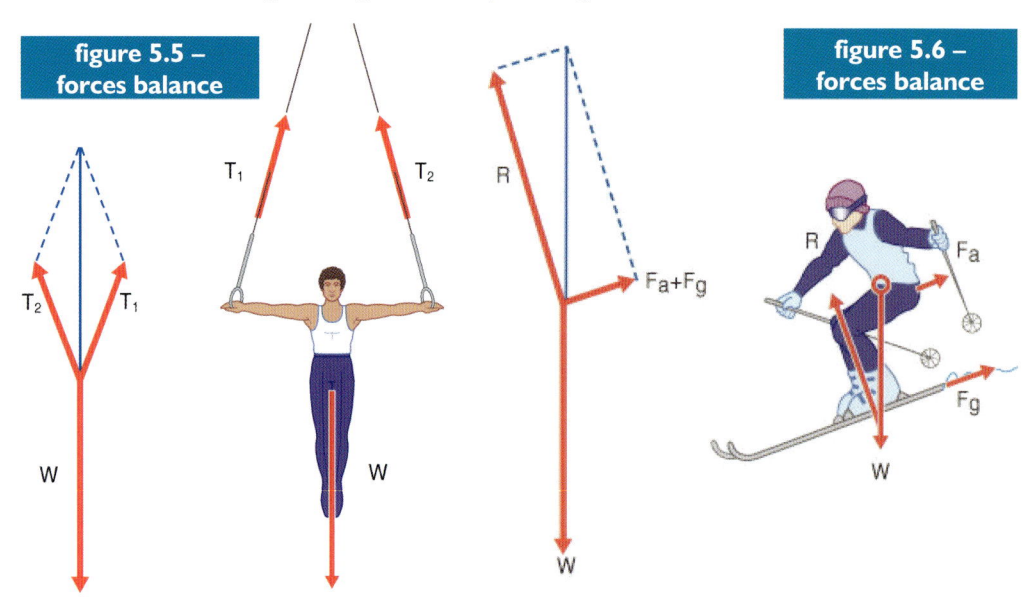

Figure 5.7 shows **resultants of forces** acting on a swimmer. His weight (W) is balanced by the upthrust of the water (U) and the forward thrust (T) cancels out the backward drag (D) of the water (again dynamic equilibrium).

figure 5.7 – forces balance

Resultants

It is also possible to calculate the size and direction of resultant vectors using trigonometry. Looking at figure 5.8, in which R (the reaction force) and F (the total friction force) are at right angles, we note that angle α lies between F and the resultant X of the two vectors as drawn. Therefore using Pythagoras theorem on figure 5.8:

X^2 = $R^2 + F^2$ and
X = $\sqrt{(R^2 + F^2)}$
 = the magnitude of the resultant ($\sqrt{}$ = 'square root of').

Also:
$\tan \alpha$ = $\dfrac{R}{F}$
and α = the angle between X and R, which gives the direction of the resultant.

Hence, looking at figure 5.8, the normal reaction force on the sprinter's foot has the value 700 N and the forward friction force 200 N, so that the resultant total reaction force on his/her foot, X, has the magnitude:

X = $\sqrt{(700^2 + 200^2)}$ = $\sqrt{(530\,000)}$ = 728 N

The angle α between X and the 700 N force will be:

α = $\tan^{-1} \left(\dfrac{R}{F}\right)$ = the angle between X and R which gives the **direction** of R.
 = $\tan^{-1} \left(\dfrac{700}{200}\right)$ = $\tan^{-1} 3.5$ = 74.06°

figure 5.8 – resultant force

Hence the resultant force has a **value** of 728 N acting at an **angle** of 74.06° to the 200 N force (horizontal). Note that this force X passes through the centre of mass of the runner and therefore would cause no toppling or rotation of his/her body during the running action.

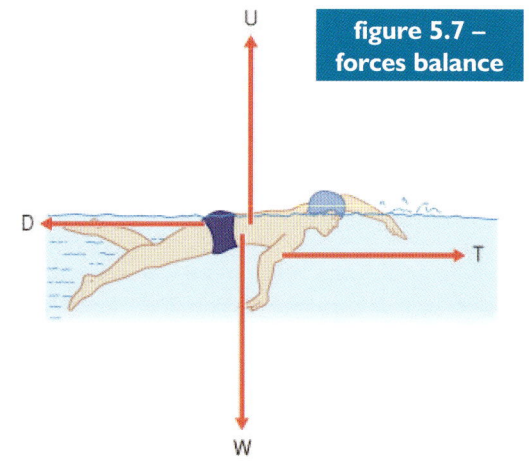

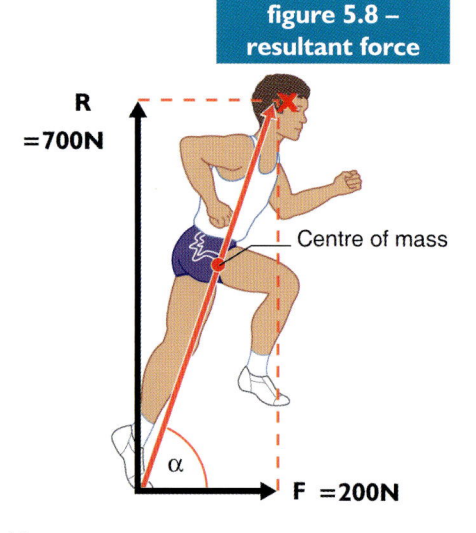

BIOMECHANICAL MOVEMENT

Components of a vector

It is possible to do the opposite of this process and split a single force into two parts at right angles to one another – this is called **taking components**. This is particularly useful when looking at **vertical** and **horizontal** components of a force, it might enable you to see how a complicated set of forces could add up or cancel out in relation to the weight of an object, which is always vertical.

The components together with the original force form a right-angled triangle (figure 5.9). Then we see that:

$$\frac{F_v}{F} = \sin \alpha \quad \text{and} \quad F_v = F \sin \alpha$$

and:
$$\frac{F_h}{F} = \cos \alpha \quad \text{and} \quad F_h = F \cos \alpha$$

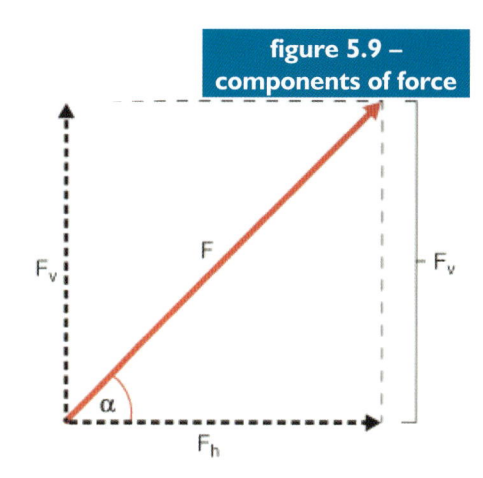

where F_v = the vertical component of F, F_h = the horizontal component of F (the original force) and α = the angle the original force makes with the horizontal.

Note that either the original force or the components can be used, but not both together.

figure 5.9 – components of force

Looking at figure 5.10 of a discus in flight with a velocity of 25 m s^{-1} at an angle of 35° to the horizontal (approximately the situation at the moment of release of an international-standard thrower), the **vertical** and **horizontal components** of this velocity can be calculated as for forces (velocity is a vector and obeys the same rules as forces):

vertical component of velocity
$$V_v = 25 \times \sin 35° = 14.34 \text{ m s}^{-1}$$
horizontal component of velocity
$$V_h = 25 \times \cos 35° = 20.48 \text{ m s}^{-1}$$

figure 5.10 – discus in flight

$V_v = 14.34$ m s^{-1}
$V_h = 20.48$ m s^{-1}

It is worth noting in this example that the vertical component changes with time (since gravity acts vertically downwards and will accelerate the discus – change its velocity – continuously in a downward direction), whereas the **horizontal component hardly changes** throughout the flight since the horizontal forces (i.e. air resistance) that would produce a change in horizontal velocity are small compared with the weight.

It is beyond the scope of this book to progress these ideas further (physics text books will provide many examples of the use and practice of the formulae).

Distance, position and displacement

Speed (a **scalar**) and **velocity** (a **vector**) are ideas that involve a body or object changing its position. For example, if an athlete starts a race – the stopwatch or electronic timer starts also – and he runs 10 m in 2 seconds, his position has changed by 10 m from the start line, the distance moved is 10 m and the average speed over this distance is 5 metres per second.

The same idea could be used in a game situation but now the position of the centre-forward might be 20 m out from the opposing goal, on a line 10 m to the left of the left-hand post. At this point he might shoot for goal and the ball travels 25m – the distance from the striker to the net at the back of the goal – in 0.5 seconds. In this case the speed of the ball would be 50 metres per second.

So, you can see that distance is usually measured from one point to another point and the position of the points tells us where they are in space (or on a pitch or court). This distinction becomes important in races or games where starts and finishes are fixed.

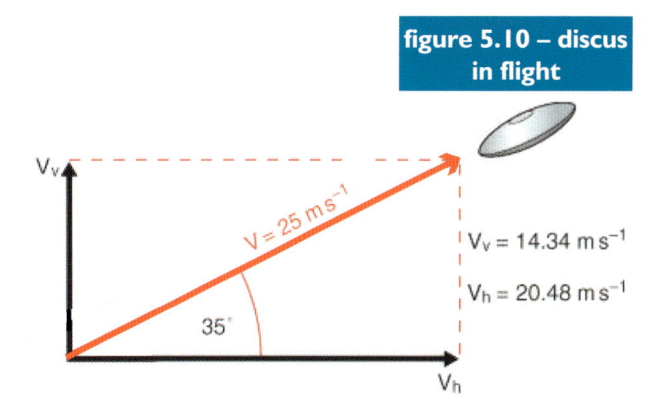

Distance, position and displacement

SECTION 4 CHAPTER 5 — LINEAR MOTION

Distance, position and displacement

The **displacement** of a sportsperson from the start of an event may also be important in some cases. For example, a triathlete may swim, cycle and run huge distances but he/she may only be displaced at most 2km from the start position. So the displacement of the triathlete is the distance (as the crow flies) between the start position and the position of the triathlete – usually the direction is also taken into account.

Speed and velocity

The difference between these two apparently similar concepts, is that velocity has direction and is therefore a vector, whereas speed is a scalar and has size only.

Both are expressed as metres per second and are defined by the same formula:
(**v = distance/time**), velocity is a vector and has value and direction whereas speed is a scalar and has value only.

Sometimes, it doesn't actually make any difference whether we use speed or velocity to describe the motion of a sportsperson or object, because he, she or it always moves in the same direction. But once the direction changes, it is important to use velocity to describe the motion. This is because the definition of **acceleration** is:

$$\text{change of } \textbf{velocity} \text{ per second}$$

So if the direction changes, so will the velocity and there will be an acceleration and a force (by Newton's Second Law).

figure 5.11 – tennis ball will have velocity

BIOMECHANICAL MOVEMENT

Weight and mass

These two ideas are often confused. **Mass** is a scalar and represents the total quantity of matter in an object. **Weight** is the force due to gravity on a mass (with a direction towards the centre of the Earth). Weight will vary slightly over the surface of the Earth depending on the gravitational field strength.

The gravitational field strength changes slightly depending on the thickness of the Earth's crust, the longitude, the proximity of large mountains, and the height above sea level. Weight is approximately 10 newtons for each kilogramme of mass (the actual figure is 9.81 N kg^{-1} but it is usual to approximate this to 10 N kg^{-1} to simplify calculations), and will act on the **centre of mass** of a body (the point which represents the averaged position of all the mass of a body), as covered in the AQA AS/A1 book section 5 page 165 in this series).

Hence if the mass of a sprinter is 50 kg, then her weight would be 50 x 10 = 500 newtons **towards** the centre of the Earth.

Weight is also the predominant force acting on an object projected into flight.

Weight

Gravity is an example of a force field (others occurring in nature are electromagnetic and nuclear fields which are not relevant to this text).

A **force field** is a means by which a force can be exerted **without touching**. So, for example, a ball in flight is accelerated towards the earth's centre continuously and therefore has a net force acting on it without being in contact with the earth.

When thinking about this, you may be confused by the fact that the air surrounds the ball (figure 5.12, since the ball is in contact with the air, which in turn is in contact with the earth). However, experiments on falling objects have been done **in a vacuum**, which confirm the concept of the 'non-touching' force.

figure 5.12 – weight acting on a ball in flight

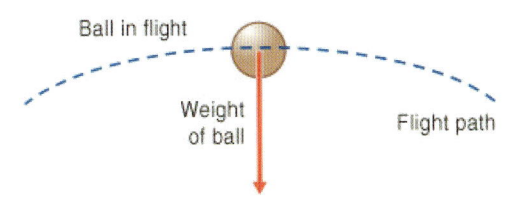

Mass

Not only is mass related to the **total quantity of matter** in an object or body, and not related to the gravity field strength, but linked closely to the idea of inertia, as explained by Newton's first and second laws of motion.

Inertia is explained as **resistance to acceleration**. The more inertia an object has, the harder it is to accelerate when a given force is applied. This is why it is a good idea for any sportsperson who has to change speed or direction rapidly or accelerate from rest to have the least body mass possible consistent with the necessary strength. **Inertia** is derived from **Newton's First** and **Second Laws**, the quantity m in the formula F = m × a relates exactly to this, so inertia is therefore a property of mass and consequently a property of all objects.

figure 5.13 – sprinters have inertia

Inertia also applies to decelerating objects or people, so that, once moving, an object requires a force to slow it down or stop it. For example, at the end of an indoor 60 m sprint, runners have difficulty in stopping (figure 5.13); this is because of the inertia of their mass.

SECTION 4 CHAPTER 5 — LINEAR MOTION

Graphs and curves of motion

Graphs of distance against time

The following graphs of **distance against time** will show the progress of an object as it moves along. In graph 5.14A, the distance remains the same as time goes along - which means that the object remains in the same place, there is **no movement**, the object is stationary, with speed zero.

In graph 5.14B, the distance changes with time - meaning that the object is **moving forward**, and eventually it comes to a halt with zero speed, so it **slows down** as the speed reduces to zero.

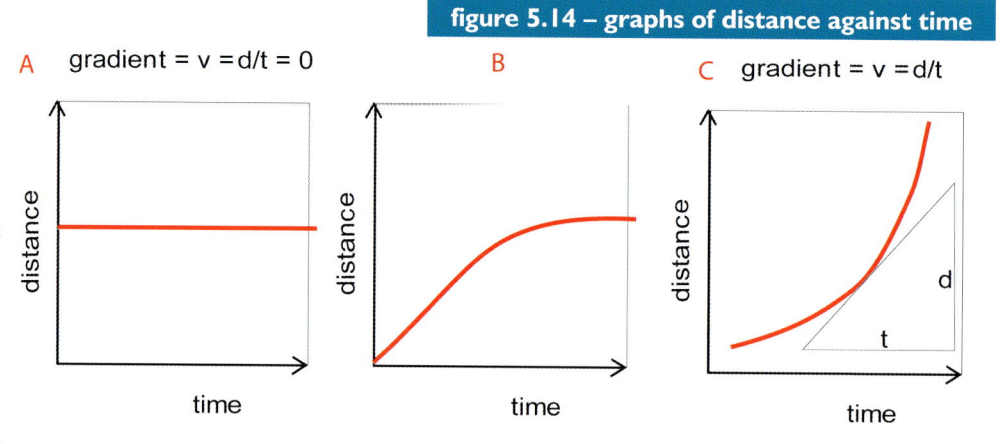

figure 5.14 – graphs of distance against time

A gradient = v = d/t = 0
B
C gradient = v = d/t

What changes is the **gradient** of the graph, and this is explained in graph 5.14C. The gradient is defined as the rate of change of speed with time and this is the gradient as shown in the graph.

$$speed = \frac{d}{t}$$

So the steeper the gradient or **slope** of the graph, the faster the movement and the greater the speed or velocity.

Graphs of speed/velocity against time

Graphs of **velocity against time** show how velocity changes with time and here, the gradient is the acceleration of the moving object

$$acceleration = \frac{change\ of\ velocity}{time\ taken\ to\ change}$$

In graph 5.15A, the velocity **remains the same**, the gradient of the graph is **zero**, therefore the body's acceleration is zero. This body has **constant velocity** and is subject to Newton's first law.

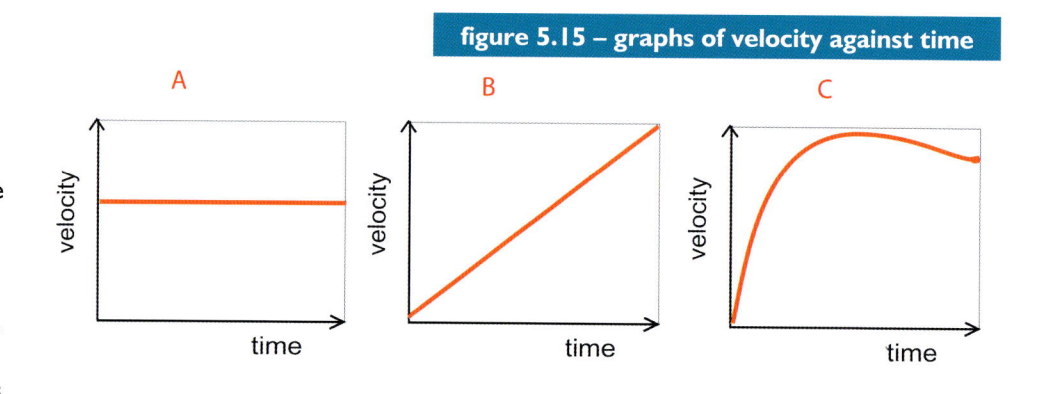

figure 5.15 – graphs of velocity against time

In graph 5.15B, the velocity changes continuously with time, and the gradient of the graph is constant, and therefore the **acceleration is constant**.

In graph 5.15C, the moving object is a 100 metre sprinter, whose **acceleration is largest** at the begining of the race, who reaches **maximum speed** at about half of the race, and who slows down slightly (**negative acceleration** or deceleration) before the end of the race.

This can be linked via **Newton's second law of motion** to the forces applied to the sprinter during the race.

BIOMECHANICAL MOVEMENT

Forces in sport

The sprinter

figure 5.16 – start, middle and end of a sprint

A B C

- At the **start of the race** (figure 5.16A), there is a steep upwards slope on her velocity time graph (figure 5.15C, page 76) which means a large acceleration. This corresponds with a large forward net force applied at the start when friction is a large forward force acting on the foot of the runner. From figure 5.16A you will see that the vertical forces cancel out, and the friction force forward is much larger than the air resistance drag force backward. This produces a large net (resultant) force forward (marked in black on figure 5.16A). This force provides forward acceleration from Newton's second law.
- During the **middle of the run** (figure 5.16B), the velocity time graph is almost level, which means that acceleration is almost zero, therefore forces cancel out.
- At the **end of the run** (figure 5.16C), the velocity time graph has a small negative slope, showing that the sprinter decelerates, and that therefore there must be a net force backwards (shown in black) causing this deceleration.

Friction

Friction is a force which acts sideways between two surfaces which tend to slide past one another. This force enables sportspeople to accelerate, slow down, swerve, walk, and run.

The magnitude of friction depends on the **grip of footwear** on floor surface, and the **nature of the surface** itself (rough, smooth, slippy, greasy and so on), for example:

- **Studs and spikes** increase friction to enable better swerving and accelerating and decelerating in games or track situations. This applies to soft or wet surfaces.
- For **dry hard surfaces**, solid smooth rubber soles can give better friction as in discus or hammer shoes, rock climbing shoes, or tennis shoes for concrete surfaces.
- In **snow and ice**, long slender footwear (skates or skis) have low forward friction, but high sideways friction.

Note that friction acts forwards on the feet of the accelerating runner (figure 5.17).

Friction depends on the force pressing the surfaces together, but not on the area of contact. For example:

- The inverted wings on racing cars increase the down force on wheels (figure 6.23, page 95). This increases cornering friction between the wheels and the ground.

figure 5.17 – friction

"ouch no friction"

friction acts forward on the foot of the accelerating sprinter

Friction   77

SECTION 4 CHAPTER 5 — LINEAR MOTION

Friction

- Friction also enables swerving by players in rugby, soccer, hockey, and tennis. The friction force then acts sideways to the direction of motion, and changes the direction of motion.
- The direction taken after a bounce by a spinning ball depends on the direction of spin and the friction between the ball and the ground.

Rolling or sliding friction

- **Rolling friction** is the term which describes the force between surfaces which do not move relative to one another, like a wheel rolling over a surface, or a foot driving and pushing without slipping. The friction can be anything from zero up to a maximum just before slipping occurs. As soon as slipping occurs, the friction force falls, and would not be enough to keep a sportsperson upright (so he or she slips over).
- **Sliding friction** occurs when the two surfaces are moving relative to one another, and is always less than the maximum rolling friction. This is why ABS (**advanced braking systems**) will reduce braking force on wheels if sensors detect the beginning of sliding.

Fluid friction

Fluid friction (or **drag**) is a term applying to objects moving through fluids (gases or liquids). The force acts in the opposite direction to the direction of motion. This term applies to the **air resistance** experienced by objects moving through air.

Reaction forces within the body

Action and reaction forces within the body are caused when any muscle contracts. The two ends of the muscle pull equally on one another. In figure 5.18 the insertion of the muscle is pulled to the left and the origin to the right. The effect this has on the body shape or relative position of the different limbs and attachments depends on which of these are able to move.

figure 5.18 – internal muscular forces

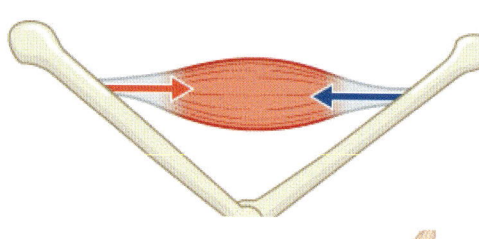

figure 5.19 – muscle contractions causing changes in body shape

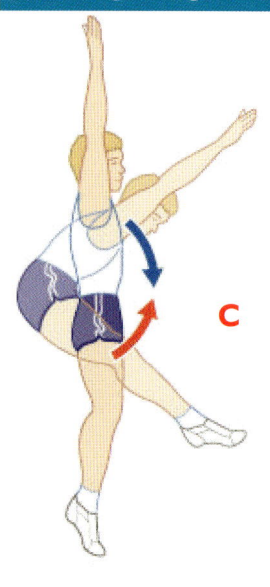

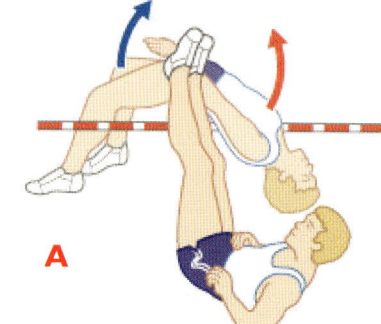

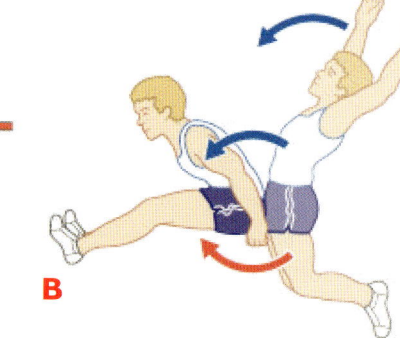

Muscle contraction within the body

Examples of muscle contraction causing changes in body shape, as origins and insertions are pulled towards one another, are shown in figure 5.18.

Figure 5.19A - bending over the bar during the high jump.
Figure 5.19B - stretching in the long jump.
Figure 5.19C - tumbling by the gymnast.
Figure 5.19D - arm action in the discus throw.

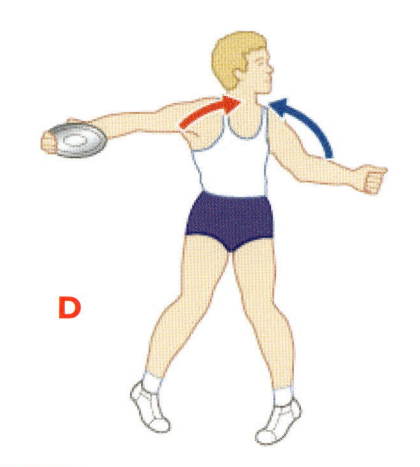

BIOMECHANICAL MOVEMENT

Reaction forces

Reaction forces are produced as a result of Newton's third law of motion, which is covered in the Year 1 text book in this series, and which is summarised here.

Newton's third law of motion describes what happens when **two bodies** (or objects) exert forces on one another. Action and reaction are equal and opposite and always occur in pairs.

Action acts on one of the bodies, and the **reaction** to this action acts on the other body. At a sprint start, the athlete **pushes back** on the blocks as hard as possible (this is the **'action'** - arrow in black in figure 5.20e), and the blocks **push forward** on the athlete (this push forward is the **'reaction force'**, arrow in red in figure 5.20e). The reaction provides forward acceleration on the athlete. In figure 5.20c, a swimmer pushes backwards on the water with hands and feet (this is the force in **black**, the **action**). At the same time, the water thrusts the swimmer forward (this is the force in red, the **reaction force**).

From figure 5.20:
- **a**, the jumper pushes down on the ground (black arrow), the ground pushes up on the jumper (red arrow - the reaction).

- **b**, the weight lifter pulls up on the weight (black arrow), weight pulls down on lifter (red arrow - the reaction).

- **c**, the swimmer pushes backwards on the water (black arrow), the water pushes forward on the swimmer (red arrow - the reaction).

- **d**, canoeist pushes backwards on the water (black arrow), reaction force thrusts the canoe forward (red arrow - the reaction).

- **e**, sprinter pushes back and down on the ground (black arrow), the ground pushes upwards and forwards on the sprinter (red arrow - the reaction).

- **f**, in cycling, the tyre on the rear wheel pushes backward on the ground (black arrow), the ground pushes forward on the rear wheel (red arrow - the reaction).

Impulse and impact

When a foot, bat or club strikes a ball, there are often **very large forces** acting on the ball during the period of contact. These cause correspondingly large accelerations of the ball as it moves from rest to its speed at the start of its flight. Since these forces act over **very short times**, when dealing with such cases it is convenient to use a different approach to that of the straightforward definition of acceleration and **Newton's Second Law of Motion**.

The same idea is applicable to tennis, squash, cricket and baseball where the ball is already moving rapidly on contact with the racket or bat. This new approach is as follows:

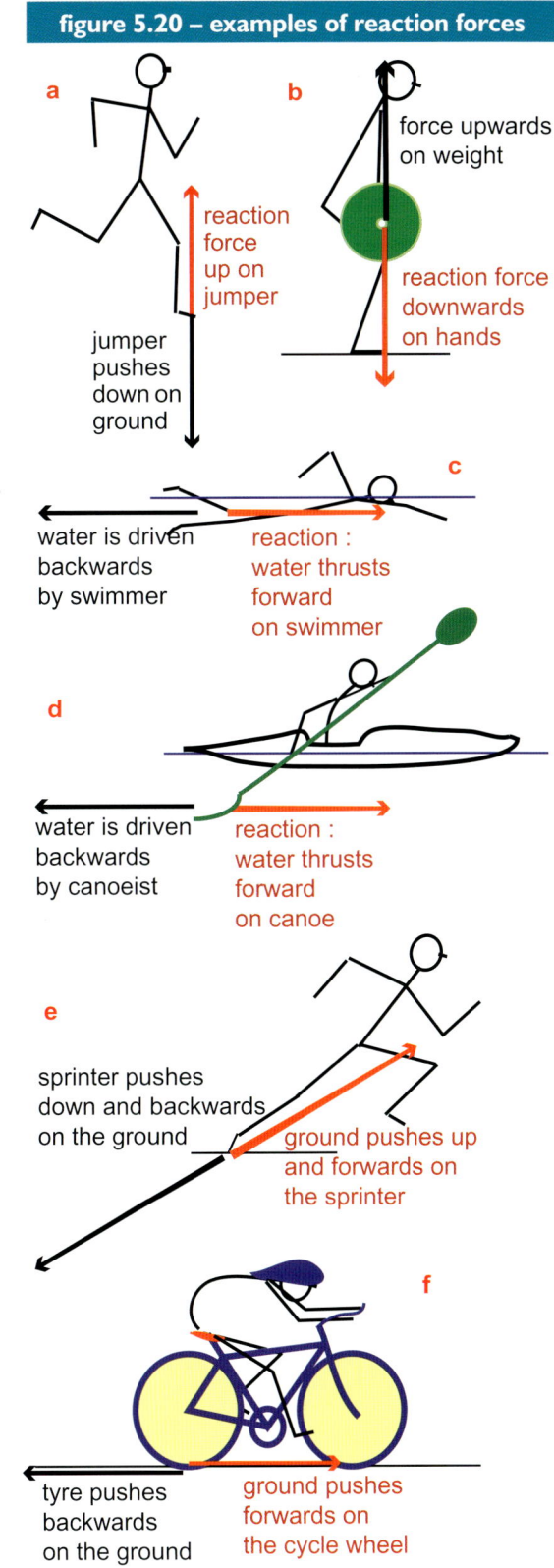

figure 5.20 – examples of reaction forces

a – jumper pushes down on ground / reaction force up on jumper

b – force upwards on weight / reaction force downwards on hands

c – water is driven backwards by swimmer / reaction : water thrusts forward on swimmer

d – water is driven backwards by canoeist / reaction : water thrusts forward on canoe

e – sprinter pushes down and backwards on the ground / ground pushes up and forwards on the sprinter

f – tyre pushes backwards on the ground / ground pushes forwards on the cycle wheel

Impulse and impact

SECTION 4 CHAPTER 5

LINEAR MOTION

Impulse and Newton's second law

Strictly, Newton's Second Law should read:

Force applied to a body = rate of change of momentum of the body

or

Force = change of momentum per second

Force = $\dfrac{\text{change of momentum}}{\text{time taken to change}}$

or

Force × time = change of momentum

This brings in two new constructs as below:

Momentum: defined by **mass × velocity**

or   momentum = m × v

and   **Impulse**: defined by **force × time**

or   impulse = F × t

Therefore Newton's Second Law becomes:

impulse = change of momentum

or   F × t = change of (m × v)

Note: this formula is compatible with our original Newton's Second Law formula since:

change of (m × v) = m × (change of v)

therefore: F × t = m × (change of v)

or: F = m × $\dfrac{\text{(change of v)}}{t}$

and: F = m × acceleration

Use of impulse in impacts

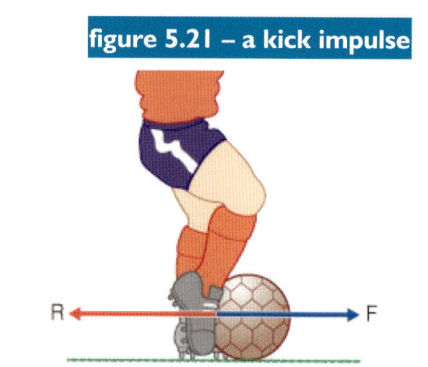

In figure 5.21 we see the force of impact on the ball (F) and its reaction on the foot of the kicker (R).
This force of impact lasts for a short time (t in the formula).

Figure 5.22 shows a graph of force of impact against time.
It shows a force of 250 N lasting for 1/50 s.
It can be seen that the product F × t has the value 250 × 1/50 = 5 Ns.

This can be equated to the area under the graph (shaded red).
The area under a force–time graph is a convenient measure of impulse.

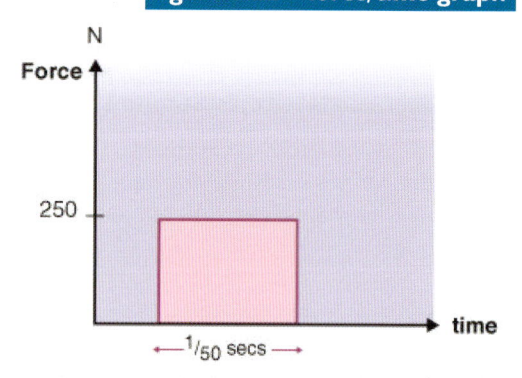

In practice, the force of impact is not constant but varies with time. It is possible to measure how F changes with time using a force sensor mounted on the ball or foot. Figure 5.23 page 81, shows how a graph of force (acting on the ball) against time would look, and the reaction force acting on the foot (which is shown as negative - meaning that it is in the opposite direction).

Impulse is defined as the area under the graph (shaded red), which represents the total force × time added up over the time of contact. Note that the maximum force is large, 500 N, and the time of contact short, 1/50 s.

impulse = area under graph

= 1/2 × 1/50 × 500   approximately

= 5 Ns.

figure 5.21 – a kick impulse

figure 5.22 – force/time graph

BIOMECHANICAL MOVEMENT

Use of impulse in impacts

The following calculation assumes that the shape in figure 5.23 is a triangle and its
area = 1/2 × base × height.

If the mass of the ball,
m = 0.5 kg,
then the change of momentum
= m × change of velocity of the ball
= 0.5 × final velocity

Therefore:
impulse = change of momentum
5 Ns = 0.5 × final velocity

and so: final velocity = 10 m s^{-1}

Figure 5.23 also shows the graph of the reaction force on the foot of the kicker with time. Note that the graph **exactly mirrors** that of the force on the ball – this fits in with **Newton's Third Law**, since at all times the **reaction force** must be exactly equal and opposite (and therefore negative) to the **force on the ball**.

figure 5.23 – force/time graph for ball and foot

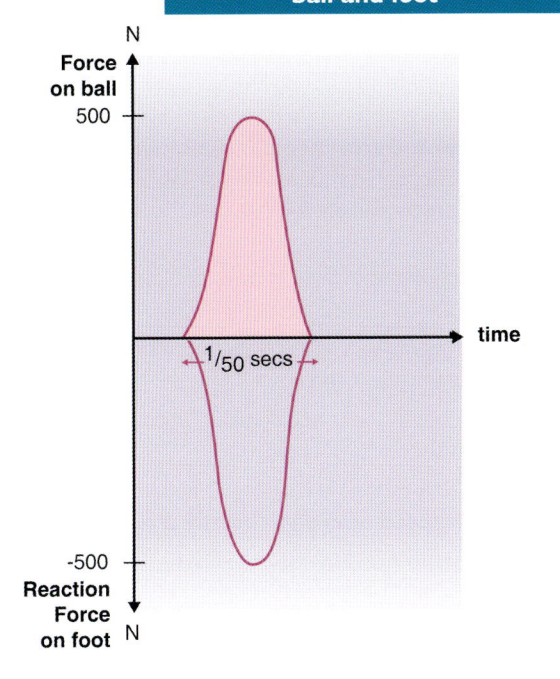

Applications of impulse

The reason that follow-through in striking a ball increases the outgoing velocity of the ball (not to mention better control of its direction) is because the time of contact is increased and therefore the impulse is increased.

When a ball is caught, the impulse is determined by the incoming mass and velocity of the ball (figure 5.24) so an increase in the length of time over which force acts on the ball will reduce the force exerted during the catch.

figure 5.24 – force changes with time

This is similar to the sprinter running into a barrier at the end of a 60 m indoor sprint, a padded barrier increases the time over which force is exerted and therefore **reduces the force** required to stop the sprinter (figure 5.25) and hence reduces the damage done to the sprinter on hitting the barrier.

figure 5.25 – force smaller when time longer

Application of impulse 81

SECTION 4 CHAPTER 5

LINEAR MOTION

Example of the application of impulse to foot impact in running

Force platforms linked to a computer have been developed to analyse scientifically impacts between the foot and the ground during foot strike of a runner during a race or at the point of take-off for a high or long jumper or volleyball or basketball player when jumping. These produce graphs of force applied against the time of contact for both horizontal and vertical forces and allow comparison of the way in which force is applied for runners or jumpers of different standards and so point the way towards improvements in technique of the less competent performer.

Figure 5.26 shows the various phases of horizontal foot impulse during a sprint.

- **a** when the runner is in contact with starting blocks or immediately at the start.
- **b** when he or she is accelerating during the first two to three seconds of a run.
- **c** when the runner is running at approximately constant speed during the middle of a run.
- **d** during the slowing down at the end of a run.

- In figure 5.26a, the area under the **force time curve** is above the horizontal axis (and hence **positive**), which means the force is acting **forwards** on the runner. The force lasts for a relatively long time, therefore the impulse is high and positive and would cause large forward acceleration and change of forward velocity of the runner.

- In figure 5.26b, some of the area of the graph is below the horizontal axis and therefore **negative** but the **overall impulse** is **positive**, meaning that the runner is still accelerating forwards but not now as much as in case **a**.

- In figure 5.26c, the **positive** area above the horizontal axis is exactly **cancelled** by the **negative** area under the axis. This means that the **horizontal impulse is zero** so the sprinter would not be accelerating or decelerating and would be running at **constant speed**.

- In figure 5.26d, the **negative** area below the axis of the graph is **bigger** than the **positive** part and hence the **overall impulse is negative**. This means that the runner will be experiencing an overall **force** (averaged over the stride) **backwards** and hence would be **decelerating** or losing speed.

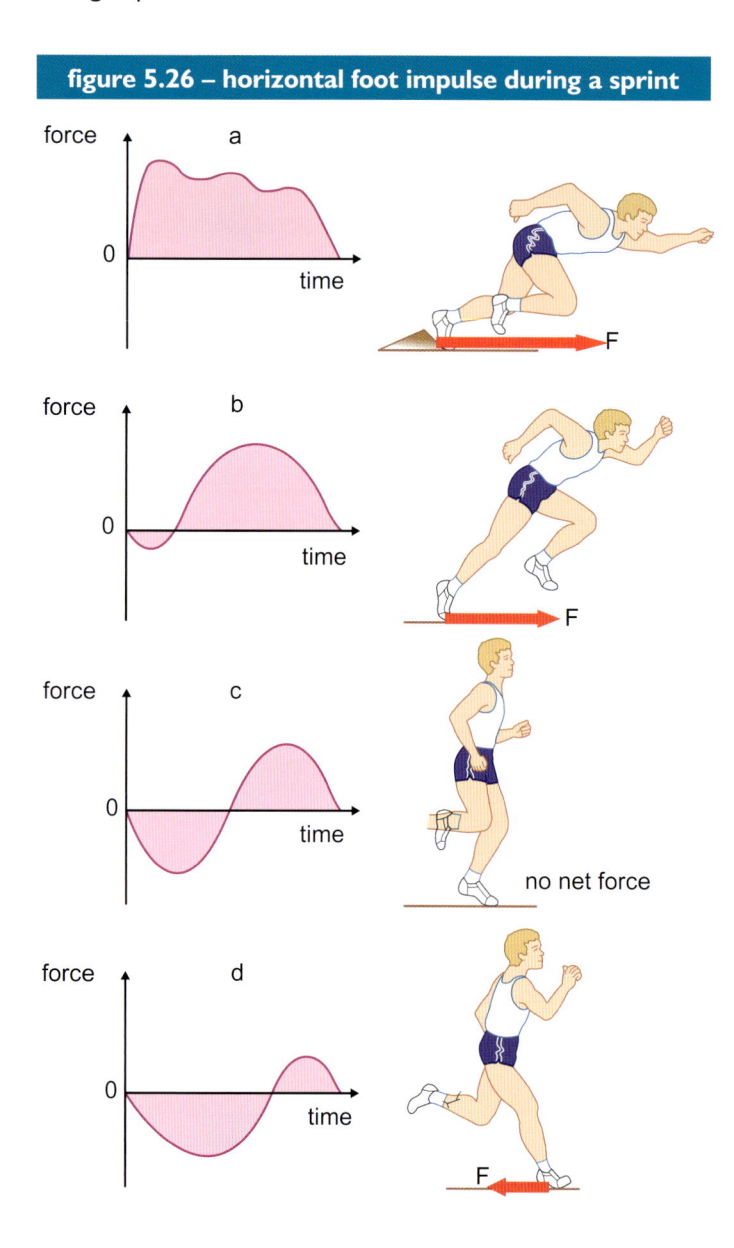

In figures 5.26 b, c and d, the parts of the graphs which show a negative impulse (area below the horizontal axis of the graph) correspond to the situation where the foot placement is in front of the runner's centre of mass and so exerts a backwards force for a short time.

This is immediately followed by the **centre of mass** moving forward over the contact foot which then applies a **forward force** on the runner and hence a positive impulse for the latter part of the foot contact.

figure 5.26 – horizontal foot impulse during a sprint

BIOMECHANICAL MOVEMENT

Example of the application of impulse to a jumper taking off

Figure 5.27A shows a graph of the **vertical** force against time for the take-off foot of a volleyball player during the plant phase of his jump. The positive area above the horizontal axis of the graph represents the **upwards** impulse and hence **force exerted by the floor on the jumper (reaction force)**.

figure 5.27 – vertical foot impulse during a jump

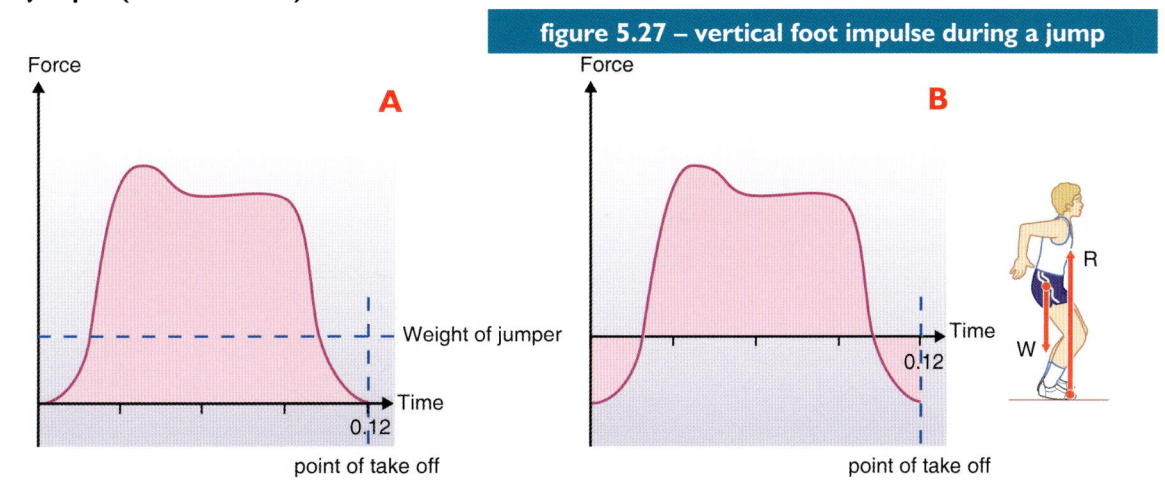

Figure 5.27B represents the **net force** acting on the jumper, taking into account his weight. Note that now the impulse is positive, large and lasts for a relatively long time which tells us that there is a large average net force acting upwards on the jumper during take-off.

This will cause the jumper to accelerate upwards and leave the ground; this upward acceleration needs to be larger and last for a long time in order to send the jumper well off the ground. So the reaction force R is much larger than W for most of the take-off process.

Conservation of momentum in collisions

In the above section the concept of **momentum** (**momentum = mass x velocity** of a moving object) was introduced as a way of looking at collisions and also as part of the fundamental description of Newton's Second Law of Motion.

Momentum is a **vector** (and has therefore both **size and direction**) and the same theory reproduced above can show that it is conserved in collisions in which no external forces act.

What this means is that if you were to calculate the momentum of two snooker balls (by **adding together** the values of mass x velocity, taking into account the direction) just before collision and then calculated it again just after the collision, you would find exactly the same result. No external forces means that the balls do not touch any other objects (cushion, cue, other balls, you) during the time of contact during the collision.

This law seems to apply **everywhere in the universe** and can be used to predict what happens during the collisions between planets and asteroids, spaceships and satellites and, on earth, rugby or football players and tacklers, moving racing cars and so on.

For example, a simple case is when a snooker cue ball strikes another head on without spin. This results in the object ball (the second ball) moving away from the collision at exactly the same velocity (speed and direction) that the cue ball had before the collision, with the cue ball stopping dead. Of course, all pool and snooker players use **spin** to position the cue ball after the collision, so what we have said here is a simplification.

Conservation of momentum in collisions 83

SECTION 4 CHAPTER 5 — LINEAR MOTION

Transfer of momentum

Another example is that of the running rugby (or football) player being able to brush off the tackle of a much bigger opponent. The momentum of the running player can be transferred to the tackler (and hence knock him over) with a skilful flick of the hips or a hand-off, particularly if the tackler is balanced, (he is not leaning into the runner). This latter point is mentioned because the law of conservation of momentum in collisions does not apply if external forces are applied during the collision. If a tackler were to lean into the runner, then he would be exerting a force from the ground into the collision and hence preventing transfer of momentum from the runner.

The case of the unspinning snooker ball striking another ball head on, causing the first ball to stop dead and the second ball to move with the same momentum as the original ball, is a direct case of transfer of momentum. The momentum of the cue ball is directly transferred to the object ball during the collision between the balls.

Most sporting situations in which collisions occur have some transfer of momentum. However, the amount of momentum transferred from a moving object (rugby player, for example) to the stationary object with which it collides (for example, the rugby tackler) depends on the relative mass of the two objects.

The skill of the running player is to transfer as much momentum as possible to the tackler in order to evade tackling and the skill of the tackler is to apply as much force as possible from the surroundings to the runner in order to minimise transfer of momentum to himself and therefore complete the tackle (figure 5.28).

figure 5.28 – rugby player and tackler

Another example of transfer of momentum would be when a racquet or bat strikes a ball. The momentum of the racquet would be much larger than that of a moving ball since its mass would be much larger. After the strike, some of the momentum of the racquet would be transferred to the ball, giving it substantial speed and direction in a way controlled by the player using the racquet.

Practice questions

1) Which of the following pairs of quantities is not a vector/scalar pair?
   a. weight/mass.
   b. reaction force/centre of mass.
   c. velocity/speed.
   d. energy/power.

2) Which of the following is a vector?
   a. gravitational field strength.
   b. centripetal force.
   c. the ratio of force to acceleration for a moving body.
   d. rate of change of speed.

BIOMECHANICAL MOVEMENT

Practice questions

3) Which one of the following is a definition of impulse?
   a. rate of change of momentum.
   b. force multiplied by the time of contact in an impact.
   c. change of momentum multiplied by time of contact.
   d. the acceleration of a body during an impact.

4) A positive impulse will cause:
   a. a forward velocity.
   b. a backward change of momentum.
   c. a forward change of momentum.
   d. a backward change of speed.

5) A rugby prop brushes off a tackle from a much smaller opponent, which one of the following statements is true about this tackle?
   a. momentum is conserved during the tackle.
   b. momentum is conserved during the tackle provided no other tackler is involved.
   c. the velocity of the tackler is increased.
   d. the velocity of the tackler is reduced.

6) a) What characterises a vector quantity? 2 marks

   b) Figure 5.29 shows the forces acting on a runner at the start of a race. Use a vector diagram to show how you could work out the resultant force acting. 3 marks

   c) Sketch a pin man drawing of a person standing still showing all the forces acting on him. 2 marks

   d) Sketch a second diagram showing the vertical forces acting on a basketballer just before take-off while performing a jump shot. Represent the relative sizes of any forces you show by the length of the force arrows on your diagram. 2 marks

   e) Use this second diagram and your understanding of Newton's laws of motion to explain why the basketballer is able to take off. If the vertical upward ground reaction force on him is 2000 N, and his weight is 800 N, estimate the net upward force acting on him. 4 marks

figure 5.29 – forces acting on a runner

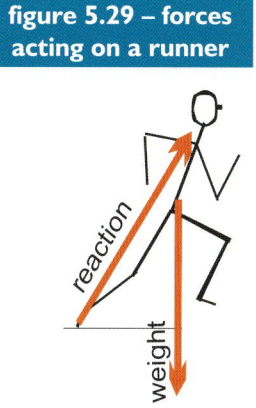

7) The four man bobsleigh develops a large momentum during the first few seconds of its run.

   a) Explain the meaning of the term momentum, and explain why the four man bobsleigh travelling at a speed of 28 ms^{-1} has a different momentum to a skier moving at the same speed. 2 marks

   b) Explain using Newton's laws of motion how the bobsleigh acquires its large momentum during the first part of a run. 4 marks

8) The follow-through is an important aspect of a forehand ground stroke in tennis.

   a) Sketch a graph of the force applied by the racquet (y axis) against time (x axis). Show the effect of a follow-through on your graph. 2 marks

   b) Explain how the use of a follow-through would affect the motion of the ball. 4 marks

SECTION 4 CHAPTER 5
LINEAR MOTION

Practice questions

9) a) In a tennis match, the ball travels towards a player at 35 ms^{-1}. The ball has a mass of 80 g and the racket head has a mass of 0.6 kg. The racket head moves towards the ball at 10 ms^{-1}. Calculate the momentum of the racket and the ball before contact. **3 marks**

b) If the player stops the racket moving on contact with the ball, calculate the velocity of the ball after contact. **3 marks**

c) The graphs in figure 5.30 show the forces acting on a runner's foot during a 100 metre sprint. For each graph, describe the resultant impulse force and the motion that occurs. **6 marks**

figure 5.30 – horizontal force acting on a runner's foot

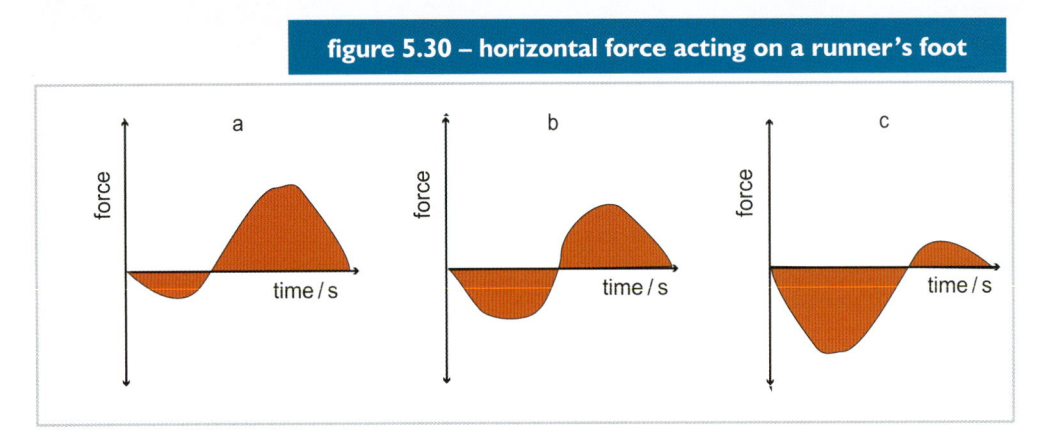

10) Tennis players have to change direction quickly during a match to recover to the centre of the court.
Figure 5.31 shows a tennis player just after hitting a forehand and then starting to recover to the centre of the court in the direction shown.

a) Draw a pin diagram of the tennis player as he pushes off the court surface to recover to the centre of the court, showing all forces acting on the tennis player at this point. All forces must be clearly identified. **3 marks**

b) Explain the factors that affect the horizontal force at this point. Apply Newton's second law of motion to explain the effect of this force on the player. **4 marks**

figure 5.31 – a tennis player moves between strokes

11) A sprinter uses her calf muscles to push on the blocks at the start of a run. Sketch a pin man diagram of the forces acting and use this to explain how this produces a forward force on her. **3 marks**

12) Explain the nature of the reaction force which provides forwards impulsion for a cyclist. **4 marks**

Answers link: http://www.jroscoe.co.uk/downloads/a2_revise_pe_aqa/AQAA2_ch5_answers.pdf

BIOMECHANICAL MOVEMENT

CHAPTER 6: Angular motion, projectile motion and fluid mechanics

Angular motion

Angular motion is defined as **the motion of a body which twists or turns about an axis** as defined in figure 6.1. The twists, tumbles and turns involved in sports movements can all be described in this way.

Three imaginary axes of rotation

An axis of rotation is defined as '**an imaginary line about which the body rotates or spins, at right angles to the plane**' – as in figure 6.1, axes labelled A, B and C.

- **Longitudinal axis**
  - Axis A on figure 6.1.
  - This axis runs vertically from the top of the head to a point between the feet.
  - Movements in the **transverse plane** about the longitudinal axis are rotational movements.
  - Examples of sporting movements would be the spinning skater and the hammer throw (figure 6.2).
- **Transverse axis**
  - Axis B on figure 6.1. This axis runs horizontally from side to side across the body between opposite hips at right angles to the sagittal plane.
  - Movements within the **sagittal plane** about the transverse axis are flexion, extension, hyperextension, dorsiflexion and plantarflexion.
  - Sports movements about this axis include sit ups, and the high jump Fosbury Flop flight phase, and somersaults (figure 6.3).
- **Frontal axis (also called the sagittal axis)**
  - Axis C on figure 6.1.
  - This axis runs horizontally from front to back between belly button and lumbar spine.
  - Movements in the **frontal plane** about the frontal axis include abduction, adduction and spinal lateral flexion.
  - Examples of sports movements about this axis are a cartwheel (figure 6.4), and the bowling action in cricket.

Planes of the body

The term **body plane** is defined as '**an imaginary flat surface running through the centre of gravity of the body**', and is used to assist in the understanding of movement of body segments with respect to one another. Within each plane the turning axis can be identified as in figure 6.1.

figure 6.1 – planes and axes

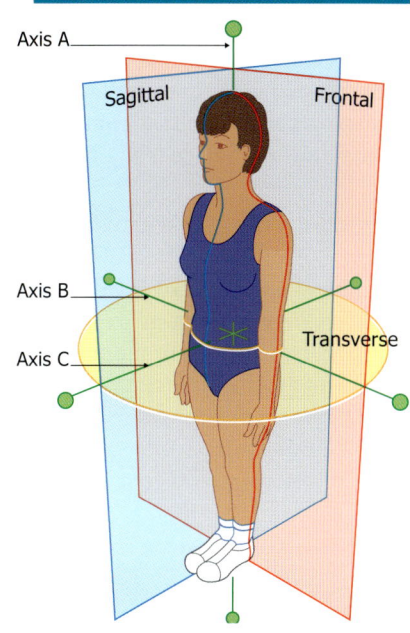

figure 6.2 – a hammer thrower turning around longitudinal axis

figure 6.3 – a gymnast tumbling around the transverse axis

figure 6.4 – a cartwheel rotating about the frontal axis

Angular motion

SECTION 4 CHAPTER 6
ANGULAR MOTION, PROJECTILE MOTION AND FLUID MECHANICS

Angle

Angle is a familiar concept to most people, so it is readily understood what is meant by 30°, 90°, 180° and 360°. In scientific terms, an angle is measured in radians. The radian as a unit of angle is defined as '**the angle subtended at the centre of a circle by an arc length of one radius**'. Suffice it to say at this point that one radian is approximately 60°.

Angular displacement

Angular displacement is defined similarly to displacement for linear systems and is the **relative angle** compared to some fixed position or line in space. For example, if a golfer starts his/her drive from the presentation position (i.e. with club just touching the ball) and backswings to the fully extended position with the club behind his/her back, the club shaft would have an angular displacement equal to the angle between the starting position and the fully extended position of the backswing. This would be a measure of the fluency and range of the swing and could be anywhere from 180° to 290° (or 3.142 to 5.06 radians).

Angular velocity

Angular velocity is the same thing as rate of spinning or twisting, and is defined as:

angular velocity (ω) = $\dfrac{\text{angle turned (in radians)}}{\text{time taken to turn}}$

This is a similar definition to that for linear velocity, except distance is replaced by angle in the formula.

Angular acceleration

Again in a similar way to linear systems, it is possible to define angular acceleration as:

angular acceleration = $\dfrac{\text{change of angular velocity}}{\text{time taken to change}}$

This concept applies to situations in which the rate of spin **changes with time**. Examples of this would be the hammer throw (in which the rate of spin increases throughout the movement up to the release of the hammer) and the tumbler, gymnast or diver (who speeds up the rate of rotation or slows it down by changing his/her body shape).

Torque

Torque is the twisting force which you could apply to a body to cause it to turn or spin. It is defined as the force applied to the body multiplied by the perpendicular distance to the axis of rotation (the moment of force about the turning axis).

This definition means that the bigger the force and the distance from the axis of turning, the bigger the turning effect.

Moment of inertia (MI)

This is the equivalent of mass (**inertia**) in the linear system, and is defined as:

moment of inertia = sum of [(mass of body part) x (distance of body part from the axis of rotation) squared] over all parts of the rotating body.

Mathematically: $MI = \Sigma m r^2$

Objects rotating with large MI require large moments of force (torque) to change their angular velocity, and objects with small MI require small moments of force (torque) to change their angular velocity or ω.

BIOMECHANICAL MOVEMENT

Moment of inertia

The formula on page 88 means that moment of inertia depends on the spread of mass away from the axis of spin, so as the body shape changes, the moment of inertia of the shape changes. The more spread out the mass, the bigger the MI.

The unit of MI is kilogramme metre squared - kgm^2.

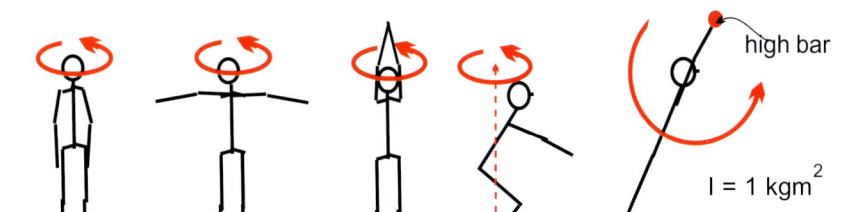

figure 6.5 – moments of inertia of different shapes

- Bodies with **arms held out wide** have large MI, the further the mass is away from the axis of rotation increases the MI dramatically.
- Sportspeople use this to control all spinning or turning movements.
- Pikes and tucks are good examples of use of MI, both reduce MI.

I | 2I | 0.8I | 5I | 70I

$I = 1\ kgm^2$

Values of moment of inertia

In figure 6.5, I is the MI for the left most pin man and has a value of about 1.0 kgm^2 for an average male person. From this diagram you can see how control of the arms will make a big difference to the value of MI, and that a tuck or pike can also **change MI** dramatically.

Angular momentum

Angular momentum is a quantity used to describe what happens when bodies spin and turn, it is defined as:

angular momentum = moment of inertia x angular velocity
= rotational inertia x rate of spin
H = I x ω

Conservation of angular momentum

The **law of conservation of angular momentum** is a law of the universe which says that angular momentum of a spinning body remains the same (provided no external forces act)

figure 6.6 – moment of inertia is very large with both arms and legs spread wide

Conservation of angular momentum **89**

SECTION 4 CHAPTER 6 — ANGULAR MOTION, PROJECTILE MOTION AND FLUID MECHANICS

Conservation of angular momentum

- This means that a body which is spinning, twisting or tumbling will keep its value of **H** once the movement has started.
- Therefore if moment of inertia (**I**) changes by changing body shape, then angular velocity (ω) must also change to keep angular momentum (**H**) the same.
- So, if MI (**I**) **increases** (body spread out more) then ω must **decrease** (rate of spin gets less).
- And conversely, if MI (**I**) **decreases** (body tucked in more) then ω must **increase** (rate of spin gets bigger).
- Strictly, this is only exactly true if the body has no contact with its surroundings, as for example a high diver doing piked or tucked somersaults in the air, but it is almost true for the spinning skater!

Sporting examples of conservation of angular momentum

- **The spinning skater**. If the arms are wide, the MI is large and the skater spins slowly. If the arms are brought in, MI is small and the skater will spin more quickly (figure 6.7).
- **The tumbling gymnast** (figure 6.8). With the body position open, the MI is large and the gymnast (or diver or trampolinist) will spin slowly. When he or she creates a tucked body position, the MI is small and he or she will spin more quickly.
- **The dancer doing a spin jump** (figure 6.9). The movement is initiated with arms held wide which would therefore have the highest possible MI. Immediately he or she has taken off, the angular momentum is conserved, and so by tucking the arms across the chest, this will create the lowest possible MI. This then means that he or she will acquire the highest possible rate of spin, so that more spins can be completed before landing.
- **The slalom skier**. The slalom skier crouches on approach to the gate and therefore will have a large turning MI. As he or she passes the gate, he or she stands straight up (reducing MI). This enables the person to turn rapidly past the gate, then he or she crouches again (figure 6.10) - increasing MI which will resume a slow turn between the gates.

Newton's laws of angular motion

The laws of angular motion are similar to Newton's laws of linear motion except that they apply to turning, spinning, or twisting system or bodies. They are:

- **Newton's first law of angular motion** states that a spinning or rotating body will continue with a constant angular momentum except when acted upon by an external force or torque.
- **Newton's second law of angular motion** states that the rate of change of angular momentum of the body will be proportional to the torque acting on it, and in the same direction (of spin) as the torque.
- **Newton's third law of angular motion** states that when a torque is applied to one body by another body, an equal but opposite in direction torque will be applied by the second body to the first body.

figure 6.7 – a spinning skater

figure 6.8 – a tumbling gymnast

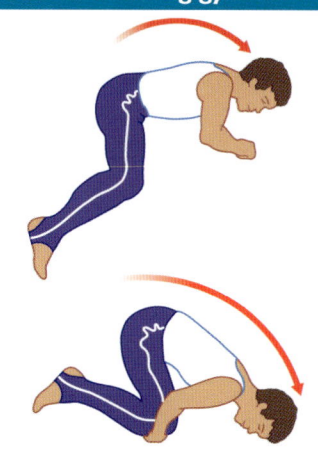

figure 6.9 – a spinning dancer

figure 6.10 – a slalom skier

BIOMECHANICAL MOVEMENT

Projectile motion

Factors affecting horizontal displacement of projectiles

This section looks at the **motion of objects in flight**, such as human bodies (during the flight phase of a jump), throwing implements (shot, discus, javelin or hammer), and soccer, rugby, cricket, tennis and golf balls.

The flight is governed by the forces acting, the weight, air resistance, Magnus effect (page 95), aerodynamic lift, and the direction of motion. If weight were the only force acting, the flight path would be **parabolic** in shape, and some flight paths are similar to this (shot or hammer, the human body in jumps or tumbles or dives as in figures 6.11, 6.12, and 6.13, where weight is the predominant force acting).

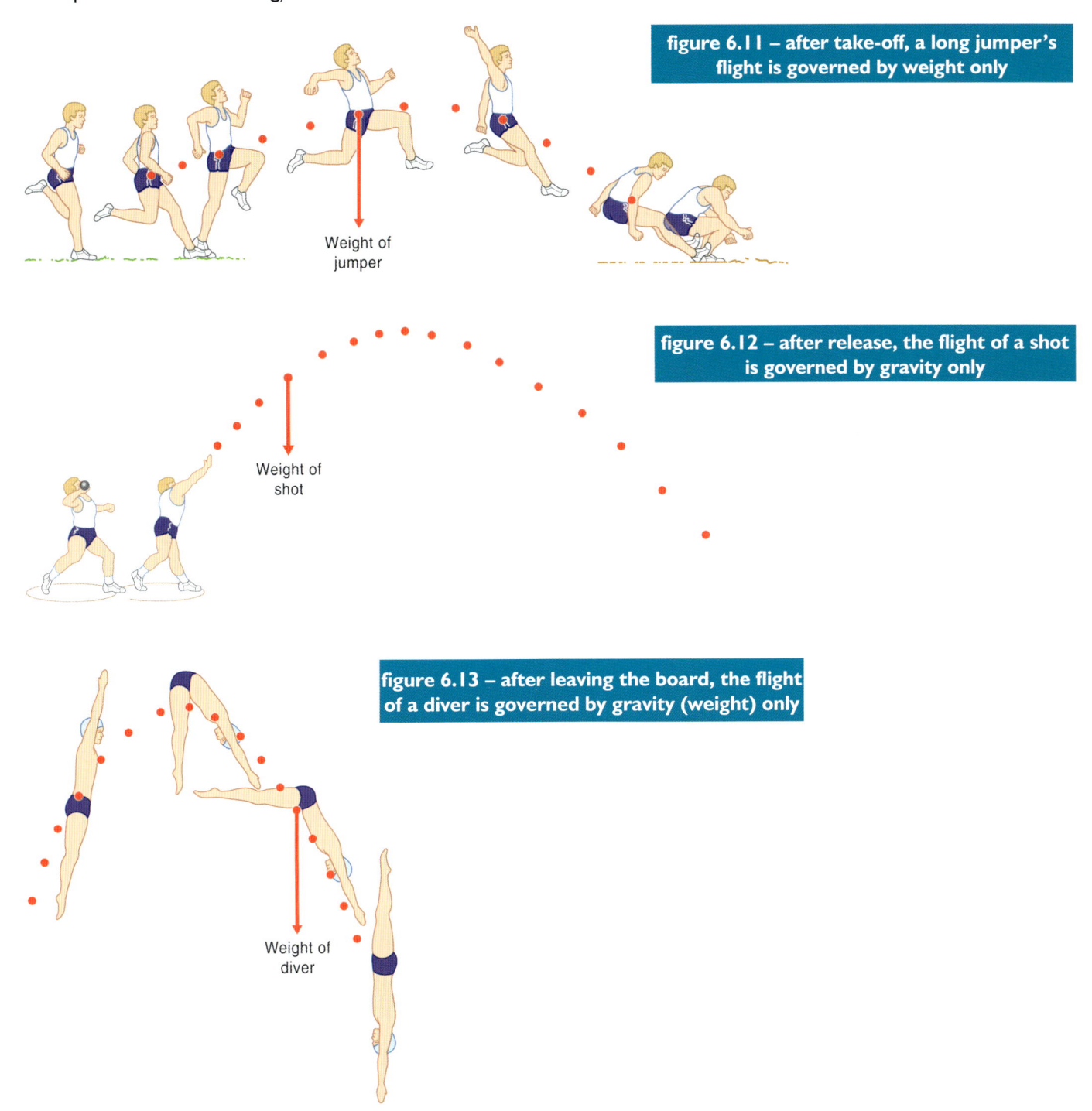

figure 6.11 – after take-off, a long jumper's flight is governed by weight only

Weight of jumper

figure 6.12 – after release, the flight of a shot is governed by gravity only

Weight of shot

figure 6.13 – after leaving the board, the flight of a diver is governed by gravity (weight) only

Weight of diver

Projectile motion | 91

SECTION 4 CHAPTER 6 — ANGULAR MOTION, PROJECTILE MOTION AND FLUID MECHANICS

Factors affecting horizontal displacement of projectiles

Figure 6.14 summarises the factors which influence the distance travelled, the **angle of release**, the **speed of release**, and the **height of release**.

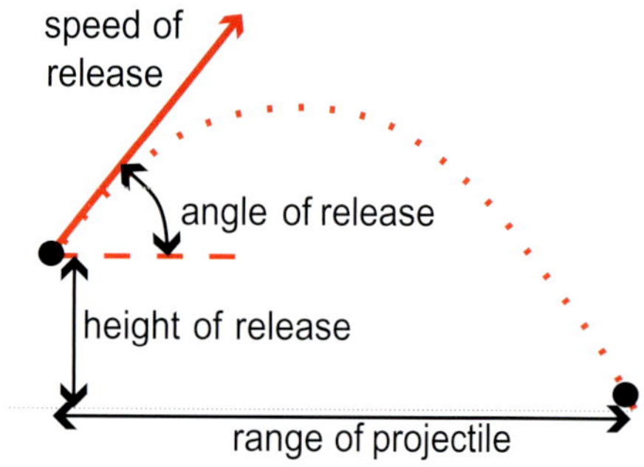

The optimum distance moved before landing is acheived at 45° release angle.

If the height of release is about 2 metres off the ground, as in the shot put (figure 6.14), then the optimum angle of release (to achieve maximum distance) will be less than 45°, probably approximately 42°.

But if the landing of the object thrown is higher than the point of release (as in the case of a basketball shot), then the optimum angle of release will be greater than 45°.

figure 6.14 – factors affecting distance travelled

The relative size of forces during flight

The forces acting during flight are: the weight of the object, the air resistance or drag, (the faster the projectile travels the greater will be the air resistance), **aerodynamic lift**, and the **Bernoulli effect** (page 94) or **Magnus effect** (page 95).

If the shapes of the flight path differ from a parabola then some combination of these forces must be relatively large compared with the weight (remembering that a flight of an object with only weight force acting would be a parabola).

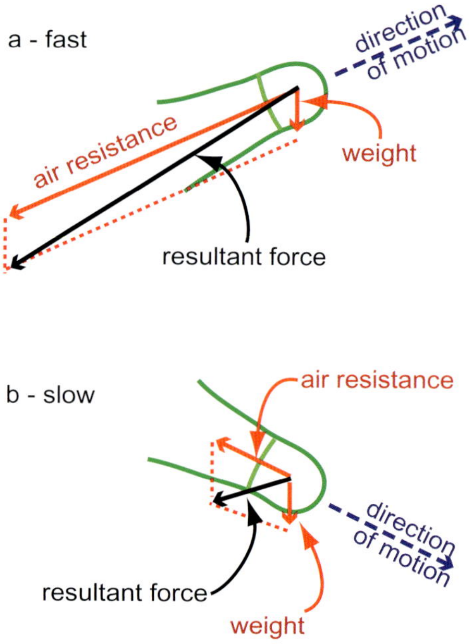

For example, the badminton shuttle

For a badminton shuttle **struck hard** (figure 6.15a), the air resistance is very large compared with the weight, because the shuttle is moving quickly. The resultant force will therefore be very close to the air resistance. This would make the shuttle slow down rapidly over the **first part of the flight**.

Later in the flight of the badminton shuttle (figure 6.15b), when the shuttle is moving much more slowly, the air resistance is much less and comparable with the weight. This pattern of the resultant force changing markedly during the flight predicts a pronounced asymmetric path.

Figure 6.16 shows a badminton shuttle's flight path, which is markedly asymmetric, because of the change of predominant force during the flight.

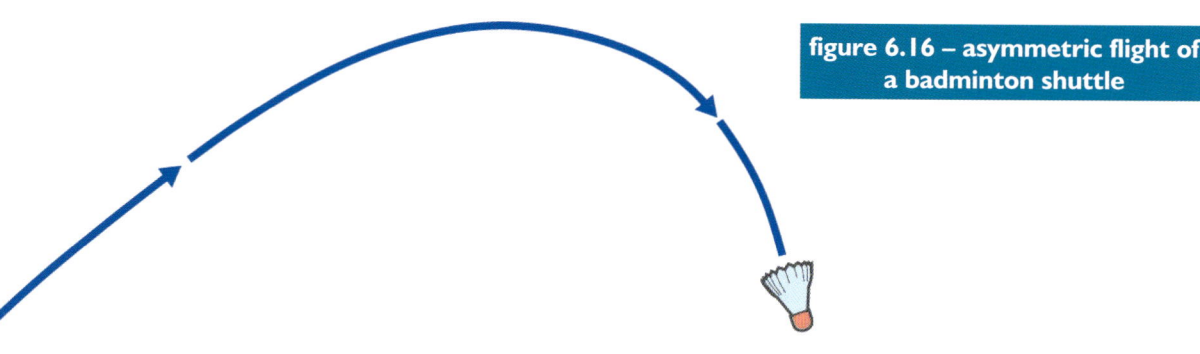

figure 6.15 – forces on a badminton shuttle

a - fast

b - slow

figure 6.16 – asymmetric flight of a badminton shuttle

92

BIOMECHANICAL MOVEMENT

Vector components of velocity during flight

Figure 6.17 outlines the **vertical** and **horizontal components** of the velocity during the flight of a projectile.

Near the start of the flight:
- There is a large **upward vertical component** v_v.
- But a **fixed horizontal component** v_h.

At the middle of the flight:
- There is zero **upward vertical component**, since the object moves entirely horizontally at this point.
- There is still a **fixed horizontal component** v_h, which is the same as at the start.

Near the end of the flight:
- There is a large **downward vertical component** v_v, which is almost the same as the **horizontal component** since the object is travelling at approx 45° to the horizontal downwards.
- There is still a **fixed horizontal component** v_h, which is the same as at the start.

figure 6.17 – components of velocity during flight

Fluid mechanics

Fluid friction force depends on the shape and size of the moving object, the **speed** of the moving object, and the streamlining effect (summarised in figure 6.18).

figure 6.18 – factors affecting fluid friction or air resistance

Drag and air resistance

In order to minimise drag, the following developments affect sport:
- The body position and shape for a swimmer.
- The shape of helmets for cyclists.
- The use of lycra clothing.
- The shape of sports vehicles (cars or bikes).

Low values of fluid friction

This discussion concerns **low values of drag** compared with other forces. Examples are:
- Any sprinter or game player for whom air resistance is usually much less than friction effects and weight. Therefore streamlining is seen as less important.
- A shot or hammer in flight, in which air resistance would be much less than the weight, and therefore the angle of release should be around 45°.

High values of fluid friction

High values of drag will occur for any sportsperson or vehicle moving through water, and hence fluid friction is the critical factor governing swimming speed.

- Body shape or cross section, and clothing (surface material to assist laminar flow, on page 94), are adjusted to minimise fluid friction.

A cyclist (figure 6.19) travels much faster than a runner and therefore has **high fluid friction**:

- He or she crouches low to reduce the forward cross sectional area.
- The helmet is designed to minimise turbulent flow.
- Clothing and wheel profiles are designed to assist streamlining.

Cross sectional area is the area of the moving object as viewed from the front. The smaller the better to reduce drag, hence cyclists crouch down, and keep their elbows in.

figure 6.19 – a cyclist needs good streamlining

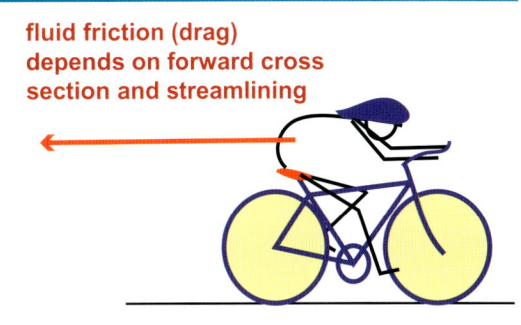

fluid friction (drag) depends on forward cross section and streamlining

Fluid mechanics

SECTION 4 CHAPTER 6 — ANGULAR MOTION, PROJECTILE MOTION AND FLUID MECHANICS

Laminar flow and drag

Fluid friction (or drag) depends on **laminar** flow, the smooth flowing of air or water past an object. Laminar means flowing in layers, and streamlining assists laminar flow. Figure 6.20 shows images of a streamlined helmet, and a non-streamlined helmet. The point of the streamlined shape is that the air moves past it in layers whereas in the case of the non-streamlined helmet, vortices are formed where the fluid does not flow smoothly. When this happens bits of fluid are flung randomly sideways which causes drag.

The drag is caused by bits of fluid being dragged along with the moving object (the cycle helmet).

Lift force

Dynamic **lift** (upward force) can be caused by the movement of the body. As the body moves forward, the angle presented by the lower surface of the body to the direction of motion (called the angle of attack) can cause the air molecules through which the object is moving to be deflected downward and hence would cause a downward force on the air through which the object passes (figure 6.21).

This **downward force on the air** would cause an **upward force on the moving object** in reaction to the downward force on the air (by Newton's third law). This is the lift.

Such a force can explain the flight of a discus.

A discus is a symmetrical object, which would therefore not be subject to the Bernoulli force which explains the flight of a wing moving horizontally through air.

The angle of attack of the discus is such as to present its lower surface to the air flow which causes the lift as explained above.

There is a distinction between a force caused as a reaction to air (or water) thrown up or sideways to the direction of motion of for example a downhill skier or a cyclist.

The Bernoulli effect

The force which gives lift to aircraft wings, and down-pressure on racing car bodies (figure 6.22, enabling greater friction between wheels and the road, and hence faster cornering speeds) is called the **Bernoulli effect**.

This effect depends on the fact that fluids which move quickly across the surface of an object cause a reduced pressure when compared with slower moving air across another surface.

Hence, in figure 6.22, the laminar flow of air across the **lower** surface of the wing (or car body shaped like an inverted wing) is **quicker**, because the air has to travel **further** in the same time as the air moving a shorter distance across the upper surface of the wing. Hence the shape of the wing is crucial to create the Bernoulli lift (in aeroplanes) or down force (in racing cars, figure 6.23 page 95).

figure 6.20 – laminar flow and vortex flow

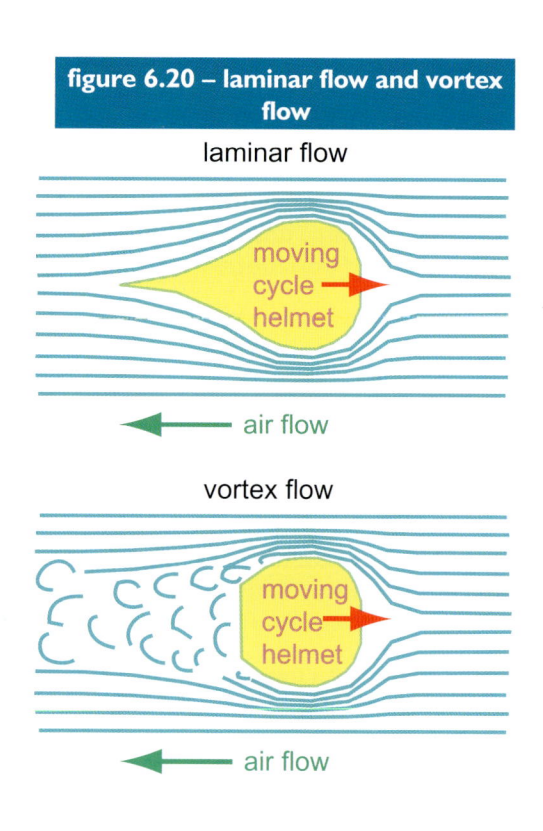

figure 6.21 – lift force on a discus

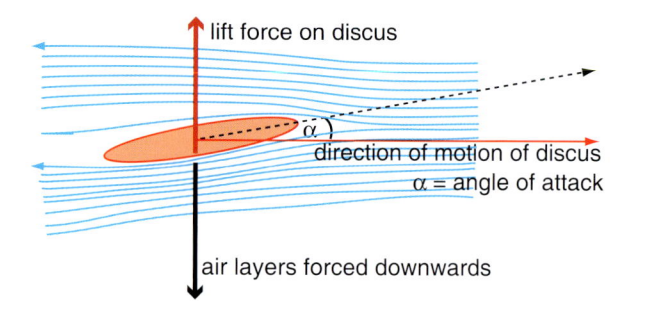

figure 6.22 – Bernoulli effect on an inverted wing

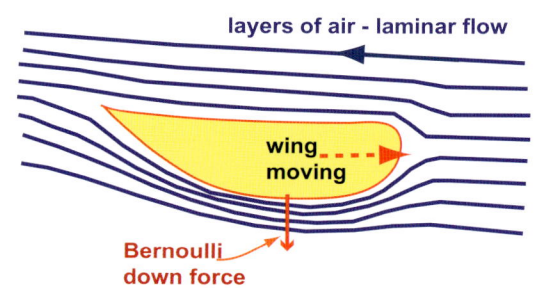

BIOMECHANICAL MOVEMENT

The Bernoulli effect

The **Bernoulli effect** has been built into racing cars to increase the down force (which would therefore increase the friction force between wheels and the ground).

So, formula 1 racing car manufacturers build this **shape into the whole car** (figure 6.23), not just the artificial wings sometimes attached to the car upper surfaces.

figure 6.23 – shape of a racing car body

The Magnus effect

The **Magnus effect** is the Bernoulli principle applied to spinning balls.

As a **spinning ball** moves through the air (from left to right on figure 6.24), the air layers which flow round the ball are forced into the path shown in the diagram. Here you can see that the air flow is **further** round the top of the ball, and hence the air flow is **faster** over the top of the ball than the bottom. This means that the **air pressure** will be **less** over the top of the ball than the lower half of the ball (following from the Bernoulli effect), hence the ball will experience a force upwards in the view of figure 6.24.

figure 6.24 – Magnus effect on a spinning ball

Hence **top-spin** as shown in figure 6.25, would cause a dipping effect on the ball in flight, the force is downward in this figure.

Similarly, **side-spin** will cause a swerve in the flight whose direction is in the same sense as the spin of the ball.

Golfers (figure 6.27, page 96) cause a ball to fade to the right or hook to the left by imparting side-spin to the ball during the strike.

The diagram in figure 6.26a show how side spin causes swerving sideways by the golfers.

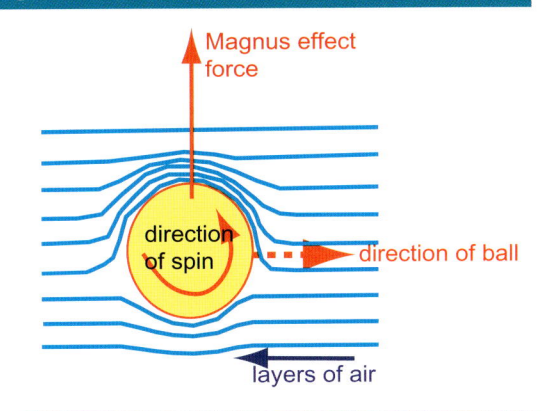

figure 6.25 – flight of a spinning ball

The sense of swerve is in the same direction as the spin on the ball.

The sports in which back spin (figure 6.26b) and top spin (figure 6.26c) are used to the maximum are raquet sports such as tennis and table tennis.

Most tennis players use the top spin effect to cause a ball to dip into the opponent's court after a very firm hit of the ball. Rafael Nadal is a prime exponent of this technique.

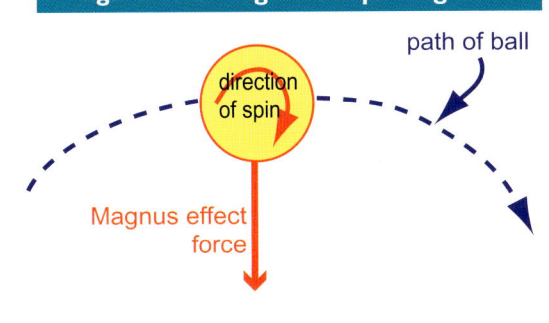

figure 6.26 – flight of a spinning ball

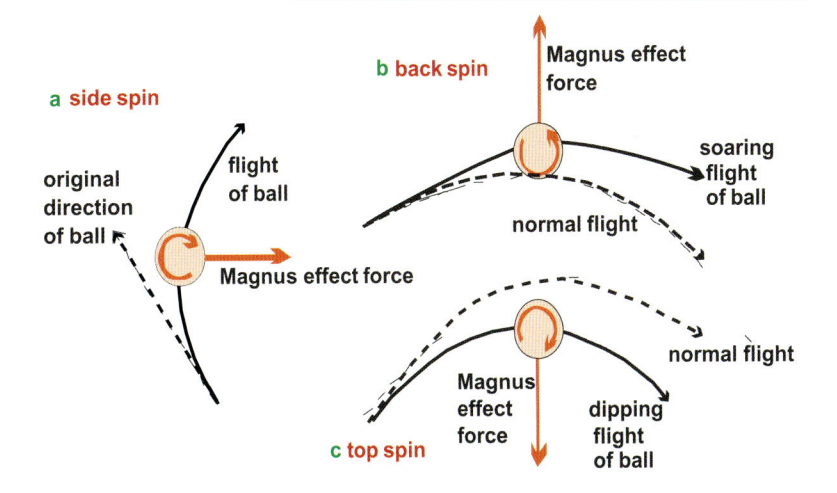

a **side spin**
b **back spin**
c **top spin**

The Bernolli effect 95

SECTION 4 CHAPTER 6

ANGULAR MOTION, PROJECTILE MOTION AND FLUID MECHANICS

figure 6.27 – golfers can control ball spin to place the ball on the green

Practice questions

1) Angle in radians is defined as:
   a. rate of turning.
   b. arc length subtending the angle divided by radius of the circle.
   c. radius of a circle divided by arc length subtending the angle.
   d. moment of inertia divided by angular velocity.

2) Angular velocity is defined as:
   a. angular acceleration divided by time taken to turn through an angle.
   b. distance moved per second in a certain direction.
   c. angle turned through in radians divided by time taken to turn
   d. moment of inertia divided by angular momentum.

3) Which sentence best explains the flight of a projectile?
   a. the projectile travels further if air resistance is large compared with its weight.
   b. a projectile ejected at 45° to the horizontal will travel the furthest.
   c. the flight path of a projectile falls from its initial direction caused by gravity only..
   d. weight and fluid friction are the only forces acting on a projectile.

4) The Bernoulli effect causes a sideways force on an object moving through a fluid because:
   a. fluids flow in a laminar pattern past a moving object.
   b. the pressure exerted by a fast moving fluid is less than that exerted by a slow moving fluid.
   c. the pressure exerted by a fast moving fluid is greater than that exerted by a slow moving fluid.
   d. an unstreamlined object will cause fluid flow to break into vortices.

5) A dancer spinning with arms out wide will spin slower than when he crosses his arms across his chest during a jump because:
   a. angular momentum is bigger with his arms out wide.
   b. angular momentum is smaller with his arms across his chest.
   c. moment of inertia of his body with his arms out wide is bigger.
   d. angular momentum is conserved during the flight of the dancer.

6) Define the term angular velocity.   2 marks

BIOMECHANICAL MOVEMENT

Practice questions

7) a) A diver can make a number of different shapes in the air. Table 6.1 shows three of these. Explain the meaning of moment of inertia (MI) in this context. **4 marks**

Table 6.1 – data for shapes of diver during flight

phase of dive	shape of diver	time during flight	MI of shape kgm²
1	Z 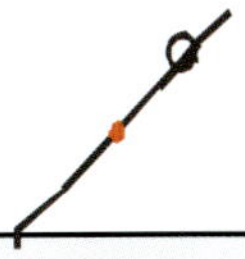	0.0 - 0.5s	18
2	Y 	0.5 - 0.7s	9
3	X 	0.7 - 1.0s	3
4	Z 	1.0 - 1.1s	18
entry	axis of rotation = ●	1.1s	

b) During a dive a diver goes through the shapes shown in table 6.1.
Explain how the rate of spinning (angular velocity) would change through the dive. **5 marks**

c) Sketch a graph of this rate of spinning against time. Your sketch need only be approximate. **4 marks**

d) State the relationship between angular momentum, moment of inertia and angular velocity. **2 marks**

e) Name the law of conservation which accounts for these variations in rate of spin. **1 mark**

f) Explain and sketch the arc described by the diver as he or she falls. **3 marks**

8) a) Describe in detail the body shape and movement within a chosen sporting situation where rates of spin are affected by body shape. **6 marks**

b) How would you stop the spinning in this situation? **2 marks**

c) Figure 6.28 shows a sportsperson's leg in two different positions. The values quoted are the moment of inertia of the leg as it rotates about the hip joint (shown as a red dot on each diagram). Explain the implications of these data for the efficiency of running style in a sprinter and long distance runner **7 marks**

figure 6.28 – shape of leg

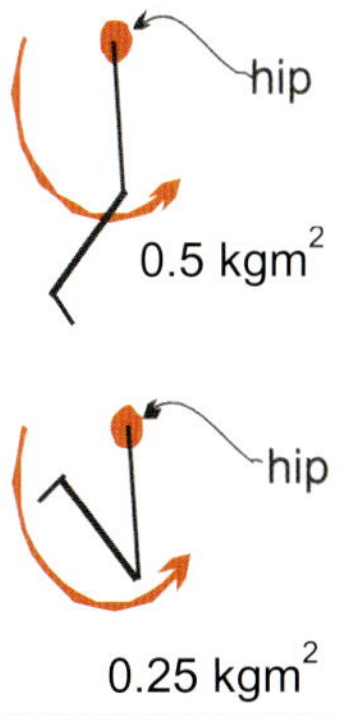

hip — 0.5 kgm²

hip — 0.25 kgm²

Practice questions 97

SECTION 4
CHAPTER 6
ANGULAR MOTION, PROJECTILE MOTION AND FLUID MECHANICS

Practice questions

9) a) Figure 6.29 shows a gymnast undertaking a forward somersault following a run up. Sketch three traces on a single graph to represent any changes in angular momentum, moment of inertia and angular velocity for the period of activity between positions 2 and 9. **3 marks**

figure 6.29 – shapes of a gymnast

b) Explain the shapes of the traces on the sketch graph that you have drawn. **6 marks**

c) Table 6.2 sets out measurements of angular velocities (rates of spin) of the gymnast at successive frames from the start of the somersault.

Estimate from this table the ratio of angular velocities at times X and Y. **1 mark**

d) If the moment of inertia of the gymnast is 8 kgm² at time X, estimate the moment of inertia at time Y, using data from table 6.2. **2 marks**

Table 6.2 – data for angular velocity of gymnast

	frame	angular velocity (degrees s⁻¹)
	1	650
X	2	750
	3	850
	4	1100
	5	1400
Y	6	1500
	7	1000
	8	850
	9	650

10) a) Figure 6.30 shows a spinning skater in various positions. Under each diagram is an approximate value for the moment of inertia of the skater spinning about his or her central vertical axis.

The angular velocity of the skater in position **W** is 2.0 revolutions per second. What is the formula for calculating the skater's angular velocity?

Calculate the angular velocity for the skater in position **Z**. **2 marks**

figure 6.30 – shapes of a skater

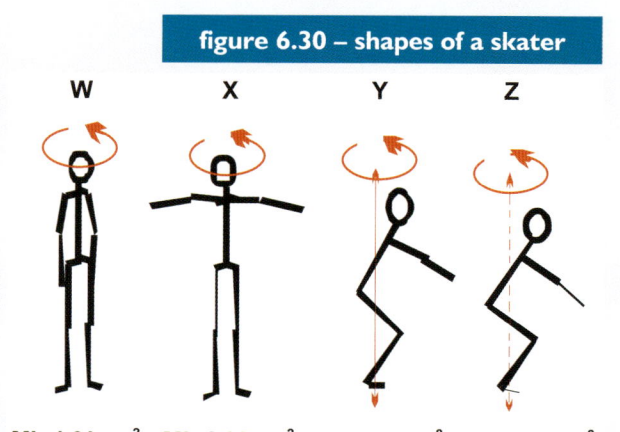

W   X   Y   Z

MI=1.0 kgm²   MI=2.0 kgm²   MI=4.5 kgm²   MI=6.0 kgm²

b) Sketch a figure showing a possible position which could cause the skater to attain an angular velocity of 3.0 revolutions per second and calculate what the moment of inertia of this shape must be. **2 marks**

c) Principles of angular momentum can be used to improve performance in a variety of sports. With the use of diagrams explain how a slalom skier turns through the gates at maximum speed. **4 marks**

d) Explain with the use of diagrams how a dancer manages to complete a triple spin in the air before touching the ground. **4 marks**

98

BIOMECHANICAL MOVEMENT

Practice questions

11) a) Using examples, explain how the shape of an object can alter its flight path. **4 marks**

   b) Explain the effect of air resistance on the flight of two badminton shuttles, one of which has been struck hard and the other gently. **10 marks**

   c) Briefly explain why the flight path of a shot in athletics is so different from the flight of a badminton shuttle. **4 marks**

12) a) Identify three physical factors (not skill factors) which govern a swimmer's speed and explain how one of these occurs. **3 marks**

   b) Describe the factors which determine the amount of fluid friction acting on a swimmer. **4 marks**

   c) Explain how you would minimise turbulent flow (high drag) of the water past the swimmer's body. **2 marks**

   d) Give three examples, each from a different sporting context, to show how fluid friction affects the sportsperson. **3 marks**

   e) How would you attempt to reduce fluid friction? **3 marks**

   f) Look at figure 6.31 showing the vertical forces acting on a swimmer during a stroke. Explain why it is difficult for a swimmer to keep a horizontal floating position. **4 marks**

figure 6.31 – forces acting on a swimmer

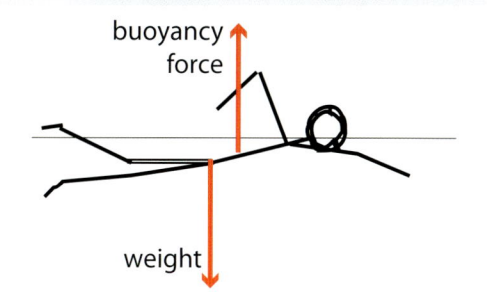

13) a) Fluid friction is a force which acts on a bobsleigh once it is moving. Identify the nature of the fluid friction in this case and explain how this might limit the maximum speed of the bob. **3 marks**

   b) Explain the term 'turbulent flow', and how the bobsleigh is used to minimise this factor. **3 marks**

14) a) Sketch a diagram to show the flight path of the shot from the moment it leaves the putter's hand to the moment it lands. **2 marks**

   b) State and briefly explain three factors (excluding air effects) which should be used by the putter to optimise the distance thrown. **6 marks**

   c) Explain why the turn in a discus throw produces greater horizontal range than the standing throw. **3 marks**

15) a) The Bernoulli effect states that a faster flowing liquid or gas exerts less pressure than a slower moving liquid or gas. Using figure 6.32, show how the Bernoulli effect explains the swerve of a spinning ball. **4 marks**

   b) Use diagrams to show how your explanation relates to the flight of a table tennis ball with side, back and top spin. **3 marks**

   c) Sketch a vector diagram of all forces acting on a table tennis ball in flight with back spin, and explain how the resultant force on the ball predicts the actual acceleration of the ball. **4 marks**

   d) Identify one sport other than a ball game, in which the Bernoulli effect plays a part. **1 mark**

figure 6.32 – Bernoulli effect on a spinning ball

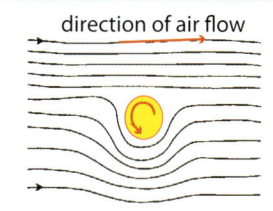

Answers link: http://www.jroscoe.co.uk/downloads/a2_revise_pe_aqa/AQAA2_ch6_answers.pdf

SECTION 4
CHAPTERS 5 & 6

STUDENT NOTES

SECTION 5

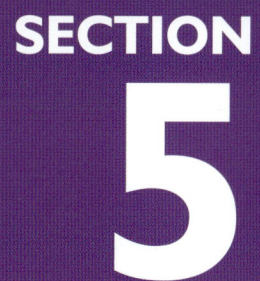

SPORT PSYCHOLOGY

CHAPTER 7
ACHIEVEMENT MOTIVATION, ATTRIBUTION THEORY, SELF-EFFICACY AND CONFIDENCE

CHAPTER 8
LEADERSHIP AND STRESS MANAGEMENT

SECTION 5 CHAPTER 7: ACHIEVEMENT MOTIVATION, ATTRIBUTION THEORY, SELF-EFFICACY AND CONFIDENCE

CHAPTER 7: Achievement motivation, attribution theory, self-efficacy and confidence

Achievement motivation

Achievement motivation is the drive to achieve success for its own sake, and is related to competitiveness, persistence, and striving for perfection.

Achievement motivation is influenced by:
- **Personality** factors, which are:
  - The need to achieve (Nach).
  - The need to avoid failure (Naf).
- **Situational** factors, which are:
  - Probability of success.
  - Incentive value of success.

Atkinson's model of achievement motivation

Atkinson and McCelland derived this idea which hinged around:
- The **need to achieve** (**Nach**) or **tendency to approach success** (**Ts**) personality type likes a challenge, likes feedback, is not afraid of failure and has high task persistence.
- The **need to avoid failure** (**Naf**) or **tendency to avoid failure** (**Taf**) personality type avoids challenges, does not take risks, often gives up, and does not want feedback.

Personality components of achievement motivation

The chart in figure 7.1 shows **Nach** against **Naf**. Most people participating in sport will occupy a small region of the chart, for example regions **A** or **B** as shown on the chart.

A = someone with a high need to achieve who will probably have a low need to avoid failure. Such a person will choose difficult, demanding or more risky tasks, for example, the hard route up a rock face (figure 7.2).

B = someone with a high need to avoid failure who will probably have a low need to achieve, will choose tasks which are less risky and more easily achieved. For example, this person will take the easy route up the rock face.

Situational factors affecting achievement motivation

The chart in figure 7.3 shows probability of success against incentive value of success, and again most people will occupy a small region (examples here are marked **C** and **D**).

C = region of the chart where a task's **probability of success** is **low** (for example, competing against the world champion), and therefore the sportsperson has to strive very hard to win. The **incentive** to **achieve success** is **very high**, and the sportsperson will be hugely pleased if he or she wins.

D = region of the chart where **probability of success** is **high** (for example, competing in local club match), and the sportsperson therefore doesn't need to try as hard to win. Hence the **incentive to achieve** is **low**, because the person expects to win easily, and of course this is not so pleasing to the performer.

STUDENT NOTE

Motivation is discussed on pages 80 and 81 of 'AS/A1 Revise PE for AQA' ISBN 978 1 901424 85 0

figure 7.1 – personality aspects of achievement motivation

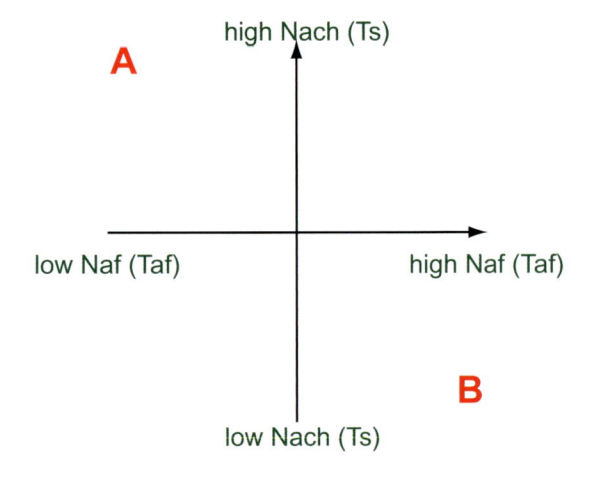

figure 7.2 – high Nach?

figure 7.3 – situational factors in achievement motivation

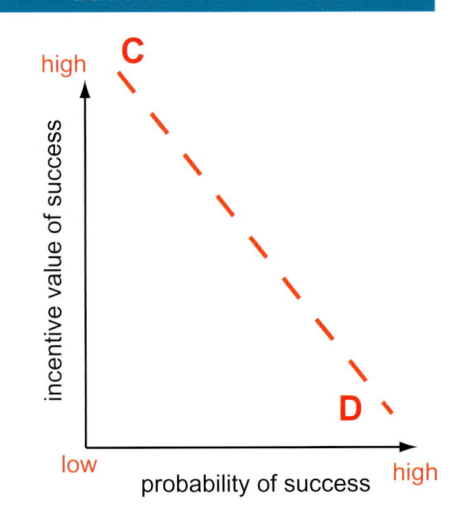

SPORT PSYCHOLOGY

Achievement goal theory

Achievement goals are aims based on how good a person is at an activity (for example sport). Individuals will create their aims in an evaluative situation, for example in a competitive situation as demonstrated by Laura Trott, Max Whitlock and Jack Laugher, multiple winners in Rio (figure 7.4).

Originally, two distinctive achievement goals were identified based on the definition of personal competence. Namely outcome (performance) oriented goals, and task (mastery) oriented goals.

- **Outcome (performance) goals** reflect ability perception relative to the performance of others. Therefore, outcome oriented athletes define their ability in terms of interpersonal and personal comparisons, namely whether they perform with perfect technique or not.
- **Task (mastery) goals** reflect perceived competence or ability in terms of an absolute standard. When someone is task-involved, her primary goal is learning and mastery of the task **for its own sake,** namely whether or not she breaks the world record.
- **Task involvement** appears when the athlete is **intrinsically** interested in the activity and judges herself to her own high standards in comparison to national or world standards.
- Therefore, **task oriented goals** rely on comparisons with requirements of the task and/or internal comparisons with one's past attainment or one's maximum potential attainment.
- There is a focus on **effort** and **improvement**.

These two **goal orientations** determine different consequences in achievement context. In general, **task orientation** is regarded as more adaptive than outcome orientation.

- Task orientation is related to selection of challenging tasks, effective study of strategies, positive attitudes toward learning, and positive emotions.
- Whereas quite often **outcome orientation** is associated with selection of easier tasks, trivial learning strategies, concern for social status, and thoughts of escape and behavioural withdrawal when difficulties are encountered.
- However, if high perceived competence is combined with high task orientation, then outcome orientation supports positive achievement outcomes.

figure 7.4 – team GB, Rio

What should the coach do to develop the need to achieve?

The prime need for a coach is to **improve need and motive to achieve** (Nach) in a sportsperson. This is the positive way to deal with motivational issues, and there are strategies he could use to **promote Nach**:
- Increase **positive reinforcement** hence increasing pride and satisfaction.
- Ensure that goals are **achievable**.
- Ensure that at least some situations **guarantee success**.
- Gradually **increase task difficulty** in line with progress.
- Ensure that tasks are **challenging**.
- Ensure that the **probability of success is good**.
- Ensure that the **incentive value of the success is high** (is the race worth winning?).

The coach should also **reduce tendency and motive to avoid failure** (Naf) by:
- **Reducing punishment** hence lowering the chance of performer worrying about failure.
- **Focusing negative feedback** on effort rather than ability.
- This avoids the performer tending to believe that causes of failure are internal (due to lack of ability for example).
- And reduces the risk of learned helplessness (page 106).
- **Avoiding** situations where defeat or **failure is inevitable** (such as performing against a much superior opponent).
- If this is not possible **redefine the criteria for success** (for example, you will have succeeded if you only lose by 2 goals).

Achievement goal theory   **103**

SECTION 5 CHAPTER 7 — *ACHIEVEMENT MOTIVATION, ATTRIBUTION THEORY, SELF-EFFICACY AND CONFIDENCE*

Attribution

Attribution is the process of giving **reasons** for behaviour and ascribing **causes** for events. For example, the player played badly today because the weather was poor.

Weiner's model

Weiner's model has four attributions, **ability**, **effort**, **task difficulty** and **luck** (see figure 7.5).

As in figure 7.5, these attributions are arranged in two dimensions, **locus of causality** and **stability** (with a possible third dimension, **controllability**).

figure 7.5 – Weiner's model of sports attribution

		LOCUS OF CAUSALITY	
		INTERNAL	**EXTERNAL**
STABILITY	**STABLE**	ability 'we were more skilful'	task difficulty 'the opposition are world champions'
	UNSTABLE	effort 'we tried hard'	luck 'the court was slippy'

Locus of causality dimension

Locus of causality is the performance outcome caused by:
- **Internal factors** under the control of the performer such as ability and effort.
  - **Ability** is the extent of the performer's capacity to cope with a sporting task.
  - **Effort** refers to the amount of mental and physical effort the performer gives to the task.
- **External factors** beyond the control of the performer such as task difficulty and luck.
  - **Task difficulty** is the term describing the extent of the problems posed by the task including the strength of the opposition.
  - **Luck** describes factors attributable to chance, such as the weather or the state of the pitch.

Stability dimension

Stability refers to the performance outcome caused by stable or unstable factors:
- **Stable** factors are fixed factors which don't change with time such as **ability** or **task difficulty**.
- **Unstable** factors are factors which can vary with time such as **effort** or **luck**.

In attribution theory, **success** is explained by internal attributions, and **failure** is explained by external attributions. **Future expectations** are related to stability. If we attribute success to stable factors, or if we attribute failure to stable factors, then we expect the same next time.

Relationship to sports achievement

- **High achievers** (such as Andy Murray, figure 7.6) tend to attribute **success** to internal factors (such as Andy's incredible state of fitness), and attribute **failure** to external factors (such as the high temperature or strong wind during the match).
- **Low achievers** tend to attribute success to external factors (such as a favourable wind), and attribute failure to internal factors (such as lack of fitness or ability).
- The process of changing attributions is called **attribution retraining**. The point of this is to change a person's tendency to ascribe reasons for success or failure so that it is more like that of a successful performer rather than an unsuccessful performer.
- Attributions affect a sportsperson's **pride**, **satisfaction**, and **expectancy of success**. Some people exhibit **avoidance** tendencies when faced with a sporting situation (they try to avoid participating), and this is called **learned helplessness**.

figure 7.6 – Andy Murray - high achiever

SPORT PSYCHOLOGY

Controllability, the third dimension

The **locus of control** covers attributions under the control of the performer (and sometimes not under the control of the performer). The locus of control dimension relates to the intensity of a performer's feelings of **pride** and **satisfaction**, **shame** and **guilt**.

- **Pride** and **satisfaction** are maximised if success is attributed to internal controllable factors like ability and effort, therefore motivation would be enhanced.
- If **success** were attributed to **external** and **uncontrollable** factors such as luck or the fact that the task was very easy, then satisfaction would be less intense and there would be less motivation.
- If **failure** is attributed to internal controllable factors such as **lack of ability** and **lack of effort**, then the overpowering emotion would be dissatisfaction and motivation would be reduced.

The self-serving bias

- This idea crops up because **successful performers** tend to take credit for success. They do this by **attributing success** to their own overwhelmingly outstanding **qualities** (natural ability, **ability** to respond to the competitive situation), thereby enhancing their feelings of pride, self-worth, and self-esteem. They also tend to **blame external factors** for failure.

- Failure is automatically attributed to **avoid internal** controllable and stable factors (even if such factors may be true). This is the **self-serving bias**, people tend to give attributions to **protect their self-esteem** rather than look for true attributions which would reflect the reality of the situation.

- **Unsuccessful performers** do not always attribute failure to external factors and therefore do not protect their self-esteem. This tends to reduce motivation.

Figure 7.7 summarises the attribution process.

figure 7.7 – the attribution process

OUTCOME: success / failure

ATTRIBUTION:
- internal external
- stable unstable
- intentional unintentional
- controlled uncontrolled
- specific global

EXPECTANCY: future failure / future success

EMOTIONS: pride / satisfaction

MASTERY ORIENTATION: attribution of success to internal stable factors / attribution of failure to external unstable factors

DECISIONS ABOUT PARTICIPATION: drive to succeed / motivation / continuation

LEARNED HELPLESSNESS: lack of motivation / reinforced failure

The link between motivation, attribution and task persistence

Table 7.1 – motivation, attribution and task choice and persistence

	high achiever	low achiever
motivation	high motive to achieve success low motive to avoid failure focuses on pride and on success	low motive to achieve success high motive to avoid failure focuses on shame and worry about failure
attributions	ascribes success to stable internal controllable factors ascribes failure to unstable external uncontrollable factors	ascribes success to unstable external uncontrollable factors ascribes failure to stable internal controllable factors
goals adopted	adopts task oriented goals	adopts outcome oriented goals
task choice and persistence	seeks challenging tasks and competitive situations and stays with them	avoids challenge, seeks very difficult or very easy tasks or competition and easily gives up
performance	performs well in front of evaluative audiences	performs badly in front of evaluative audiences

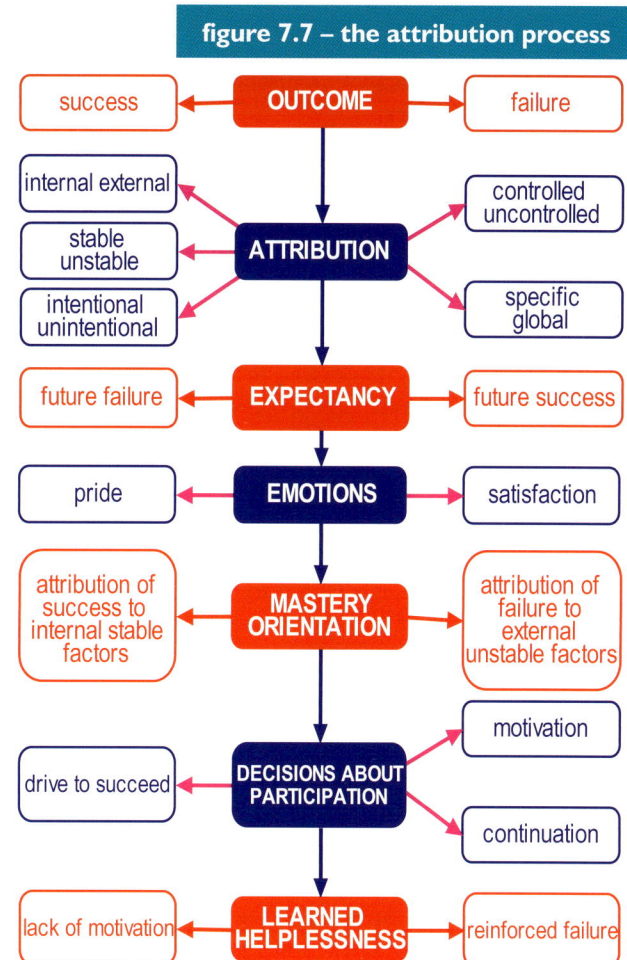

The self-serving bias

SECTION 5 CHAPTER 7
ACHIEVEMENT MOTIVATION, ATTRIBUTION THEORY, SELF-EFFICACY AND CONFIDENCE

Learned helplessness (LH)

Repeated failure (or lack of success) can lead to a state known as **learned helplessness**.

This is explained as a **belief** acquired over time that one has no control over events and that failure is inevitable (for example, if a batsman repeatedly gets a duck, he may feel that he no longer has the skill to succeed at sport). It is characterised by a feeling of **hopelessness** in which a person with the physical potential to achieve highly at sport no longer feels that it is possible for him or her to do so (figure 7.8).

This is what is behind the common belief that if you fall off a bike, you must get back on straight away, otherwise you may never do so.

figure 7.8 – get back on the bike straight away

General and specific learned helplessness

- **General (global) learned helplessness** occurs when a person attributes failure to internal and stable factors, and this feeling of failure is applied to all sports. For example, the comment 'I am useless at all sports'.
- **Specific learned helplessness** occurs when a person attributes difficulties to internal and stable factors, and this feeling is applied to one specific sport. For example, the comment 'I am good at soccer but useless at racquet games'.

Attribution retraining strategies

Figure 7.9 summarises the process which must be undertaken if learned helplessness is to be avoided or recovered from. Following failure, low achievers need to learn to attribute success and failure to the same reasons as high achievers, namely:

- Success should be attributed to stable internal factors.
- Failure should be attributed to unstable external factors.

This would raise the **self-efficacy** (page 107) of the performer for his or her sport.

Hence attribution retraining will influence how the performer deals with a situation. During this process, the coach can provide encouraging feedback and set realistic achievable goals.

The positive and negative applications of attribution theory on performance and sustaining a balanced, active lifestyle is summarised in table 7.1 on page 105.

figure 7.9 – attribution retraining

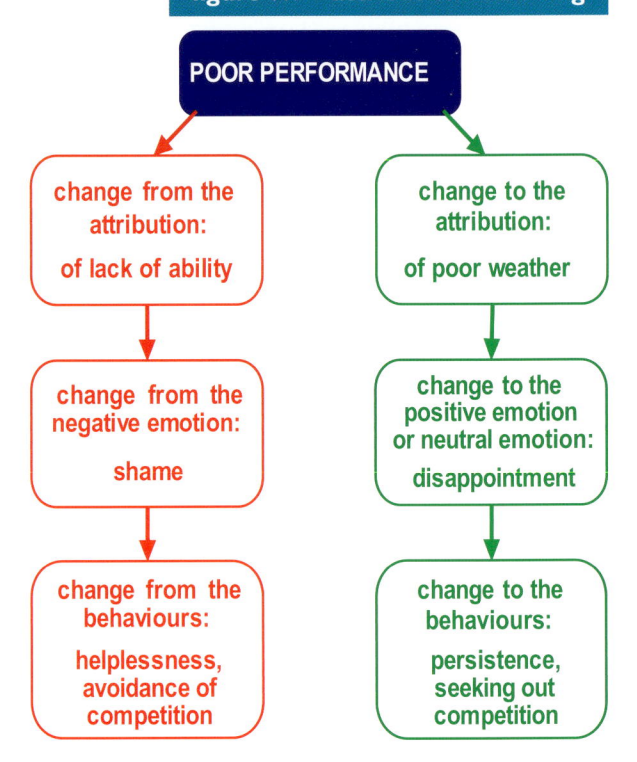

POOR PERFORMANCE

change from the attribution: of lack of ability → change from the negative emotion: shame → change from the behaviours: helplessness, avoidance of competition

change to the attribution: of poor weather → change to the positive emotion or neutral emotion: disappointment → change to the behaviours: persistence, seeking out competition

figure 7.10 – failure needs retraining

figure 7.11 – a confident save

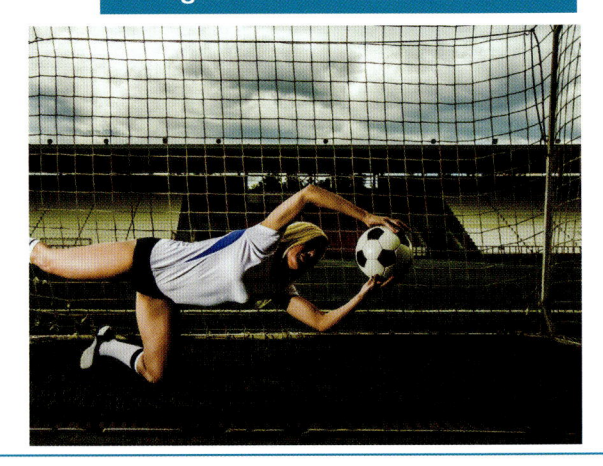

106

SPORT PSYCHOLOGY

Self-confidence and self-efficacy

Confidence

Confidence is an element of mental preparation for sports performance, as outlined in figure 7.8, page 106.

Confidence affects us by:
- Arousing **positive** emotions.
- Facilitating **concentration**.
- Enabling **focus** on the important aspects of a task.

Confidence (figure 7.12) arouses positive emotions which allow the athlete to:
- Remain **calm** under pressure.
- Be **assertive** when required.
- **Concentrate** easily.
- **Focus** on the important aspects of a task.
- Set challenging but realistic **goals**.
- Increase **effort**.
- Devise effective game **strategies**.
- Keep psychological **momentum**.

Self-confidence and self-efficacy

Self-confidence is a feature of a sportsperson's attitude to his or her sporting activity which boosts personal self-worth and self-belief as outlined in figure 7.13. This belief centres around the notion that he or she can win or perform well.

Self-efficacy is a situational form of self-confidence. It is specific to the sport or activity which a person is undertaking.

Sport-confidence

A confident player plays to win even if it means **taking risks**, will take each point or play at a time, and **never gives up** even when defeat is imminent.

Self-esteem

Self-esteem is the **regard** you hold for yourself. Everyone has a concept of his or her person (**self-concept**). If you like your self-concept (who you think you are), then you have self-esteem. Self-confidence is different.

Self-confidence is the **belief in your ability** to perform a task - it is not a judgment. You can have self-confidence, but not self-esteem, and vice versa. Optimally, you want both high self-confidence in your abilities and self-esteem.

Self-esteem should be based on **who you are as a person** instead of how well you can perform in your sport or how high you go in a sporting career. Think about this: if you take away the part of you who is an athlete, how would you describe yourself? What are your personal characteristics that describe you? This is what self-esteem should be based on.
If you feel like you struggle with self-esteem, have hope, since this is a learned capability and it can change with practice, and the will to improve.

figure 7.12 – self-confidence

figure 7.13 – self-confidence and self-efficacy

Self-efficacy and confidence | 107

SECTION 5 CHAPTER 7 — ACHIEVEMENT MOTIVATION, ATTRIBUTION THEORY, SELF-EFFICACY AND CONFIDENCE

Self-efficacy

Bandura's self-efficacy model (figure 7.14) outlines **four** factors relevant to the self-efficacy of a sports performer.

Performance accomplishments

- **Performance accomplishments** consist of **past experiences**, for example, a previously performed skill at dribbling a soccer ball.
- If this is successful, then this leads to greater self-efficacy at this particular task in the future.

Vicarious experiences

- **Vicarious experiences** consist of what has **been observed in others** performing a similar skill (the sports performer experiences the same feelings of mastery and competence by watching another person perform a skill as if he or she has performed the skill himself or herself).
- For example, observing another player in your team dribbling a soccer ball. This is most effective if the model is of similar age or ability and is successful. This may lead to greater self-efficacy.

Verbal persuasion

- **Verbal encouragement** can lead to greater self-efficacy if the person giving encouragement is of **high status** compared with the performer.

Emotional arousal

- If **arousal** is too high, then **state anxiety** (anxiety produced by the specific situation of an activity - otherwise known as **A-state**) can be too high.
- This could lead to low self-efficacy. Mental rehearsal or physical relaxation techniques could lead to greater confidence and a calmer approach - this also contributes to greater self-efficacy.

figure 7.14 – self-efficacy (Bandura)

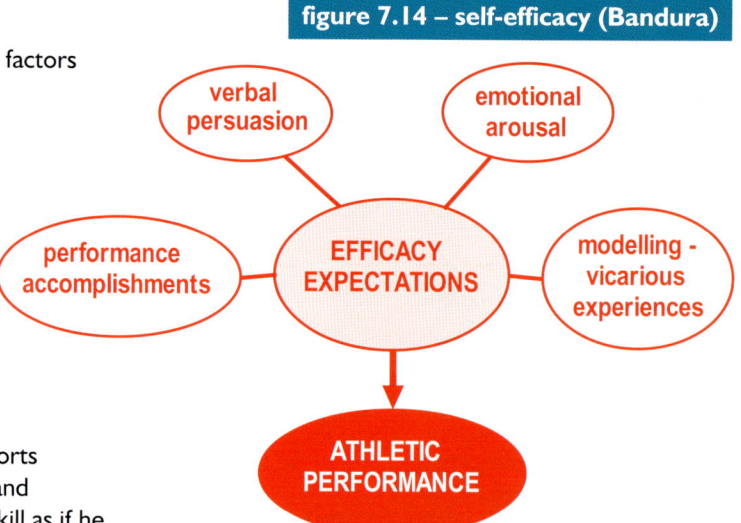

Vealey's model of sport confidence

Vealey's **sport confidence** is the level of belief a person has in his or her ability to be successful at sport.

- Success in sport could be related to winning (**outcome orientation**), or performing well (**performance orientation**).
- Different performers have different ways of enhancing sport confidence. Their **competitive orientations** can be varied according to the situation and whether a performer is motivated towards a performance goal or an outcome goal.

Table 7.2 – **sport confidence**

factors influencing sport confidence	definition
trait sport confidence	the level of sport confidence a person usually has
competitive orientation	the perceived opportunity to achieve a performance or outcome goal
state sport confidence	the level of sport confidence a performer has in a specific sport situation
objective sporting situation	the performance takes into account the situation in which performance occurs

SPORT PSYCHOLOGY

Vealey's model

Trait sport-confidence example, a discus thrower is generally confident about making a throw (figure 7.15).

Competitive orientation example, the discus thrower is motivated by a challenging competition to throw well.

State sport-confidence example, the discus thrower feels confident because the wind is in the right direction.

Objective sporting situation, the discus thrower competes well in the World Championships.

Relationship of confidence to attribution

A performer's attribution of success or failure will relate to sport confidence. Attributing success to factors like ability and effort will increase a performer's sport confidence, by increasing his or her future expectancy of success.

Results of research

- **Males** (in the general population) have a higher sport-confidence than **females**.
- **Elite performers** have high sport-confidence.
- Elite sporting females have the **same level** of sport-confidence as elite sporting males.
- Therefore elite sporting females are **less affected** by **traditional female stereotyping** and roles.
- Elite performers are more **performance oriented**, which means that their feelings of confidence are based more on how well they perform than whether they win or lose.

Lack of confidence

Lack of confidence can cause **stress** under pressure. What tends to happen is that attention and concentration tend to focus on outside stressors such as mistakes (falling during an ice-skating or gymnastics programme), or spectators (shouted comments or applause on a neighbouring court).

- What also tends to happen is the setting of **goals** which are either **too easy** or **too hard**.
- Lack of confidence also causes the athlete to try to **avoid mistakes** (fear of failure or tendency to avoid failure, see page 102 about achievement motivation).
- Non-confident athletes find it difficult to reverse negative psychological momentum, so that once things start to go wrong it is difficult to think positively.

Over-confidence or false confidence

Over-confidence is dangerous because it can lead to inadequate preparation (the athlete thinks he or she is better prepared than is actually the case, figure 7.16).

Low motivation and low arousal can occur, which are difficult to correct when competition is under way.

figure 7.15 – discus throwers need to be confident

figure 7.16 – over-confidence can lead to injury

Lack of confidence   109

SECTION 5 CHAPTER 7 — ACHIEVEMENT MOTIVATION, ATTRIBUTION THEORY, SELF-EFFICACY AND CONFIDENCE

Strategies for the coach in building self-efficacy

Coaches can raise a performer's self-efficacy, resulting in a more positive and successful performance, as suggested in Bandura's self-efficacy theory (page 108):

- Build upon **successful experiences** by reminding performer of past successes. A previous performance is the strongest factor affecting self-efficacy and there is no reason why it cannot be repeated.
- Observe a **good demonstration** from a performer who shares the same characteristics, such as ability, gender and age, as the young performer. For example, a gymnast of similar age and standard, performs a forward roll on the beam. This performer will feel 'If she can do it, so can I'. Such a demonstration reduces worry and develops confidence.
- Use **role models** (figure 7.17) to inspire and motivate performer of potential long-term goals.
- Use **specific positive feedback**, such as words of encouragement and support, that may be related to a previous performance. The aim would be to convince the athlete of his or her ability to accomplish the task. Therefore, saying 'You can do it!' is not as effective as saying 'You successfully long jumped 4 metres, you can do 4.2 metres.' This positive talk or persuasion will elevate self-belief.
- **Break down complex skills** (whole-part-whole learning) into smaller specific components that challenge the performer but are within his or her current ability level, thus allowing the performer to have successful experiences which will over time increase the performer's self-efficacy.
- Use **mental rehearsal** or **imagery** techniques to reinforce skill learning (page 117).
- Control of **arousal levels** of the performer's internal feelings and physiological state, for example, increased heart rate and sweating. This may include **cognitive** and **somatic** strategies.

figure 7.17 – Johanna Konta role model

Homefield advantage

Homefield advantage describes the benefit that the home team is said to gain over the visiting team. This benefit has been attributed to:

- The **psychological effects** supporting fans have on the competitors or referees.
- The psychological and **physiological** advantages of playing at home in familiar situations.
- The **disadvantages** away teams suffer from changing time zones or **climates** or from the rigors of **travel**.
- And, in some sports, to **specific rules** that favour the home team directly or indirectly.
- As **spectator density** increases, homefield advantage increases.
- The **nearer the spectators** are to the performers, the greater the homefield advantage.
- The more **hostile the spectators** are to the visiting team, the greater the homefield advantage.

These benefits keep **uncertainty** and therefore **arousal** levels **low**. However, the pressure may be high when playing at home due to the home spectators' expectation of winning. If an individual or team performance does **not live up to** the pre-game expectation, a home crowd might boo or chant, causing player **inhibition** and choking, with a catastrophic effect on individual performances.

The gold medal count in the London Olympics 2012 was of 29 gold medals (one of which was won by Jessica Ennis figure 7.18).

This remarkable result was in part due to superb performances at the home games over and above the performers' expectations. **Huge spectator attendances** helped boost the confidence of all performers not just the medalists. This **facilitation** was a factor in the homefield advantage of the games.

figure 7.18 – Jessica Ennis wins in London 2012, homefield advantage

SPORT PSYCHOLOGY

Practice questions

1) Which one of the following best explains achievement motivation?
   a. a person will seek out risky tasks which will have great rewards.
   b. a person will fear risky tasks but loves to take on easy tasks.
   c. a person will fear risky tasks and will give up his or her sport.
   d. a person will will have great self satisfaction from succeeding at risky tasks.

2) A coach could reduce the tendency to avoid failure in his or athletes by:
   a. increasing the punishment (using sendings off or fines) when they fail.
   b. focusing negative feedback on the athlete's effort.
   c. avoid situations where defeat is inevitable (not competing agaianst much better opponents).
   d. ridicule the athlete for poor performance.

3) Weiner's model of attribution refers to:
   a. stable factors, such as efforts and luck.
   b. unstable factors sucuh as ability or task difficulty.
   c. future expectations are related to unstable factors.
   d. success is best explained by internal attributions.

4) Bandura's model of self-efficacy does not include:
   a. performance accomplishments.
   b. excitement-arousal.
   c. vicarious experiences.
   d. verbal persuasion.

5) Vealey's model of sport confidence includes:
   a. competitive orientation.
   b. a nurtured personality.
   c. confidence at all sports.
   d. a subjective outcome.

6) A thrower prepares for a qualifying competition, but suffers from stress and tries too hard and so performs badly. Which theory explains this behaviour?
   a. catastrophe theory.
   b. multi-dimensional anxiety theory.
   c. inverted U theory.
   d. drive theory.

7) a) What do you understand by the term achievement motivation? Explain the different types.   3 marks

   b) How could a coach use the different types of achievement motivation with a group of beginners?   2 marks

8) a) Describe the characteristics of the positive motive: 'the need to achieve'.   4 marks

   b) Describe an example from sport of someone who has a high motive to avoid failure.   3 marks

   c) Identify factors which could affect the use of motives to achieve and to avoid failure in sporting situations.   3 marks

9) How would you promote the need to achieve motive, rather than the need to avoid failure motive?   8 marks

SECTION 5 CHAPTER 7
ACHIEVEMENT MOTIVATION, ATTRIBUTION THEORY, SELF-EFFICACY AND CONFIDENCE

Practice questions

10) a) Figure 7.19 partly illustrates Weiner's model of attribution. Explain the term attribution using a sporting situation. **2 marks**

   b) Explain the terms locus of causality and stability when applied to attribution theory. **4 marks**

   c) Redraw the model and place on it relevant attributions for each of the four boxes. **4 marks**

   d) What attributions would you encourage if your team were playing well but often losing? **5 marks**

figure 7.19 – Weiner's model of attribution

	locus of causality	
	internal	external
stable		
unstable		

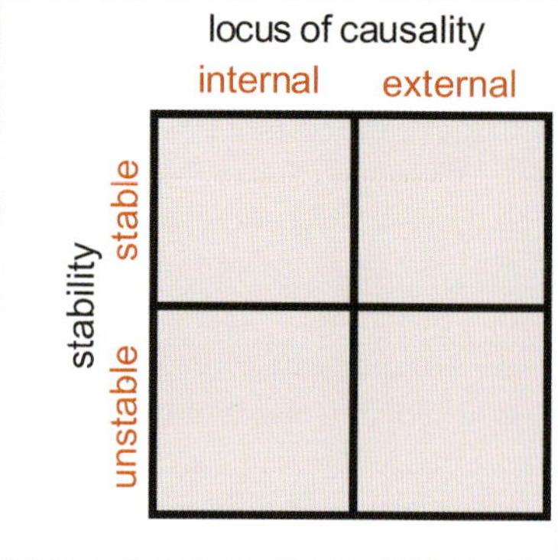

11) a) Many young people claim to be hopeless at gymnastics. Suggest three reasons why these youngsters might have a negative attitude to gymnastics. **3 marks**

   b) What is meant by learned helplessness (LH) and how is it caused? **3 marks**

   c) How would you attempt to attract beginners to a gymnastics class, and then change any negative attitudes? **4 marks**

12) Those who achieve little in sport often attribute their failure to factors outside their control and learned helplessness can result.
Using examples from sport, explain what is meant by learned helplessness and identify how self-motivational techniques may help to limit the effects of learned helplessness. **6 marks**

13) a) What is meant by the term self-efficacy when applied to sports psychology? **1 mark**

   b) Bandura suggested that self-efficacy is influenced by four factors. Identify and apply these factors to a sport of your choice. **8 marks**

   c) As a coach of a sports team, how would you raise an individual's level of self-efficacy? **4 marks**

14) Drawing on your knowledge and understanding of sports psychology, examine the theories and methods that you might use to raise the levels of confidence of a sports performer. Illustrate your answer with practical examples. **15 marks**

Answers link: http://www.jroscoe.co.uk/downloads/a2_revise_pe_aqa/AQAA2_ch7_answers.pdf

SPORT PSYCHOLOGY

CHAPTER 8: Leadership and stress management

Leadership

Leaders play an important role influencing groups and individuals as well as setting goals. In terms of sport, leaders include team captains, coaches, managers and teachers. Successful teams have strong leaders.

A leader can influence the behaviour of others towards required and desired goals and will influence effective team cohesion. He or she will also help fulfil the expectations of a team, and will develop an environment in which a group is motivated, rewarded and helped towards its common goals. Recognised characteristics of successful leaders are summarised in figure 8.1.

Carron suggested that leaders emerge in two ways:

- **Emergent leaders** come from within a group because of their skill and abilities or through nomination or election.
- **Prescribed leaders** are appointed by a governing body or agency outside the group.

figure 8.1 – leadership chacteristics

CHARACTERISTICS OF EFFECTIVE LEADERS: knowledgeable, motivational, respectful, communicative, patient, firm, consistent, fair, fearless, forgiving, confident, engaging, empathetic, organised

The Chelladurai continuum

The **Chelladurai continuum** theory covers the notion that there are three types of leader, and that an actual leader may adopt all three of the types in different situations depending on the circumstances. These three types of leader are:

- The **autocratic authoritarian** leader who makes all the decisions.
- The **democratic** leader who shares the decisions (with members of a group or team), and seeks advice from the group itself. He or she will be prepared to change his or her mind based on this advice.
- The **laissez-faire** leader who lets others make decisions and is prepared to go along with whatever they decide.

Effective leadership

Table 8.1 effective leadership

	autocratic style	democratic style	laissez-faire style
what is it?	the leader commands, and other team members have no input	team members discuss with leader what to do	leader has the same role as rest of the team, he or she is passive, but provides support where necessary
characteristics	leader makes all decisions leader tells them all what to do	team members give input social development encouraged	team members take responsibility for decisions lleader has very little input
when is it effective?	dangerous situations team performing badly team members not familiar with tactics or skills	small groups team members are highly skilled team members are all capable of being leaders	most people think this does not work but may function for very experienced team members

Leadership 113

SECTION 5 CHAPTER 8 — LEADERSHIP AND STRESS MANAGEMENT

Theories of leadership

These theories centre around the **nature** or **nurture** debate.

The 'great man' or trait theory

This is the '**nature**' theory, that leaders are born not made, and have relevant innate personality qualities.

Social learning theory

This is the '**nurture**' theory, in which leaders learn their skills through watching and imitating other people (models). This theory says that leaders are formed throughout life by social or environmental influences.

According to this idea, learning to be a leader starts by observation of a model, then continues by imitation or copying of the behaviour of the model. The effectiveness of this process would depend on the model having high status.

figure 8.2 – Kate Richardson-Walsh

Kate Richardson-Walsh (figure 8.2) was the inspirational captain of the women's hockey team which won gold at the Rio Olympics 2016. She had 375 caps for her country and was captain for 13 years. She is an example of a highly successful leader.

Fiedler's contingency theory

Fiedler's theory states that there is a continuum between:

- **Task-centred leadership**, which would be best for the most favourable or least favourable situations.
- **Person** (or relationship) **centred leadership** which would be best for moderately favourable situations.

Whether or not the task-centred or person-centred approach should be used depends on whether relationships are warm, if the task has a clear structure, or if the leader is powerful and people will do exactly what he or she says.

There would also be the pressure of time which might affect the choice of leadership style.

Factors affecting leader effectiveness

Figure 8.3 summarises the three broad groups of factors affecting the effectiveness of a leader with any given group or team.

Leader characteristics

The following **leadership qualities** will determine a leader's effectiveness (this is expanded in figure 8.1 page 113):

- Ability to communicate.
- Respect for group members.
- Enthusiasm.
- High ability.
- Deep knowledge of the sport and techniques or tactics.
- Charisma.

figure 8.3 – factors affecting leader effectiveness

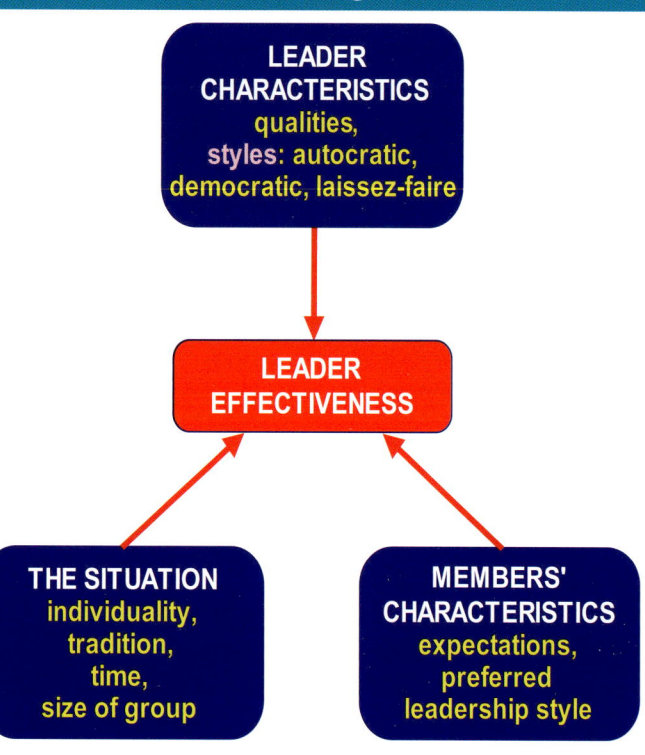

LEADER CHARACTERISTICS
qualities, styles: autocratic, democratic, laissez-faire

→ **LEADER EFFECTIVENESS**

THE SITUATION
individuality, tradition, time, size of group

MEMBERS' CHARACTERISTICS
expectations, preferred leadership style

SPORT PSYCHOLOGY

Situational factors within leadership

- If things are going **well** for the team, or things are going **badly** (for example there are poor facilities or no support), then a leader needs to be **task-oriented**.
- On the other hand, if things are going **moderately well**, then a leader needs to be **person-centred**.
- In **team sports**, a leader should be **directive** (task-oriented) and would organise and structure group tasks according to a plan (tactics or game strategy).
- In **individual sports**, however, we would look for a person-oriented leader, who would empathise with athlete problems and be sympathetic to individual difficulties.
- The **size of group** will affect leadership style, since the more members in a group, the less likely individual needs will be taken into account.
- If a **decision needs to be made quickly** (for example in a dangerous rock climbing situation), then an **autocratic** style of leader would be essential to ensure that the correct action is taken immediately (people will need to be told what to do to avoid danger).
- **Tradition** can sometimes play a part in which style of leadership should be used, since within some groups, group members might tend to resent change. Sometimes change is essential, and it would be necessary to be **autocratic** and **task-centred** to implement change (the leader would not try and explain why change is needed, just that it needs to be done for the good of the team).

Members' characteristics within leadership

A good leader will adapt to the expectations, knowledge and experience of group members.

- If members of a group are **hostile**, then a leader would adopt an **autocratic** style.
- If members of a group are **friendly**, then the leader would adopt a more **democratic** and **person-centred** style.

Problems arise if the strategies for preparation used by a leader do not match group expectations (for example, if members of a team do not feel that the proposed strategy will achieve a win in the next match against a particular opposing team).

Chelladurai's multidimensional model

Chelladurai set out the model in figure 8.4, which sets out the links between **leader**, **situation** and **member** characteristics, and **required**, **actual** and **preferred** leader behaviour. All these factors will affect the eventual performance of a team or group, and the satisfaction gained or perceived by both group members and the leader him or herself.

The point made by the model is that all the factors discussed above are linked in a real situation.

Chelladurai's five types of leader behaviour

Training and instruction behaviour

This behaviour is aimed at improving performance. This type of leader behaviour is strong on **technical** and **tactical** aspects.

Democratic behaviour

This approach is one in which the leader allows decisions to be made **collectively**.

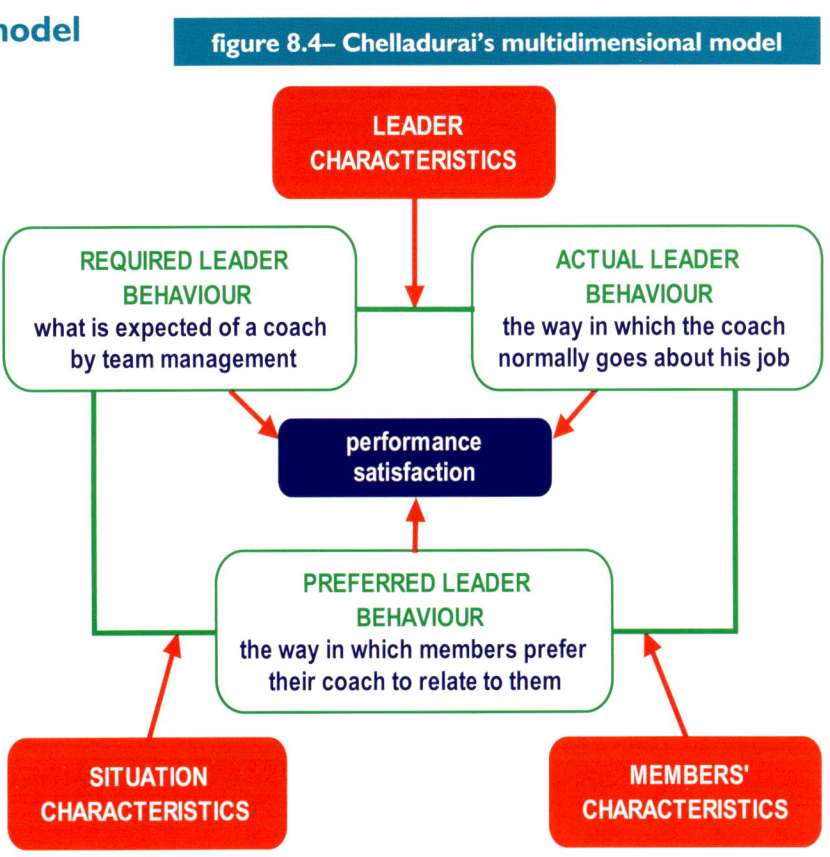

figure 8.4– Chelladurai's multidimensional model

LEADER CHARACTERISTICS

REQUIRED LEADER BEHAVIOUR
what is expected of a coach by team management

ACTUAL LEADER BEHAVIOUR
the way in which the coach normally goes about his job

performance satisfaction

PREFERRED LEADER BEHAVIOUR
the way in which members prefer their coach to relate to them

SITUATION CHARACTERISTICS

MEMBERS' CHARACTERISTICS

SECTION 5 CHAPTER 8 — LEADERSHIP AND STRESS MANAGEMENT

Chelladurai's five types of leader behaviour

Autocratic behaviour
This approach is one in which a leader uses his or her **personal authority**. This type would be least preferred if the leader or coach **does not show** that he or she is aware of sportspeople's needs and preferences.

Social support behaviour
This approach is one in which concern is shown for the **well-being of others**. This might be preferred by youngsters.

Rewards behaviour
A leader uses **positive reinforcement** to gain the **authority** of leadership.

Stress management

Stress can be used positively in sport, but at the same time it can result in a **bad experience**.

Stress and **anxiety** are closely linked, with stress being a major cause of health issues in our society. Figure 8.5 outlines the main factors associated with stress and stressors.

Stress is a response of the body to any demands made on it. The symptoms of stress are **physiological**, **psychological** or **behavioural** (see table 8.2 below for details).

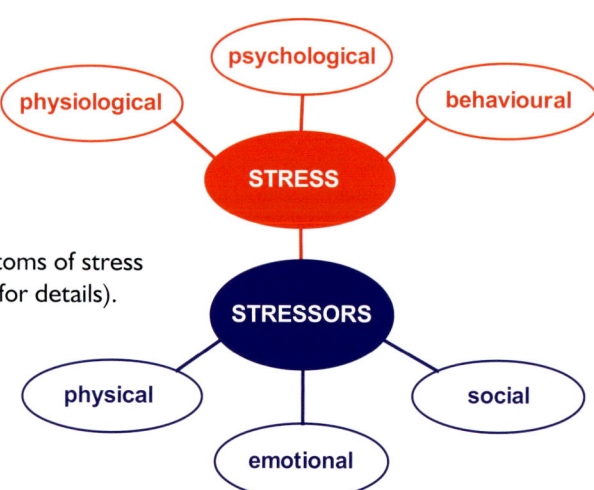

figure 8.5 – stress and stressors

Stress and stressors

Stressors are the cause of stress and are:

- **Social**, including the disapproval of parents or peers, the effects of an audience, a 'win-at-all-costs' attitude, excessive expectations from pre-match pep talks.
- **Chemical** or **biochemical**, in which damage is inflicted by ingestion of harmful substances.
- **Bacterial**, which would be an illness caused by micro-organisms.
- **Physical**, in which a person would suffer injury, pain or exhaustion.
- **Climatic**, in which extremes of weather are experienced, such as hot weather for endurance activities, or rain and cold on bare skin.
- **Psychological** or **cognitive**, in which there is a mismatch between the perception of the demands of a task and the ability of a person to cope with these demands.
- **Physiological** or **somatic**, which produces a physiological response such as increased heart rate.

Symptoms of stress

Table 8.2 – **symptoms of stress**

physiological symptoms	psychological symptoms	behavioural symptoms
increased heart rate	worry	rapid talking
increased blood pressure	feeling overwhelmed	nail biting
increased sweating	inability to make decisions	pacing
increased breathing rate	inability to concentrate	scowling
decreased flow of blood to the skin	inability to direct attention appropriately	yawning
increased oxygen uptake	narrowing of attention	trembling
dry mouth	feeling out of control	raised voice pitch
cold clammy hands	negative self-talk	frequent urination
constantly feeling sick	apprehension	dazed look in eyes

SPORT PSYCHOLOGY

Control of stress and anxiety

Stress and anxiety management techniques become important for sports performers when performances fall, or failure is experienced.

Cognitive and somatic relaxation techniques

Cognitive techniques use the power of **thought** to redirect attention away from failure or perceived failure. A performer will take **control** of emotions and thought processes, will **eliminate negative feelings**, and will develop **self-confidence** (self-efficacy, page 93).

Somatic relaxation techniques are used to control the **physiological** symptoms of stress and anxiety.

Cognitive relaxation techniques

Psychological skills training

Psychological skills training (PST), refers to the total experience of training at the following various techniques for improving cognitive relaxation. The point is that such activities have to be repeated (trained) if they are to be effective. Most top sports clubs and national teams employ sports psychologists to supervise and direct this training.

Mental rehearsal

Mental rehearsal or practice describes the mental or cognitive rehearsal of a skill by a performer without actual physical movement. The performer will consciously imagine a performance, sometimes whlie being prompted by a coach, with attention to technical or tactical issues.

This process helps **concentration**, and helps the performer to focus on strengths and weaknesses. This technique is used by most top level sportsmen, and is often prompted by a video or talk from a coach.

The point of this in stress or anxiety control is that it brings an activity away from the actual performance, and therefore away from any anxieties associated with the performance itself. Figure 8.6 outlines the main features of this process.

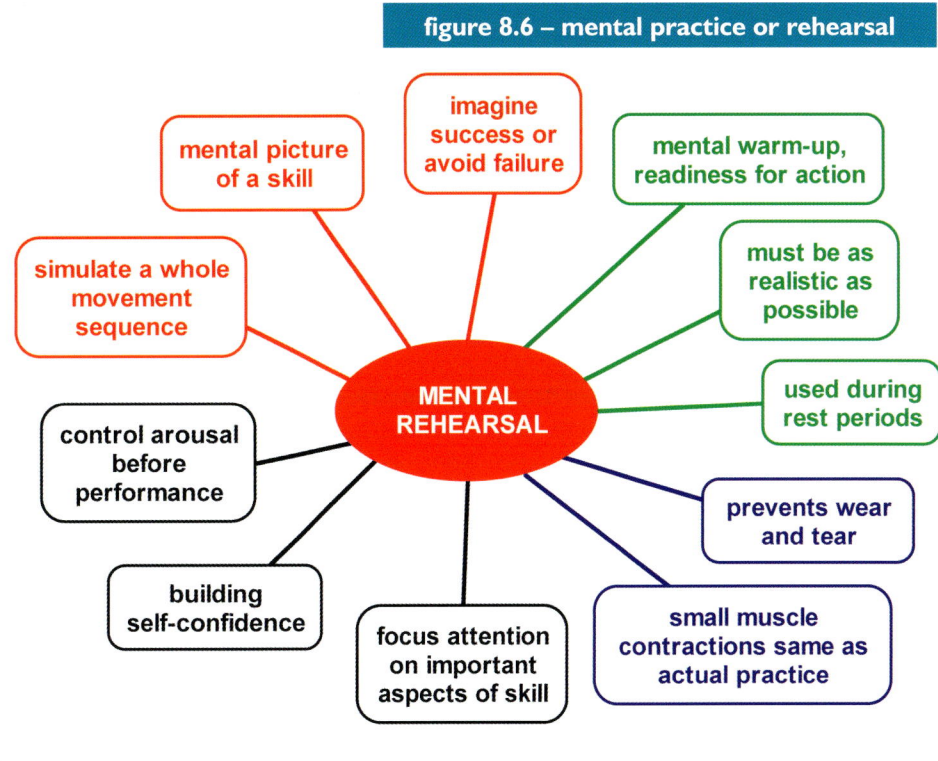

figure 8.6 – mental practice or rehearsal

MENTAL REHEARSAL
- mental picture of a skill
- imagine success or avoid failure
- mental warm-up, readiness for action
- must be as realistic as possible
- used during rest periods
- prevents wear and tear
- small muscle contractions same as actual practice
- focus attention on important aspects of skill
- building self-confidence
- control arousal before performance
- simulate a whole movement sequence

Cognitive relaxation techniques 117

SECTION 5 CHAPTER 8 — LEADERSHIP AND STRESS MANAGEMENT

Visualisation

figure 8.7 – visualisation

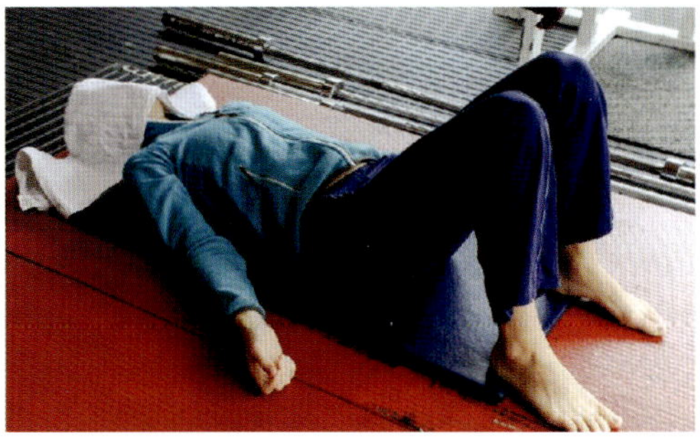

The process of visualisation asks a performer to rerun a past experience, or an experience in training in a simlar way to mental reghearsal (figure 8.7). This will continue with a preview of hoped-for success in a future performance. Again, this activity can be prompted by a coach and will intend to remove the stress and anxiety associated with the actual performance, particularly without the stress of a negative audience or aggression from other players The intention will then be to rebuild a new performance without such features.

Imagery relaxation

Imagery relaxation, in which a performer will think of a place with associations of warmth and relaxation, then imagine the activity or technique.

This process involves practice in non-stressful situations, and will be used prior to competition.

Attentional control

Attention

Attention relates to:
- **Amount of information** we can cope with, since the amount of information we can attend to **is limited**, and therefore we have limited **attentional capacity**.
- **Relevance of the information**. The performer must therefore attend to only **relevant information**, and **disregard irrelevant** information. This is called **selective attention**.

Selective attention

This is the process of sorting out **relevant** bits of information from the many which are received. Attention passes the information to the **short-term memory** which gives time for **conscious analysis**. A good performer can **focus totally** on an important aspect of his or her skill which **can exclude other elements** which may also be desirable. Sometimes a performer may desire to concentrate on several different things at once.

When some parts of a performance become **automatic**, the information relevant to those parts does not require attention, and this gives the performer **spare attentional capacity**. This allows the performer to attend to new elements of a skill such as tactics or anticipating the moves of an opponent.

The coach will therefore need to help the performer to make best use of spare attentional capacity, and will also need to **direct the attention** of the performer to enable him or her to **concentrate** and reduce the chance of **attentional switching** to irrelevant information or distractions.

Concentration

Concentration is **a state of mind in which attention is directed towards a specific aim or activity**. Concentration and **attentional focus** (**control of attention** towards a task) are essential components of a sportsperson's armoury of mental techniques to assist performance.

Use of cognitive techniques to assist concentration

Cognitive techniques such as imagery and mental rehearsal or relaxation can be used to direct the sportsperson's mind towards a specific task (page 100). These techniques can be used to manage the stress of the situation, or to manage anxiety in a productive way.

SPORT PSYCHOLOGY

Attentional narrowing

Attentional narrowing (figure 8.8) occurs when some parts of a performance become automatic. The information relevant to those parts then does not require attention, which gives the performer spare attentional capacity. This **spare capacity** will allow the performer to attend to **new elements** of a skill such as tactics or anticipating the moves of an opponent.

The **coach** will need to help the performer to make best use of spare attentional capacity, and direct the attention of the performer to enable him or her to concentrate. This would reduce the chance of **attentional switching** to irrelevant information or distractions.

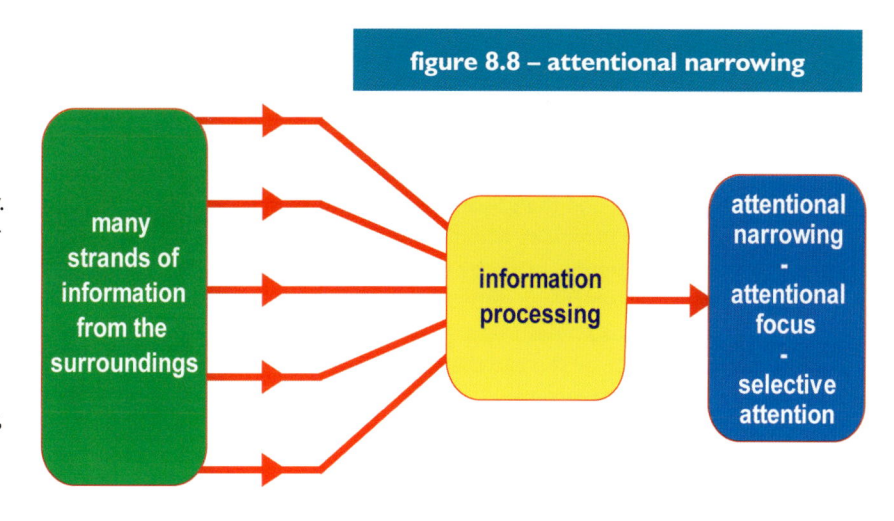

figure 8.8 – attentional narrowing

Attentional control training (ACT)

Attentional control training is a personalised programme which targets a performer's specific concentration problems. It assesses the demands of the sport, the situation, and the personality of the performer.

Cue utilisation

Cue utilisation (Easterbrook's theory) describes a situation in which cues can be used by the sportsperson to direct attention, and to trigger appropriate arousal responses.

This would enable attentional focus at a relevant moment. Sometimes, **narrowing of attentional focus** by an aroused player will cause lack of awareness of broader play issues.

Nideffer's attentional styles

On the graph in figure 8.9, the axes represent attentional styles that are narrow to broad and internal to external, and a particular event or sports activity will have a mixture of all four styles.

The following attentional styles are highlighted:
- **Narrow (A)**, in which a player concentrates on one aspect of the game, for example the goalkeeper who has predominantly closed skills.
- **Broad (B)**, in which a player concentrates on the whole game, with all players' positions and movements. This applies to open skills of this type.
- **Internal (C)**, in which a player decides to concentrate on his own technique.
- **External (D)**, in which a player focuses on the position of his opposite number.

figure 8.9 – attentional styles

Thought stopping

Thought stopping is an intervention technique that is used when negative thoughts or worry (about failure) begin. At that point, a performer should immediately think '**stop**', and substitute a **positive thought**.

Positive self-talk

- **Positive self-talk** is a procedure where a person will talk through the process of a competitive situation, talking positively and building self-confidence.
- It creates a **positive** message tied to a belief.
- It can also reduce **cognitive state anxiety**.
- It is crucial for **concentration**.

Nideffer's attentional styles

SECTION 5 CHAPTER 8 — LEADERSHIP AND STRESS MANAGEMENT

Somatic relaxation techniques

Biofeedback

- **Biofeedback** is the process of monitoring skin temperature (cold if stressed, warm if unstressed), and the galvanic skin response in which the electrical conductivity of skin increases when moist (tense muscle causes sweating).
- A further measurement is made by electromyography, in which electrodes are taped to specific muscles which can detect electrical activity and hence tension in muscle.
- The point is that these measures are perceived by the sportsperson during a performance, and he or she can then alter his or her behaviour to reduce the symptoms of stress or anxiety.

Centring

- **Centring** involves the control of physiological symptoms of stress by focusing on control of the diaphragm and deep breathing.
- The famous John McEnroe (famous for throwing tantrums on court and shouting at the umpire 'you can't be serious', then going on to win Wimbledon titles, figure 8.10), used centring to bring himself down from a major row with a court official to playing the perfect serve or shot - within 10 seconds!

figure 8.10 – John McEnroe used centring

Breathing control

- **Breathing control** - deep controlled breathing - will direct attention away from a stressful situation, and enable redirection of attention to a desired one.

Progressive muscle relaxation

- **Progressive muscle relaxation** (also known as PMR), sometimes called **self-directed muscle relaxation training**, enables a performer to focus on each of the major muscle groups in turn, then to allow breathing to become slow and easy. The athlete will visualise the tension flowing out of a muscle group until it is completely relaxed. Eventually a sportsperson will be able to combine muscle groups, and achieve total relaxation quickly.

Practice questions

1) Which one of the following is not an aspect of the trait theory of leadership?
   a. leaders are born not made.
   b. people have innate leadership qualities.
   c. people's leadership qualities can be nurtured.
   d. people's leadership qualities are enduring.

2) What is meant by emergent leaders?
   a. they are appointed by a governing body.
   b. they are appointed by the national coach.
   c. they are elected by the team.
   d. they are motivated by internal desires to do well.

3) The social learning theory of leadership is best described as:
   a. leaders learn their skills by watching others.
   b. leaders are formed throughout life by social or environmental influences.
   c. the high status of a sporting model will influence a leader most.
   d. people have innate leadership qualities.

4) Which one of the following is not a type of leader according to Chelladurai?
   a. a task centred leader.
   b. an autocratic or authoritarian leader.
   c. a laissez-faire leader.
   d. the democratic leader.

SPORT PSYCHOLOGY

Practice questions

5) Which one of the following is the best example of a stressor?
   a. bacterial infections.
   b. disapproval by parents or peers.
   c. injury suffered during a game.
   d. extremes of weather.

6) A somatic relaxation technique does not involve:
   a. progressive muscle relaxation.
   b. centring.
   c. deep breathing.
   d. mental rehearsal.

7) a) What is meant by a leader and what sort of qualities would you expect to see in a leader within the context of sport?   4 marks

   b) Using psychological theories describe how an individual becomes a leader.   4 marks

8) a) Name three leadership styles.   3 marks

   b) What factors should be taken into consideration when deciding upon which leadership style to adopt?   6 marks

9) Fiedler's Contingency Model suggests that the effectiveness of a leader can change depending on the situation.
   Use sporting examples to explain this theory.   4 marks

10) Explain the link between selective attention, concentration on a sports task, and the idea of attentional narrowing.   8 marks

11) Describe how a coach might use cognitive techniques to assist concentration.   6 marks

12) Explain how Nideffer's attentional styles describe how a sportsperson can direct attention to a relevant aspect of a game or sport.   8 marks

13) With reference to sporting performance, explain how cognitive and somatic stress differ.   5 marks

14) a) Discuss the possible relationships between stress and performance in sporting activities.   7 marks

   b) High levels of arousal have often been linked with stress.
      Sketch a graph showing the relationship between the performance of a complex skill and level of arousal.   2 marks

   c) Add a second curve to your graph showing how the performance of a simple skill might be affected by arousal.   2 marks

SECTION 5 CHAPTER 8 — LEADERSHIP AND STRESS MANAGEMENT

Practice questions

15) Look at figure 8.11 of Chelladurai's multidimensional model of leadership.

   a) Explain each part of the model using examples from sport. **5 marks**

   b) Behaviour of the group associated with leadership can be viewed from three perspectives. Briefly name and explain each of these perspectives. **5 marks**

   c) Discuss the statement 'Good leaders are born not made', and explain whether you agree or disagree in the light of psychological theory. **5 marks**

figure 8.11 – Chelladurai's multidimensional model

- **LEADER CHARACTERISTICS**
- **REQUIRED LEADER BEHAVIOUR** — what is expected of a coach by team management
- **ACTUAL LEADER BEHAVIOUR** — the way in which the coach normally goes about his job
- **performance satisfaction**
- **PREFERRED LEADER BEHAVIOUR** — the way in which members prefer their coach to relate to them
- **SITUATION CHARACTERISTICS**
- **MEMBERS' CHARACTERISTICS**

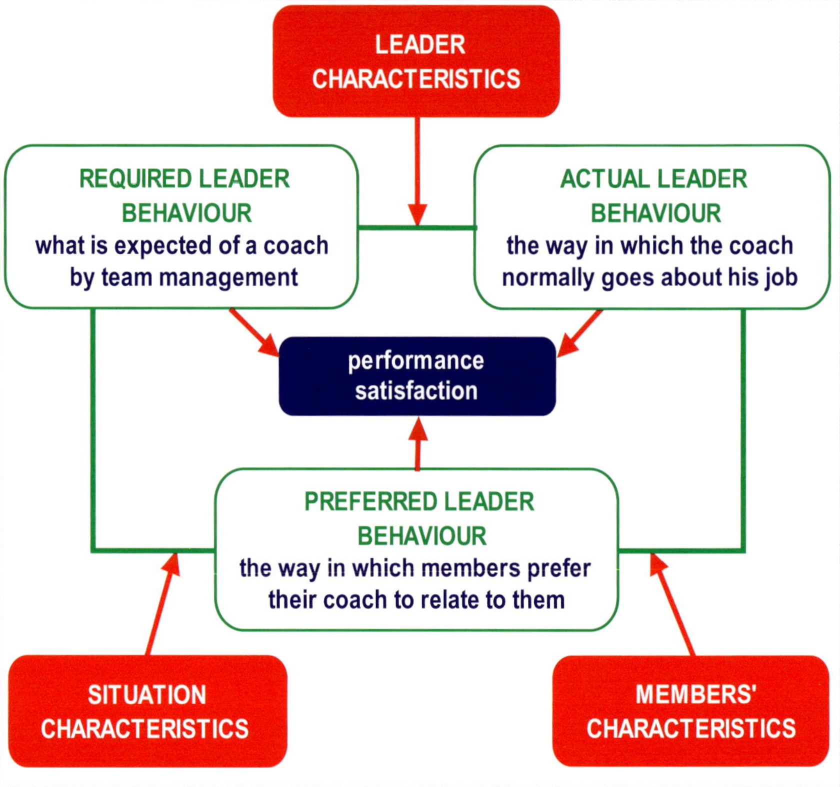

16) a) What is meant by the term stress? **2 marks**

   b) Explain two psychological symptoms of stress. **2 marks**

   c) Identify three main stressors in the context of sport. **3 marks**

   d) What is the difference between state and trait anxiety? **2 marks**

   e) What coping strategies should the anxious performer draw upon? **5 marks**

17) Give examples of positive self-talk and explain why it is important. **4 marks**

18) Describe the main physiological signs associated with increased levels of stress and explain what the technique of imagery involves and how it can help stress management. How can a coach and performer ensure that imagery is effective? **15 marks**

Answers link: http://www.jroscoe.co.uk/downloads/a2_revise_pe_aqa/AQAA2_ch8_answers.pdf

SECTION 6

SPORT AND SOCIETY

CHAPTER 9
CONCEPTS OF PHYSICAL ACTIVITY AND SPORT

CHAPTER 10
DEVELOPMENT OF ELITE PERFORMERS IN SPORT

CHAPTER 11
ETHICS AND VIOLENCE IN SPORT

CHAPTER 12
DRUGS IN SPORT, SPORT AND THE LAW AND COMMERCIALISATION

CHAPTER 13
THE ROLE OF TECHNOLOGY IN PHYSICAL EDUCATION AND SPORT

SECTION 6 CHAPTER 9 — CONCEPTS OF PHYSICAL ACTIVITY AND SPORT

CHAPTER 9: Concepts of physical activity and sport

Physical activity

Physical activity is taken to be **gross motor movement**, where major parts of the body are highly **active**. It is a necessary feature of modern society, valuable in itself, but important as part of the broader concept of having a **healthy lifestyle**. We therefore need to link a **healthy lifestyle** with **physical exercise** as it should exist in physical and outdoor recreation, physical and outdoor education, and various levels of sport.

Sports development continuum

The **Sports Development Continuum** (also known as the **sports development pyramid**, figure 9.1) is a model that represents a person's involvement in sport by what stage they are at. It also highlights the route a performer can take to become an elite performer.

This model has four stages.

Foundation

The **foundation** level begins with the early development of competence and skills, such as coordination, balance and agility. This basic level starts at an early age during school and is highly influenced by teachers and family. Many people try things out in many different activities (figure 9.2).

figure 9.1 – sports development pyramid

- elite — national standard, public recognition
- performance — coaching & development done at club & regional levels
- participation — increasing leisure options promoted via extra-curricular sport
- foundation — learning basic skills, knowledge & understanding, often delivered in PE programmes in schools

Participation

The **participation** level involves participating for fun and enjoyment, with a basic level of competence. **Individual sports** and team games become more important at a **basic** level of competition. This usually starts within secondary PE games lessons and during extra-curriculum time, where students are further encouraged to play in team/school sports and join a sports club to improve their basic skills, have fun and socialise.

Performance

The **performance** level is for a small group from the participation level who have the desire and the ability to perform at a higher level. Individuals are motivated to improve performance by training and playing in a structured and competitive way.

It involves **commitment** of the individual to play and improve performance at club, county and semi-professional levels where winning becomes more important.

Excellence

The **excellence** level is formed when an even smaller group emerges from the performance group who potentially have the **talent** and **ability** to reach a stage of excellence which would be described as **elite** performance.

This excellent or elite level represents international top level performance and is discussed from page 136 onwards.

figure 9.2 – foundation

SPORT AND SOCIETY

Physical recreation

Physical recreation is **the recreational pursuit of a range of physical activities, where the level of challenge is well within the capacity of all those participating. This is physical exercise in a recreational environment, which has a positive effect on maintaining a healthy lifestyle**.

This definition can also include outdoor recreation. Outdoor recreation has a number of unique features as recreational physical exercise in a natural environment.

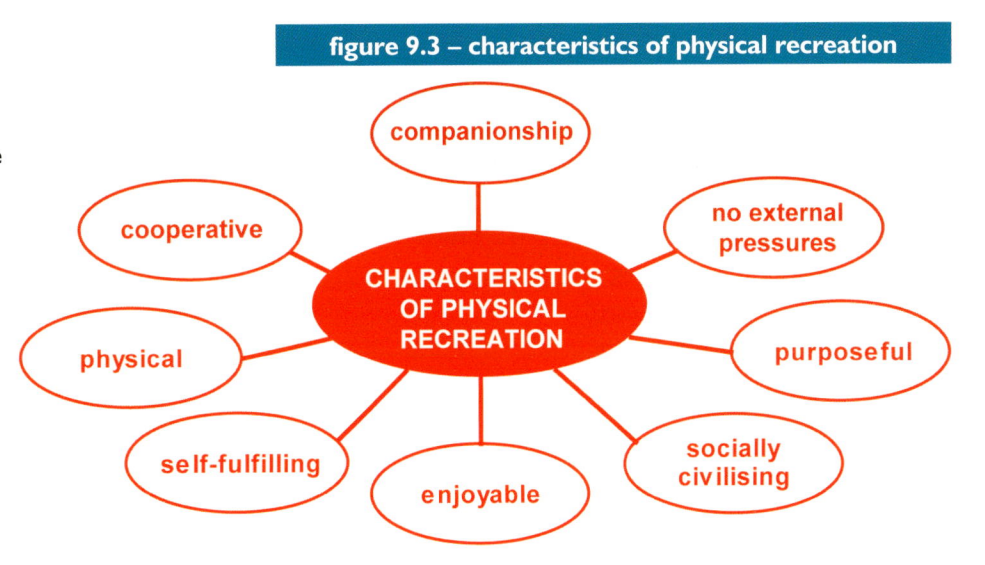

figure 9.3 – characteristics of physical recreation

CHARACTERISTICS OF PHYSICAL RECREATION:
- companionship
- no external pressures
- purposeful
- socially civilising
- enjoyable
- self-fulfilling
- physical
- cooperative

Physical recreation can be considered as **active leisure**. The term active leisure normally identifies with committed forms of recreation, which often fit into identifiable groups. This may include art classes, music and poetry groups or historical society membership, as well as physical recreation and outdoor recreation.

Characteristics of physical recreation (figure 9.3)

The sorts of activities included under the labels of physical and outdoor recreation include all physical activities which involve recreational rather than sporting values. But the recreational dimension is often identified in the title chosen for the activity. For example, bathing rather than swimming, jogging or riding rather than racing.

> **STUDENT NOTE**
>
> Note that **effort** and **prowess** would be among the main characteristics of a competitive **sporting** game or activity. Friendly participation would be firmly left to the non-serious recreational performer.
> It is important to note that the recreational approach could be more pleasant and long-lasting than the intensity of sporting activities.

Physical activity at a recreational level may not be competitive. Examples would include hitting a ball over a net, a kick-about, or a low-level match in which friendly participation is the whole point of the activity.

It means that:
- Those involved tend to **cooperate** rather than compete.
- Those involved tend to re-create **pleasant** experiences and refresh body and mind through **companionship** (figure 9.4).
- There are elements of **physical vigour** and commitment.
- It depends on the individual and is moderated by **long-term participation** objectives and to meet the capacity of the whole group.
- It is in a sense **non-utilitarian**, in that the gain lies more in **intrinsic** involvement rather than extrinsic rewards.

figure 9.4 – bowling as recreation

Characteristics of physical education **125**

SECTION 6 CHAPTER 9 — CONCEPTS OF PHYSICAL ACTIVITY AND SPORT

Objectives of physical recreation

The objectives of physical recreation and outdoor recreation are:

- To engage in a **physical challenge**, which is pleasurable and has lasting health value.
- To involve the use of activities and skills, which maintain our general fitness.
- To give us **experiences**, which provide pleasure and satisfaction.
- They should be **self-realising** in a lifetime context.
- To endorse long-term friendships.
- To be culturally rewarding.

These objectives mean that physical recreation is more than an activity. It is an experience which can be life enhancing and last throughout a lifetime (figure 9.5).

figure 9.5 – active leisure

Benefits of physical recreation

The **benefits** of **physical recreation**, as with other forms of **active leisure** (figure 9.6) are:

- Allows individuals to have time to **relax** and **recover** from work and areas of responsibility.
- It is normally an **enjoyable**, way of pursuing healthy physical activities.
- A person would be happy to undertake these activites in a non-serious atmosphere.
- There can be considerable **health values** arising from an active physical experience.
- There is skill learning and the **social contact** of friendship groups.
- The freedom associated with these activities can help the development of **self-esteem** and give **creative opportunities** to individuals as well as groups and clubs.
- There is the opportunity of progressing to performance and elite levels.

figure 9.6 – rock climbing as physical recreation

STUDENT NOTE

Note that these recreational freedoms are dependent on equality of **opportunity**, **provision** and **esteem**. Whilst it is important to fight for equality, it is equally important to consciously make healthy lifestyle choices where possible, for example by walking, jogging or taking the stairs rather than the lift.

Sport

Sports and pastimes are commonly used terms which describe a variety of sporting activities. Modern sport has many of the features and values which have evolved from the traditions built many centuries ago. Regular **institutionalised sport** was a 19th century European development of **athleticism** and **modern olympism**. In both cases, sport reflects the culture to which it belongs, and therefore **cultural variables** play a large part in its development.

Sport is **an institutionalised competitive activity that involves vigorous physical exertion and the use of relatively complex physical skills, where participation is motivated by a combination of intrinsic satisfaction associated through the activity itself, and external rewards earned by high level performance.**

126

SPORT AND SOCIETY

Sport

The advantage of this rather complex definition is that it identifies the physical exercise and physical skills criteria in physical recreation and physical education. This is within the two levels at which sport can operate, as a recreational activity and as an experience involving excellence.

Characteristics of sport

The characteristics of sport are summarised in figure 9.7.

- Within the definition of sport, the term **'institutionalised'** means the acceptance of a standard set of behaviour and rules that are regulated by a code of conduct/officials, in addition to rationalised activities such as highly organised training sessions and competitions.
- Accepting the code of conduct develops attributes such as **sportsmanship**, **fair play** and **high morals**, striving for personal excellence – **'to do one's best'** - fundamental principles of Olympism.
- Physical prowess requires **vigorous physical exertion** and mastery of **complex skills**
- **Friendships** are forged in a competitive environment a vital experience shared – a team is able to win gracefully and lose generously.
- **Regularity** and **organisation** are needed to give the structure that enables the performer to commit and develop within the sport.
- **Intrinsic** rewards result from personal achievement and satisfaction.
- **Extrinsic** rewards result from winning cups, prize money and titles.
- **Mental toughness** to consistently perform at the upper range of an individual's talent and skill regardless of competitive circumstances.

figure 9.7 – sport

The characteristics and benefits of physical recreation are carried into sport and adjusted to meet the stringent requirements of sporting excellence.

It is important to make the point that to achieve sporting excellence there must be:
- The **organisational** support including a professional administration.
- An efficient **selection** process.
- Top **facilities** and centres of excellence (figure 9.8).
- An elite system of **coaching** and **funding**.

Objectives of sport

The objectives of sport vary according to the performer's place on the continuum from recreational sport to sporting excellence. But if you assess these at a personal level, then each performer should set out to do his or her best (this is the meaning of **prowess** and **effort**, key features of how a performer should approach **sport** as opposed to **recreation**).

In **physical terms**, the objectives of sports are:
- To give the maximum **effort**.
- To make the most of your skills and tactical knowledge.

figure 9.8 – sport at university – the Loughborough HIPAC

Objectives of sport | 127

SECTION 6 CHAPTER 9 — CONCEPTS OF PHYSICAL ACTIVITY AND SPORT

Objectives of sport

In **behavioural terms**, the objectives are:

- To encourage cooperation as a team and yet **compete** as hard as you can.
- To work on **strategies** and problems arising from competitive challenges.
- To learn to **play fair** in competitions and games as part of your personal development.
- To help others, particularly if you have a **leadership** role.
- To **control your emotions** under pressure.
- To help you to **express** yourself.
- To recognise that sport is about **commitment**.
- To feel good, to be **creative**, to value the activity.
- To **appreciate** the performance of others.

These are the **noble objectives of sport**. Sadly, there is also the negative side of the coin, where the code of '**win-at-all-costs**' is dominant, and abuse and cheating become the dysfunctional behaviour alternative. Despite greed and the excessive ambition of individuals and nations, the **Olympic Code** is worth saving.

Benefits of sport

The **physical benefits** of sport are summarised in figure 9.9. These benefits allow individuals to recover from the stress of work by pursuing **healthy** sports in a happy atmosphere, as well as learning physical **skills** through friendly **competition**.

However, as the intensity of the sporting experience increases (towards **excellence**), so does the importance of **physical endeavour** and the need for **physical effort and prowess**.

The intrinsic **personal benefits** of sport also involve:

figure 9.9 – benefits of sport

- Elements of **recreational** opportunity, where the **freedom** to choose what sporting activity to do is a rewarding experience.
- Participation, in itself, can be fulfilling in the **enjoyment** sense, but also in terms of **personal achievement**.
- An experience of partner and team sport is likely to increase **social skills** in pressure situations.
- In the more formal coaching environment, **personal benefits** of sport, and particularly high level sport, include qualities of **leadership**, and sound competitive and **co-operative** attitudes.
- **Decision-making**, opportunities to learn about oneself and others in competitive situations.
- Benefiting from at least an occasional taste of **excellence**.

The potential **moral benefits** of sport arise from competition, and so it should always be performed with a spirit of **sportsmanship** and **fair play**.

SPORT AND SOCIETY

Physical education and school sport

A definition of physical education is '**the formal educational process of acquiring knowledge and values through physical activity experiences**'. Therefore physical education is an area of educational activity in which the main concern is with **vigorous bodily movement**.

A definition of sport is '**an activity involving physical exertion and skill in which an individual or team competes against another or others.**'

School sport is the **structured learning** that takes place beyond the curriculum within the school setting. Again the context for learning is physical activity. The school sport programme has the potential to develop and **broaden** the foundation learning that takes place in physical education. It also forms a vital link with **community sport** and activity.

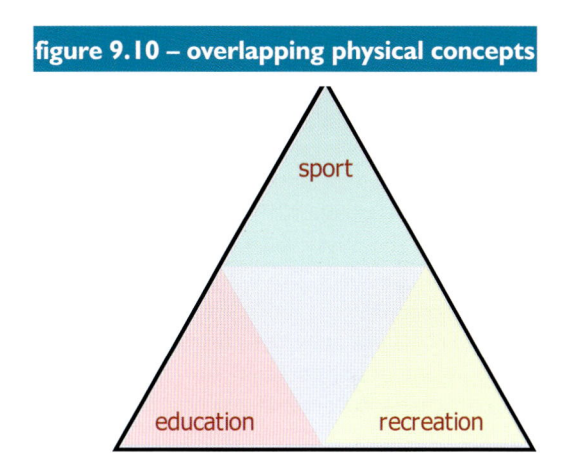

Our initial notions about what happens within physical activities in a school lies in the overlapping boundaries between **curriculum** physical education and **extra-curriculum** sport and physical recreation during the school day (figure 9.10). Both curricular and extra-curricular activity should imply desirable knowledge and values as part of the **formal curriculum** of any school or college. There is also **playtime activity**, which can add recreational opportunities in a play environment, and should therefore be taken into account as part of the school experience.

A **National Physical Education Curriculum Document** identifies certain activities which should be taught in all schools (figure 9.11).

Athletics, gymnastics and dance, games and contests, outdoor activities and swimming are important areas of study, where **opportunity** and **provision** allows.

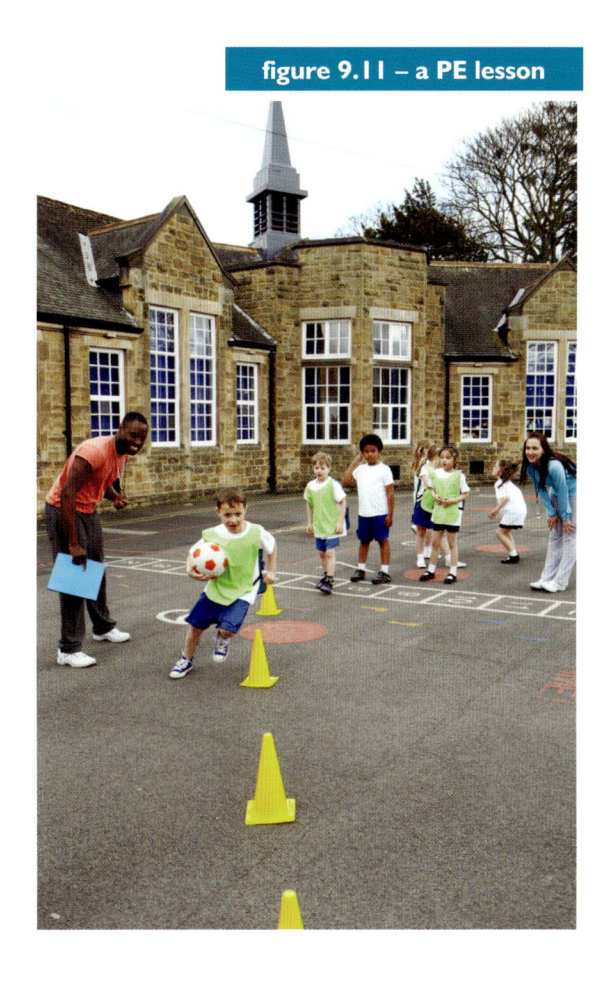

The document also recognises that the health, fitness, and safety awareness of individuals are essential elements within this experience. This hopefully leads to a **healthy lifestyle** being established among **young people**, with a view to the retention of lasting **interests and values**.

Characteristics of physical education

- Takes place within an institution.
- Is compulsory.
- Brings conformity through structured lessons.
- Taught by qualified teachers.
- Consists of four key stages.
- Starts at the foundation level in Primary schools through to participation level in Secondary schools
- Aims to impart knowledge and values through physical activities concerning bodily movement.
- Provides examinations at KS4 such as GCSE PE and BTEC Sport Level 2.

figure 9.10 – overlapping physical concepts

figure 9.11 – a PE lesson

SECTION 6 CHAPTER 9 — CONCEPTS OF PHYSICAL ACTIVITY AND SPORT

Objectives of physical education

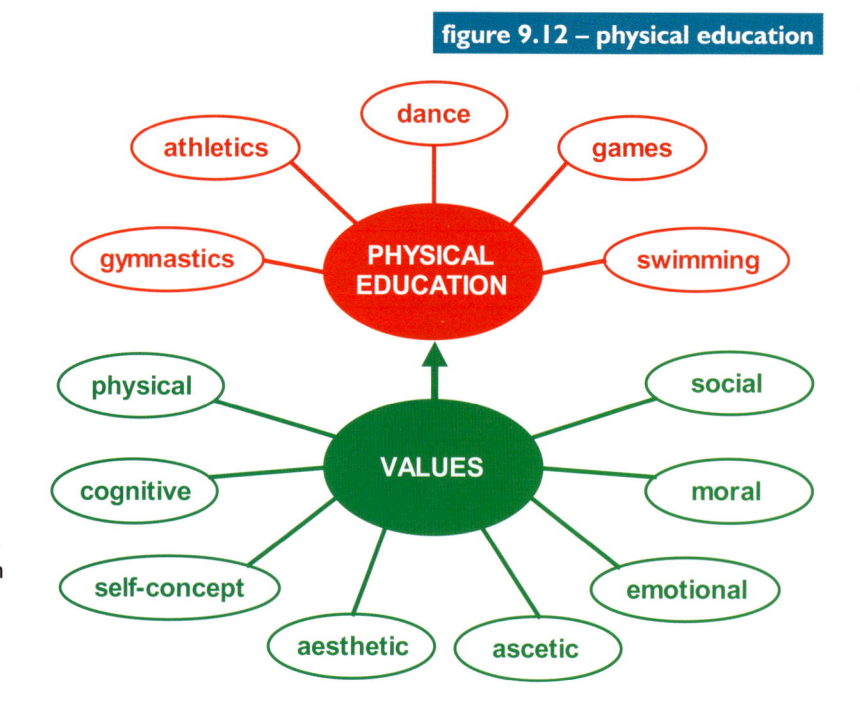

- Presents physically **challenging** experiences within an educational institution.
- Develops the **practical** skills to be able to participate in activities and the social skills to work with others as part of a team, develops cooperation and leadership.
- There are physical and educational values from such a curriculum programme, such as self-analysis, and **character building**.
- Extra-curriculum sport allows an emphasis on competitive experiences and develops values such as **fair play** and **sportsmanship**.
- Physical recreation should represent a broad band of physical activity outside the curriculum (figure 9.10, page 129) as well as during breaks.
- Most of the physical activities on the curriculum are **compulsory**, but extra-curricular activities are optional.
- Such optional activities normally involve free time and the opportunity for children to participate in personal choices.

Extra-curricular activities should still be seen to be part of the ethos of the school. The general aims of this subject area are to enthuse young people into the value of these physical experiences at both curriculum and extra-curriculum level and thus encourages a healthy lifestyle.

Values and activities are summarised as long-term objectives in figure 9.12.

figure 9.12 – physical education

PHYSICAL EDUCATION: athletics, dance, games, swimming, gymnastics

VALUES: physical, social, cognitive, moral, self-concept, emotional, aesthetic, ascetic

Benefits of physical education

The benefits of physical education (figure 9.13) are:

- All children have regular, compulsory physical activity which ensures a level of vigorous health related exercises.
- The activity includes strengthening, mobilising and co-ordinating activities designed to establish sound levels of **health and fitness**.
- **Skills and techniques** are taught in all the required physical activities.
- Children are coached at their optimum level.
- Children are also given opportunity for **competitive experiences** in individual activities and games.

figure 9.13 – benefits of physical education

BENEFITS OF PHYSICAL EDUCATION: skills and techniques, competitive experiences, enjoyment, effort and prowess, personal control, self-realisation, ethical judgements, strategy building, decision making, problem solving, understanding, cooperation, leadership, health and fitness

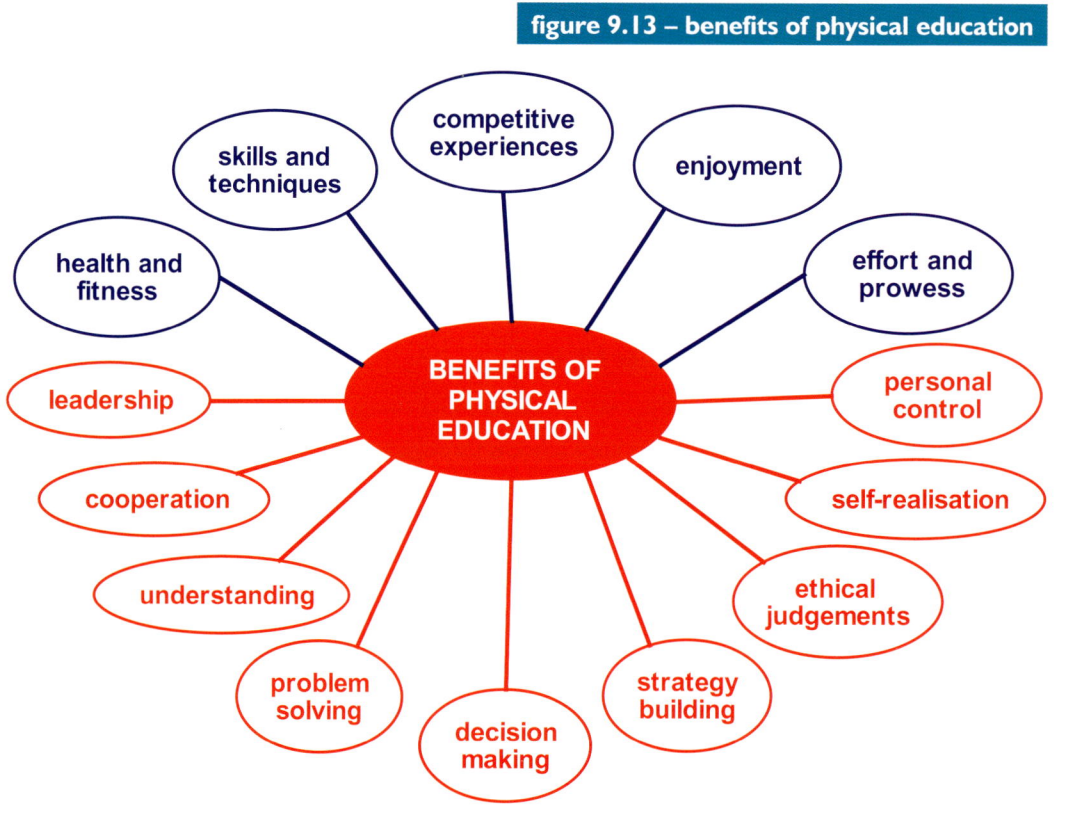

SPORT AND SOCIETY

Benefits of physical education

- Best achieved in an **enjoyable** atmosphere with the objectives of promoting **health**, **effort** and **prowess**.
- **Social** skills can be developed through the experience of performing in groups and teams.
- Qualities of **leadership and response to leadership** are combined to develop a respect for others.
- This involves the development of sound **competitive** and **co-operative** attitudes.
- **Cognitive** benefits arise from the considerable mental involvement in **understanding** skills and tactics and **decision-making**, when performing them in physical activities as part of a process of **problem solving** and **strategy building**.
- Acceptable values can be learnt through the acceptance of rules and regulations as part of a **moral code**.
- Involvement in physical activities presents opportunities for **ethical judgements**, reflected in a willingness to resist the **temptation** to break rules and practise gamesmanship.
- The opportunity is given to learn about **oneself** in critical situations and develop an awareness of others, potentially stimulating the development of **self-realisation** and **socialisation**.
- **Emotional** benefits can occur, where **personal control** is necessary in excitable competitive situations.
- The opportunity for **self-expression** is given in many creative situations.
- Physical education can be a **medium** where there is an opportunity for **creativity** and an **appreciation** of successful performance by others and as such a **taste of excellence**.
- There is an alternative test of self, where an individual or team **experiences success** as a result of a high level of **commitment** and a strong element of **vitality**.

figure 9.14 – school children experience a wide range of sports

Outdoor education

It is important to establish what outdoor education has in common with the other physical education activities and then why it should be looked upon as a different and valuable experience.

As part of physical education, a definition of outdoor education is '**the formal educational process of acquiring knowledge and values through outdoor activity experiences**'. This is an area of educational activity in which the main concern is with vigorous bodily movement. The difference is its location in the natural environment of water and mountain and the challenging nature of this experience.

Characteristics of outdoor education

As with physical education, there are **overlapping** boundaries between:
- **Curriculum**, which may be compulsory lessons or extended field weeks.
- **Extra-curriculum**, where club groups may operate.
- **Playtime activity**, where this is safe to do so.

SECTION 6 CHAPTER 9 — *CONCEPTS OF PHYSICAL ACTIVITY AND SPORT*

Characteristics of outdoor education

The **national physical education curriculum** recognises that outdoor activities are valuable physical and educational activities. All children should experience these activities where opportunity and provision allows. This type of activity can lead to a **healthy lifestyle** being established among **young people.**

In addition to the **characteristics** of physical education, with its unique combination of the **physical**, **educational** and **recreational** values, outdoor education offers **adventure in a challenging natural environment**. Figure 9.15 should give you the key words associated with this form of education, with particular focus on the relevance of **discovery**, **challenge**, **excitement** and **risk**.

The **objectives** of this educational area build on these characteristics, but also more general objectives already outlined for physical education.

figure 9.15 – outdoor education

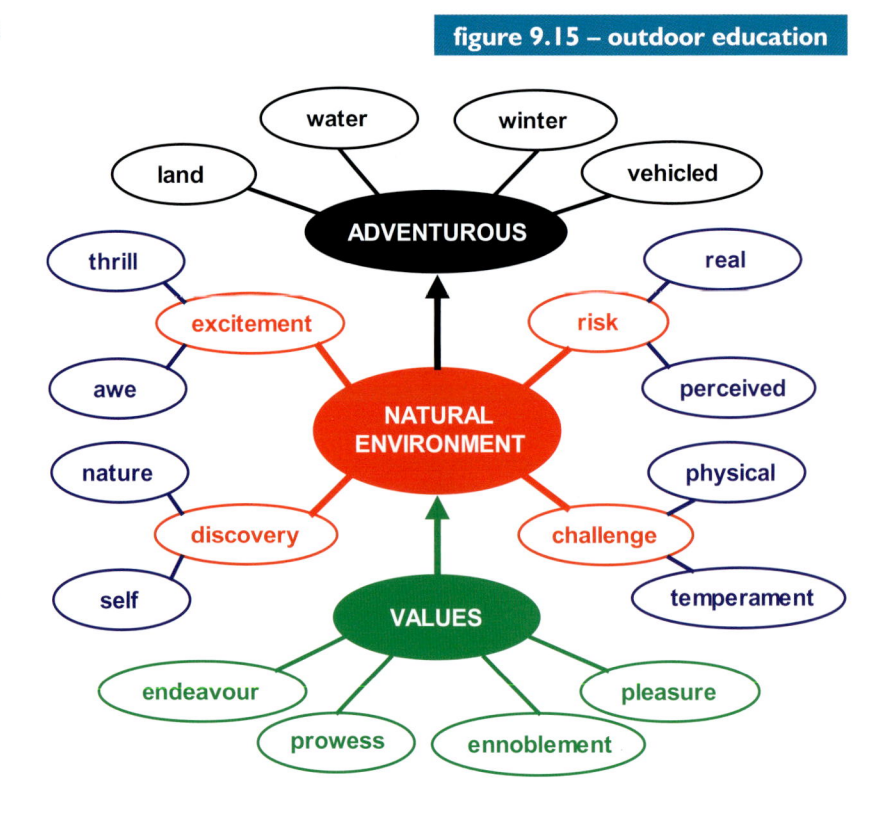

Benefits of outdoor education

In **physical terms**, it is suggested that the outdoor education experience:
- Expands the **boundaries of health** as a result of spending time in the fresh air.
- Presents situations requiring **unexpected physical challenges** and a different kind of **physical prowess**.
- Involves an additional dimension by taking children out of the school and urban existence into the less predictable natural environment.
- Set at a challenging level, **risk** has to be estimated and reduced to what is perceived risk rather than real, by qualified staff.

It is argued that many of the **educational benefits** (figure 9.16) are enhanced in this challenging and often beautiful environment.
Particularly:
- **Leadership** skills.
- **Problem solving**.
- **Strategy building**.
- The opportunity to learn about **oneself** in critical situations.
- An awareness of others.
- The emotional experience of the **thrilling**, but also **awesome** moments.
- The additional quality of experiencing and learning to appreciate the **natural world** and its beauty.
- Through individual and **group experiences**.
- Which require a high level of **commitment**.

figure 9.16 – benefits of outdoor education

132

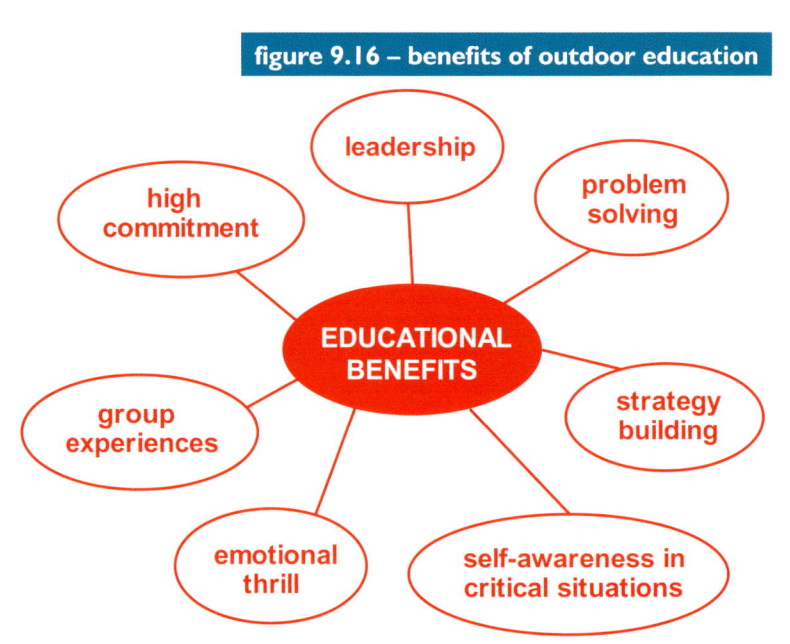

SPORT AND SOCIETY

Benefits of outdoor education

The UK is a sporting nation, but one with a tendency to watch rather than play. The primary role of **physical education** is to inculcate physical activity values in a way which encourages a life-long commitment to healthy physical exercise in society. However, what is started in the school must continue to be promoted in an adult society which values a healthy lifestyle.

Similarities and differences between these concepts

Table 9.1 – comparison between concepts of sport, physical recreation, physical education and school sport

Sport	Physical recreation	Physical education	School sport
non-compulsory	non-compulsory - no external pressures to take part	compulsory in state schools	is voluntary and so provides an element of choice
is competitive	informal and relaxed and based the free time basis of active leisure & recreation	follows a highly structured set curriculum	is competitive
has set rules and regulations	more socially orientated	raises physical activity levels from foundation to participation levels	often takes place during extra-curricula/free time
more task orientated	is viewed as a chosen hobby at the participation level	taught by teachers during the school day	involves training sessions, game tactics & strategies
involved skilful physical movements and teamwork skills	coaches available to develop skill base	introduces children to a wide variety of activities from non-competitive to competitive sports	emphasis on winning at participation level
practice is undertaken to improve and get better in sport	is fun and enjoyment based	emphasis is on taking part	practice is undertaken to improve and get better in sport
and often supervised by coaches	self regulated	teacher in charge	involves teachers and coaches
committment	voluntary	taking part	involves commitment from participants
vigorous involvement, so requires a level of fitness	improves health and fitness	improves understanding of how to improve health and fitness	improves health and fitness
often has prize money or extrinsic rewards for winners	intrinsic motives		
offers a pathway from participation to performance to elite level	mainly at participation level	raises physical activity from foundation to participation level	offers a pathway from participation to performance level
offers companionship and social cohesion	offers companionship and social cohesion	offers companionship and social cohesion	offers companionship and social cohesion

Whilst the UK is producing athletes with **sporting prowess**, it is increasingly a nation of **spectators**, supporting from the stands or glued to television. There is a problem of **obesity** in British society and the population needs to become more physically active. The focus of society needs to change. This can be achieved through a better controlled **diet**, regular visits to fitness clubs, continuing the **physical skills** learnt at school, or joining sport or rambling **clubs**.

The rewards are of feeling **better**, making new **friends** and probably living longer.

SECTION 6 CHAPTER 9 — CONCEPTS OF PHYSICAL ACTIVITY AND SPORT

Practice questions

1) Which one of the following best describes the characteristic of physical recreation?
    a. based on the performance level of the continuum that involves regular training and is more competitive.
    b. provides escape the pressures of life.
    c. often has prize money/extrinsic rewards for winners.
    d. is compulsory.

2) Most sports players accept that, when they participate in physical activities, they should observe appropriate codes of behaviour or etiquette. Which of the following is the best example of good etiquette when performing a physical activity?
    a. shaking hands with your opponent at the end of a match.
    b. obeying the referee in football.
    c. shouting 'well played' to one of your team mates.
    d. politely questioning a decision made by the referee in basketball.

3) Which one of the following is not a characteristic of sport?
    a. offers a pathway from participation to performance level.
    b. involves commitment from participants.
    c. can be competitive or non-competitive.
    d. embraces Olympism values.

4) The Sports Development Continuum is a model that represents a person's involvement in sport by what stage they are at. Which one of the following choices shows the correct route for sport's development?
    a. foundation, participation, excellence and performance.
    b. performance, foundation, participation and excellence.
    c. foundation, participation, performance and excellence.
    d. participation, foundation, performance and excellence.

5) From the following choices, identify the main benefit of an outdoor education programme.
    a. participants are presented situations requiring unexpected physical challenges.
    b. participants are introduced at the foundation level on the sports development continuum.
    c. participants enjoy the highly structured rules and regulations.
    d. participants are motivated by extrinsic rewards.

6) Explain how an individual would benefit from participating in a sports team. 4 marks

7) Identify possible physical objectives of a major game, swimming or athletics as part of your Physical Education programme. 3 marks

8) What are the main educational qualities of outdoor education? Illustrate your answer using a specific outdoor activity. 3 marks

9) Identify four characteristics of sport using a game to illustrate each of them. 4 marks

10) a) Discuss the main similarities and differences between physical recreation and sport. 4 marks

    b) How can a school provide opportunities to participate in physical recreation and sport? 3 marks

    c) Outline the basic requirements needed to undertake sport or recreation. 3 marks

SPORT AND SOCIETY

Practice questions

11) In what ways are the characteristics of physical education and those of sport different?   6 marks

12) Many schools offer their pupils the opportunity to participate in non-competitive activities. What are the benefits of taking part in non-competitive outdoor and adventurous activities, such as skiing?   5 marks

13) Outdoor education is a means of approaching educational objectives through adventurous activities in the natural environment.

    a) Select an outdoor adventurous activity and explain it in terms of four levels of adventure.   5 marks

    b) Use Figure 9.17 to explain values associated with an outdoor adventurous activity of your choice.   4 marks

figure 9.17 – an outdoor activity

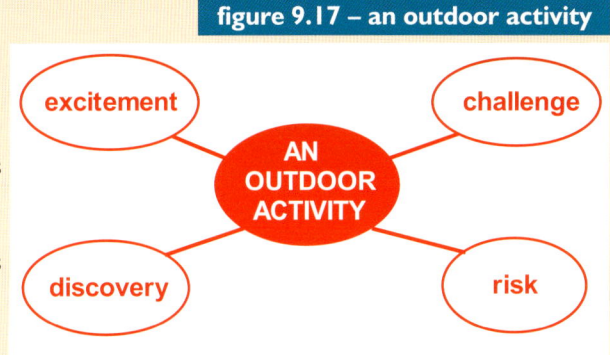

AN OUTDOOR ACTIVITY: excitement, challenge, discovery, risk

14) a) Using your school as an example, explain figure 9.18 in terms of curriculum PE, extracurricular programmes and recreational activities.   6 marks

    b) Why is a pyramid such a useful analogy?   2 marks

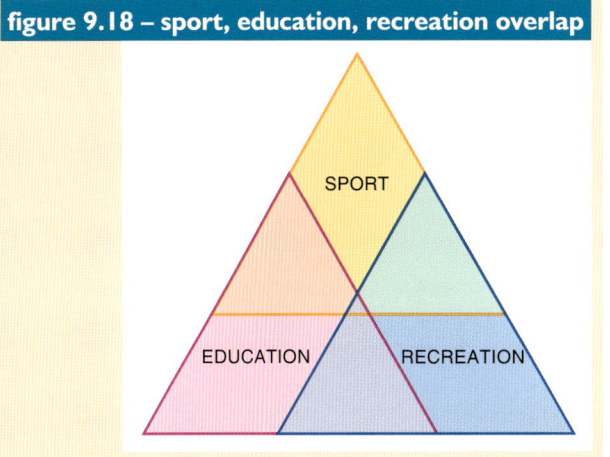

15) How can a school physical education programme act as a pathway for individuals to participate in a more structured form of sporting activity?   3 marks

16) Discuss the benefits and problems associated with participating in sporting activities.   15 marks

figure 9.18 – sport, education, recreation overlap

SPORT / EDUCATION / RECREATION

Answers link: http://www.jroscoe.co.uk/downloads/a2_revise_pe_aqa/AQAA2_ch9_answers.pdf

SECTION 6 CHAPTER 10 — **DEVELOPMENT OF ELITE PERFORMERS IN SPORT**

CHAPTER 10: Development of elite performers in sport

Excellence is defined as a '**special ability beyond the norm, to which many aspire but few go onto achieve**'. Excellence suggests a specialism of one activity and in sport is judged by international standards.

Talent is a **natural ability to be good at something, especially without being taught**.

Talent identification is the **recognition** of talent in an individual.

Identification and development of talented individuals

The early identification and development of talented individuals is considered increasingly important. What is needed to become an elite athlete is a rare combination of **nature** (genetic makeup) and **nurture** (the process of socialisation - observing and watching others).

Elite athletes have **talent** in abundance, **work hard** and have the right **psychological** profile.

Identifying attributes that characterise exceptional performers can help talented individuals to progress from **participation** to **elite** level performance (figure 9.1 page 124).

Personal factors (figure 10.1)

Motivation
Motivated by high competitive drive (i.e. the will to be the best - **intrinsic** motivation). Elite athletes possess a deep need to always improve, taking their performance to the next level.

Initiative
Driven athletes don't wait to be given permission to do something. They are the **leaders** in all they do, setting the standard for excellence.

Determination
All challenges have solutions. Elite athletes are actively looking for the opportunities to help them reach their goal. Failure is not an option.

figure 10.1 – development of talent - personal factors

- physical prowess
- motivation
- pain tolerance
- initiative
- strength based approach
- DEVELOPMENT OF TALENT - PERSONAL FACTORS
- determination
- self confidence
- tough-minded
- self efficacy
- high skills
- strong commitment

Tough-Minded
Athletes are expected to do things which stretch them all the time. Tough-minded athletes acknowledge the discomfort, but don't let it stop them.

Taking risks, and pushing through their comfort zone, is part of the champion mindset.

Strength Based Approach
Elite athletes know where they excel and use that to their advantage and are able to find the best approach based upon their strengths and develop the skills necessary to minimize weaknesses.

Strong commitment
This refers to a willingness to give time and energy to something that a person believes in. Instead of viewing obstacles as problems, elite athletes approach them as **challenges** to be overcome. The goal is the primary focus. Even when no one is looking, they continue to push themselves to be the best they can.

SPORT AND SOCIETY

Self-efficacy
This is an athlete's self-confidence at his or her specific sport which can affect his or her motivation and ultimate performance, and affects the effort and persistence put into an activity.

Self-confidence
This is a general feeling of trust in one's abilities, qualities, and judgement.

Physical prowess
Physical prowess and natural sporting ability are essential ingredients for elite athletes.

High tolerance to pain
The sportsman should be able to push the body to the limits.

High skill levels
Skills should be consistent.

Social and cultural factors
Figure 10.2 provides a summary of the social and cultural factors that are required to support progressions from talent identification to elite performance.

figure 10.2 – development of talent - social and cultural factors

SOCIAL AND CULTURAL FACTORS: family and friends, socio-economic status, media coverage, coaches and mentors, educational providers, equity in sport, friendship groups

Family and friends
Primary social groups include parental support and encouragement which is highly related to children's enjoyment, their perceived competence and enthusiasm for physical activity.

Parents of committed athletes are usually willing and happy to attend their children's training sessions and competitions, in addition to paying for equipment, travel, coaching and medical costs. Family and friends are their biggest fans and their presence at competitions is valued greatly by participants.

Socio-economic status
Socio-economic status (SES) is a critical factor when it comes to opportunities, defined in terms of individual, household and neighbourhood characteristics. All sports are available if you can afford them, but become inaccessible and are not available to those with little money.

Financial support, via lottery funding and local grants, is not available until a talented individual has been recognised and so the individual's socio-economic status is a key determining factor that influences the progression from talented individual to elite performer.

Sports coaches
Coaches assist athletes in developing their full potential, and athlete **mentors** provide **role models** to create aspiration and provide support for young people to achieve their personal best in sport or life.

They give extra motivation and encouragement through their enthusiasm and knowledge for the sport, providing the talented athlete is prepared to accept this guidance and make time to train and compete. Young talented individuals are expected to follow rules and norms dictated by management and coaching staff (figure 10.3).

figure 10.3 – coaches are important

Social and cultural factors

SECTION 6 CHAPTER 10 — DEVELOPMENT OF ELITE PERFORMERS IN SPORT

Friendship groups
The social element of sport is critical to engaging and retaining sports participants. Young talented athletes can be distracted by peers outside of the sporting environment. Team sports foster indentity and friendship, a shared culture of norms and values.

Sport equity
Female athletes have been under-represented in most sport's top flight for most of the twentieth century in most sports and have been prohibited from competing on equal terms with men through sexism and stereotyping (exceptions are in equestrian events).

Black and disabled athletes have been largely excluded from many of the key areas of society including sport.

The majority of talented sports individuals are from **middle class** and relatively affluent households, and there are disproportionately few from lower classes and deprived groups and areas.

Sport Equity is about **fairness** in sport, equality of access, recognising inequalities and taking steps to address them. National governing bodies (NGBs) are tasked to address such inequities by increasing participation at all levels. Initiatives such as **This Girl Can** (figure 10.4) and **Street Games** (figure 10.5), could be the starting point where a talented athlete becomes engaged in sport.

STUDENT NOTE
Barriers to participation are discussed in AS/A1 Revise PE for AQA ISBN 9781901424850, pages 126-127.

figure 10.4 – This Girl Can

Education providers
Rio Olympics 2016: Where did the Team GB medal winners **go to school**? Overall, just under 70% of the medal-winning athletes were educated at state-maintained schools.

A handful of athletes, including Tom Daley, the diver, were given scholarships to attend independent schools. The interesting statistic here is that **private schools** only educate 7 per cent of pupils and yet are responsible for just over 30% of the medal winning performances.

Grass roots initiatives include creating links between schools and clubs with access to specialist facilities and coaching. This is where a talented individual can progress from **participation** to **performance** level. In addition, school or county sports organisations run trials to select county sports teams, who in turn select their most promising players for regional trials, who in turn recommend players for **national** trials.

Structured levels of competitions, such as the **English Schools Track and Field Championships**, provide competition from grass roots participation level to national finals.

figure 10.5 – StreetGames

Such national competitions have common characteristics of an Olympic Games including opening ceremony with flag bearers, a band and competitors parading around the arena. Talented individuals are often spotted by NGBs at national finals.

Structured levels of competitions are reflected within the sporting pyramid model (a process of progression from mass participation to elite level of performance).

Media
The impact of the media is extensive. It gives insight into the effort needed for success at elite level, and a belief in fair play. It can raise the status of a sport and therefore help to promote the sport and inspire young people to participate at all levels.

Role models attract intense media coverage and can inspire future sports stars (figure 10.6).

figure 10.6 – David Beckham works with youngsters

SPORT AND SOCIETY

Organisations providing support and progression from talent identification to elite performance

The providers of excellence in sport are mainly:
- The Government **Department for Culture, Media and Sport.**
- **UK Sport.**
- **Sport England.**
- **British Olympic Association.**
- **Disability Sport England.**
- **British Paralympic Association.**

Figure 10.7 depicts the organisations involved in UK Sport.

UK Sport

- UK Sport is an agency that operates under **government** direction.
- The primary role of UK Sport is to strategically invest **National Lottery** and **Exchequer** income to maximise the **performance** of UK athletes in the Olympic and Paralympic Games and the **global events** which precede them.
- Decisions are made on a **four year basis** wherever possible to cover a complete Olympic or Paralympic cycle but are focussed on an **eight year performance development mode**l.
- Success is measured by the **medals won**, the number of medallists developed, and the quality of the systems and processes in place to find and support the nation's most promising **future champions**.

To achieve this UK Sport invests around 70 per cent of its income through two channels:
- **Central funding** for sporting **National Governing Bodies** (NGBs), enabling them to operate a **World Class Programme** (WCP – more detail on page 140 onwards).
- Ensuring athletes have access to outstanding support personnel and training environments to prepare them to compete against the best in the world.
- Funding is in the shape of an Athlete Performance Award (APA). This award, funded by National Lottery income, is paid directly to the athletes and contributes to their living and sporting costs.
- UK Sport also runs a number of world leading centralised **strategic** support services including the development of **world class coaches** and **talent identification** campaigns to fast track future medallists in to the right sports.
- The UK Sport coaching team seeks to ensure the delivery of quality coaching to athletes on **UK Sport's World Class Performance Pathway**, a system devised to identify, develop and refine talented British athletes.
- To achieve this, the **UK Sport World Class Coaching Strategy** must deliver targeted and innovative programmes and interventions specific to the needs of world class coaches.
- Coaching is one of a number of key elements of the high performance system, and alongside other key performance support services such as **Sports Medicine** and **Sports Science, Performance Lifestyle** and **Research** and **Innovation**, plays a crucial role in ensuring the ongoing success of British athletes.
- UK Sport works in conjunction with partners, such as the English Institute of Sport (EIS), by providing trained and accredited **Performance Lifestyle** practitioners to work with athletes to develop the necessary skills needed to cope with the unique demands of being an elite performer.

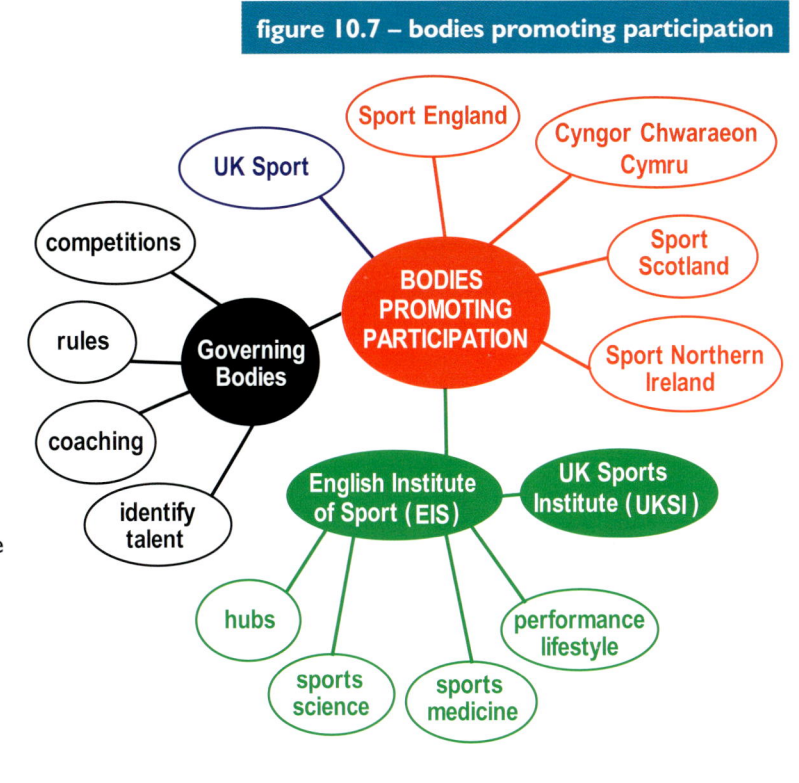

figure 10.7 – bodies promoting participation

figure 10.8 – sports coach UK

UK sport

SECTION 6 CHAPTER 10
DEVELOPMENT OF ELITE PERFORMERS IN SPORT

UK Sport

- **Lifestyle Support** is designed to support, advise and mentor talented athletes in managing their personal development and lifestyle.
- **Performance Lifestyle** aims to help the individual to develop skills to effectively manage all their commitments including sport (training and competition) and non sport (family, education and employment).

UK Sports Institute

UKSI provides world class facilities and coordinated support services. For example, the National Sports Centre at Bisham Abbey (figure 10.9) where GB women's hockey is based.

Its Athlete Medical Scheme provides the UK's top Olympic and Paralympic athletes with free medical care. It also organises and sponsors world class coaching conferences, which present the UK's top coaches with opportunities to gain new insights and skills to develop future World, Olympic and Paralympic Champions.

UK Sport and UKSI devolve their regional responsibilities into the Home Country Institutes, for example, the English Institute of Sport (EIS).

figure 10.9 – GB women's hockey, Rio 2016

National Institutes of Sport - English Institute of Sport (EIS)

The EIS aims to develop and produce performers at the **elite level** of the sport development pyramid, and who will therefore become part of the lottery funded **World Class Programme**. The WCP has three levels (figure 10.10).

Membership of a WCP group or National Squad carries great intrinsic and extrinsic esteem (in terms of adulation from the press and people who follow the sport) and ensures high **motivation** to succeed.

EIS has a network of world class services that support athletes on the WCP:

figure 10.10 – World Class Programme

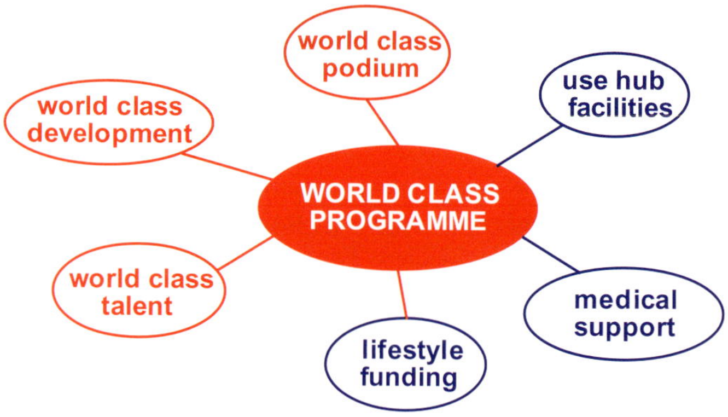

Regional multi-sport hub sites
- The 'hubs' (multi-sports High Performance Centres) provided by the Institutes of Sport for elite sportspeople, are intended to be located within 1 hour travel time of a million people, and 30 minutes travel time for 250,000.
- What is happening is that Governing Bodies are insisting that members of the World Class Performance groups locate themselves near to a hub, so that coaching and medical support can also be provided simply and at less cost.
- For example, UK Athletics have created their national hub for elite athletes at Loughborough University (figure 9.8, page 127).
- An evolving network of **satellite centres** (page 141).

Lifestyle funding
- The **Performance Lifestyle Programme** which provides supplementary career and education advice.
- The EIS's talent development work aims to identify, recruit and progress the most promising young athletes and put in place the systems, pathways and support to facilitate their transition from **talented junior** to **elite international performer**.

SPORT AND SOCIETY

Sports science and medical support systems.
- Top quality support by **strength and conditioning** specialists, medical support teams such as **physiotherapist** and **sports massage** personnel (figure 10.11).
- **Sports science** specialists, and sport psychology experts assist and advise on most situations facing the aspiring talented performer.

figure 10.11 – medical support

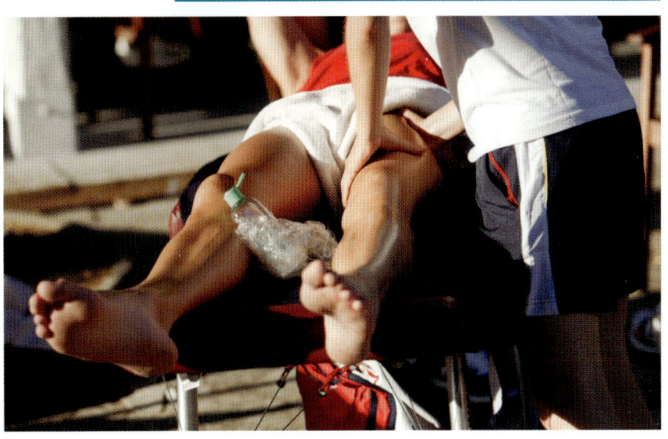

The main point of this activity is to provide a **worry-free environment** for the sportsperson to train for up to **6 hours per day for 6 days of the week** (allowing for some rest and recovery time).

In terms of sporting excellence, pre-supposing an individual has the talent to achieve excellence, then he or she must have the **opportunity** provided by facility **provision** near enough to be feasible for regular **travel**.

National Governing Bodies of Sport

NGBs are tasked with **overseeing** their sport and **organising** their existing and future direction.
These bodies are responsible for:
- Establishing the **rules**.
- Organising **national competitions**.
- **Coaching** within each individual sport.
- Selecting individuals for **funding**.
- Picking **teams** for **international** competition.

NGBs, together with local partners, are working together to create a new **satellite club** on each school setting, linked to an existing community 'hub' club, and run by coaches and volunteers from that hub club. By being located on a school site, the satellite club is within easy reach of young people, but is distinct from school physical education as it is run by community volunteers.

Sports clubs

Sports clubs **affiliate** to NGBs and provide opportunities for young talent to gain **competitive experience** in leagues and national competitions.
Most sports clubs nurture their talent, offer financial concessions, provide quality **coaching** and services to develop their young athletes. For example, athletics' clubs charge as little as £2.00 to use a **stadium facility**, **equipment** plus **coaching**.
In contrast other sport clubs, such as tennis and golf, charge for coaching and often make it financially inaccessible for the many who do not have enough disposable income.
NGBs operate within the **international governing body** umbrella, for example, the **IAAF** for athletics, and **FIFA** for soccer.

Whole Sport Plans and NGBs

Whole Sport Plans are the delivery contract between **Sport England** and each of the 46 funded **National Governing Bodies** for Sport (NGBs). Each NGB is required to produce a whole sport plan which should include everything relating to its particular sport, through the full range of abilities from **participation** at the basic level, to **elite** level.

The plan must state how that sport will achieve Sport England's '**start, stay and succeed**' objectives, and use 60% of NGB **funding** on the **14-25 year old age group**. The intention is to create a sporting habit for life.

SECTION 6 CHAPTER 10 — DEVELOPMENT OF ELITE PERFORMERS IN SPORT

Whole Sport Plans and NGBs

To be eligible for Whole Sport Plan funding, NGBs must also meet high standards of **governance** and **financial control**. Sport England has invested £493m into 46 sports between 2013 and 2017. Payment is by results, with withdrawal of funding to governing bodies that fail to deliver agreed objectives.

Of the £22 million received by UK Athletics, Sport England allocated £8.8 million of the total investment for UK Athletics to get more people involved in informal running. **Park run** is an example of a successful grassroots scheme which satisfied this criteria.

UK Athletics wants to increase the number of talented athletes who could go on to elite and world class level (figure 10.12 of Dina Asher-Smith who went from bag carrier in London 2012, to fifth in the Rio Olympics 2016) by focusing on increasing and enhancing **coaching**, as well as improving the domestic competition opportunities for talented **disabled** athletes.

figure 10.12 – Dina Asher-Smith

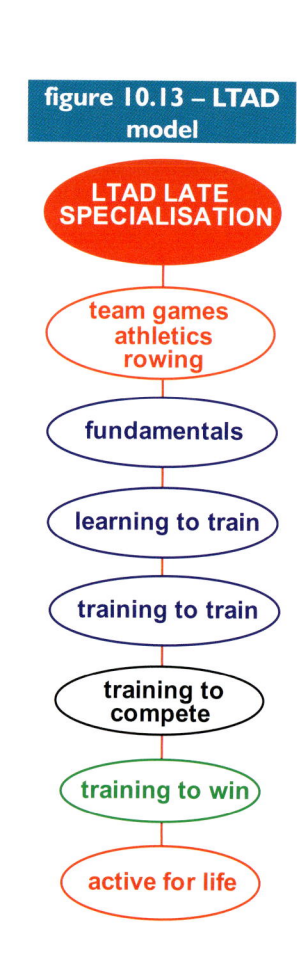

Talent development and support services

Investment in elite sport within Britain has increased considerably since 1996. If such investment is to have a positive impact on British sport, it is apparent that some of it must be targeted towards athletes that have the greatest potential of producing successful performances at major international events.

There are two predominant methods that broadly capture athletes who are currently identified within sport:

- **Natural selection** is aimed at identifying talented individuals that are already participating within a sport due to the recognition of performance or scouting.

- **Scientific selection** is a more proactive procedure by which identification of the talented occurs as a result of testing individuals on values that are associated with expertise within a certain sport.
  - For example, the physical, physiological and psychological attributes that affect performers within sprinting or weightlifting.
  - By using scientific research to identify the optimum environment for nurturing these criteria, resources can be targeted at those individuals that have the greatest potential of becoming outstanding performers.

Working in partnership, UK Sport, National Institutes of Sport and NGBs are tasked with **identifying** and **developing** sporting talent.

Talent identification programmes (TIPs)

- **TIP UK** is part of the World Class Programme and promotes competitions such as the British School Games with its competitive environment.
- Access to **Talented Athletic Scholarship Scheme** (TASS, government funded to support athletes on academic courses) and **Advance Apprenticeship in Sporting Excellence** (AASE) provide a structured training and development route across a number of sports for talented young athletes (aged 16-19), who have a real chance of excelling in their sport, either by competing on the world stage or securing a professional contract.

Long-Term Athlete Development (LTAD)

LTAD is a model used by majority of NGBs in the UK that was developed by Istvan Balyi in 2001. Figure 10.13 outlines the six stages of the late specialisation model. The philosophy of this LTAD model is as follows:
- It aims to **retain** athletes for life as well as develop them.
- It hopes to match desire and talent of a performer to an appropriate training environment.
- In turn, this should lead to increased retention and increased success.
- It hopes to establish a clear development pathway for athletes.

figure 10.13 – LTAD model

- LTAD LATE SPECIALISATION
- team games athletics rowing
- fundamentals
- learning to train
- training to train
- training to compete
- training to win
- active for life

SPORT AND SOCIETY

The effectiveness of TIPs

- Recruiting talented athletes on such schemes increases the chances of producing **more medals** on the world stage.
- Gives talented athletes considerable material benefits, **financial support**, including time to train, access to **professional coaches** who provide highly structures training programmes, and the use of top **facilities**.
- Assess to high tech sports science and **sports medicine therapies**.
- Promotes the use of a system which is **scientifically** based in terms of screening, training, diet and sports medicine.
- Talented youngsters are directed towards sports that most suit their **strengths**.
- Selection is based on **natural talent** and not socio-economic background, thus ensuring equal opportunities to the talent pool.

Disadvantage of using TIPs

- Selectors/scouts need to be able to look beyond the immediate success and characteristics, and look at the components such as age-related speed and balance, which are better predictors of potential performance.
- There is the possibility that **late developers** are not spotted.
- Early versus late specialisation needs to be considered on an individual basis.
- Talented athletes have **no guarantee** of realising their potential. They could get injured on the way.
- Identifying future potential is difficult, as predictions are being made regarding how well an athlete may develop, rather than just assessing their current ability.
- **Growth** and **maturation** have a marked effect on an athlete's ability at a given time, and need to be taken into consideration.
- Talented individuals that are effective at a young age will not necessarily be the same ones that are effective in future years.
- A sports person's **attitudes** and **psycho-behavioural** characteristics are difficult to detect in a trial situation, and so these characteristics should be monitored from within the development programme.
- From recruiting many talented athletes, statistics show that only a few athletes reach elite performance level.
- Such TID programmes are **expensive** to run and are very inefficient in terms of creating global successes.
- There are only a **finite number of talented individuals** and the more popular sports may attract the best from this talent pool. For example, UK rugby has an established high profile that attracts tall strong players that could be good throwers.

EIS Performance Pathways

Performance Pathways build and sustain highly effective systems for talented athletes to ensure success at future Olympic and Paralympic Games.

The EIS Performance Pathways work in partnership with UK Sport World Class Programmes to identify and develop talented athletes and to construct the underpinning support systems through the following four work areas:

- **Pathway Frontline Technical Solutions**: delivery of tailored solutions to identify and develop talented athletes that meets the needs of each individual sport such as talent recruitment, talent transfer and development of curriculums.

- **Pathway Education**: provision of educational opportunities for development of coaches and managers covering topics unique to the elite developing athlete.

- **Pathway Analytics**: the use of diagnostic tools that robustly measure and benchmark the effectiveness of their performance pathway. This includes the Performance Pathway Health Check (PHC) which provides a support system that provides a set of procedures that can be used to review current systems and practices which support the development of world class athletes and future medal winners.

SECTION 6 CHAPTER 10
DEVELOPMENT OF ELITE PERFORMERS IN SPORT

EIS Performance Pathways

- **Pathway Strategy**: assists individual sports to develop and implement an aligned pathway vision and strategies from foundations level to elite podium level.

An example of an EIS initiative is the **Army Elite Sports Programme** (AESP) - a joint collaboration with the British Army and UK Sport. Launched in 2014 ASEP aims to identify future Olympic medallists for the Tokyo 2020 Olympics and beyond (figure 10.14). The AESP is funded by a £1.4m donation the British Army received for providing some of the security at the London 2012 Olympic and Paralympic Games.

In terms of impact, the EIS Performance Pathways have worked in partnership with 20 Olympic and Paralympic sports, over 100 world class coaches, run 12 national athlete recruitment campaigns and assessed over 7000 athletes.

figure 10.14 – soldiers practise shooting

UK Sport's World Class Performance Programme, Gold Event Series and TID

World Class Performance Programme (WCPP)

Funded by the National Lottery through UK Sport, the WCPP selection is based upon the potential to win medals at an Olympic or Paralympic Games and has two distinct levels:

World Class Podium (WCP)
WCP supports sports and athletes with realistic medal capabilities at global events.
This group of elite athletes should be standing on the medal podium at the next world or global games for their sport.

World Class Podium Potential (WCPP)
WCPP supports sports and athletes at the stage of the pathway immediately beneath WCP, who have demonstrated realistic medal winning capabilities for future Olympic or Paralympic Games. Athletes at WCPP level are typically four to six years away from the podium.

Gold Event Series

The Gold Event Series was an initiative produced by UK Sport and the Department for Culture Media and Sport (DCMS) as part of wider plans to develop the Government's support for hosting major international sporting events, and continue the momentum generated by London 2012.

- £27 million from the National Lottery has been used to fund this flagship programme which aims to bring over 100 of the world's most prestigious sporting events to the UK, including 36 World and European Championships between 2013 and 2023.
- Providing an opportunity for 2.5 million spectators to continue to experience world class Olympic and Paralympic sport on home soil.
- Generating approximately £287 million additional expenditure in host cities and regions across the UK and over 250,000 overseas visitors
- Successful bids include the World Athletics Championships in 2017 in the Olympic Park (figure 10.15).

figure 10.15 – the Olympic Park, World Championships 2017

144

SPORT AND SOCIETY

Talent Identification and development

TID programmes have already been discussed on page 142.

Talent identification programmes usually **examine**, **judge** and **assess** a performer from watching them compete in a competitive situation. If the player is deemed 'good enough' they are invited to an academy for a trial period.

Academies are special training centres set up by clubs to help them develop young players.

England pathway for netball – an academy development

Satellite academies (figure 10.16): County Netball Associations (on behalf of England Netball) manage and deliver about 15 sessions per year. Young netballers to learn how to train on their own, and to understand, experience and practice some of the different components required in a training programme.

County academies: County Netball Associations manage and deliver the training programmes set by England Netball (15-30 sessions per year) providing athletes with the support and skill set they need to progress to the next level of the pathway, the Regional Academy.

Regional Academies: are located across the country and operate year round individualised training environments for athletes, delivering between 3-4 hours per week of coaching. There will be up to 20 athletes in each of the Regional Academies, some of whom will also attend National Academy training and may be part of the U19/U17 England Squads.

Regional Performance Academies: are located across the country and operate year round individualised training environments for athletes, delivering between 5-7 hours per week of coaching. There will be up to 20 athletes in each of the Regional Performance Academies, some of whom will also attend National Academy training and may be part of the U19/U17 England Squads.

figure 10.16 – England talent pathway for netball

The **National Academy** operates via centralised and weekend camps, bringing together the best U17 and U19 players in England for extra coaching and training. It also provides athletes with an opportunity to access similar support services that are available to senior athletes, for example, individualised strength and conditioning programmes, on-site physiotherapy, performance lifestyle and medical services.

Prior to tours and Netball Europe, U19 and U17 squads will be selected from the National Academy.

The TID system used by **professional football clubs** involves the use of **scouts** who work for or are attached to the clubs monitoring competitive matches. The criterion typically used assesses players on their techniques, balance, personality and speed.

Once recruits have entered the club system, clubs can build up a sustainable system that enables talent transfer within an aligned pathway vision (delivering tailored solutions to build sustainable programmes) that will **develop talent** from novice to elite performers.

This process can be supported by pathway analytics as explained above, such as the **Pathway Health Check** (PHC) devised by Sport England, which reviews the athlete's progress, fitness levels achieved and whether the athlete is transitioning well between junior and senior levels.

Rowing and Start

In contrast to soccer TID, some sports aim to identify **raw talent** as a starting point, providing **physical attributes** are met. For example, **British Rowing TID programme** indentify, recruit and develop individual with no prior experience to become Olympic rowers through their Start programme.

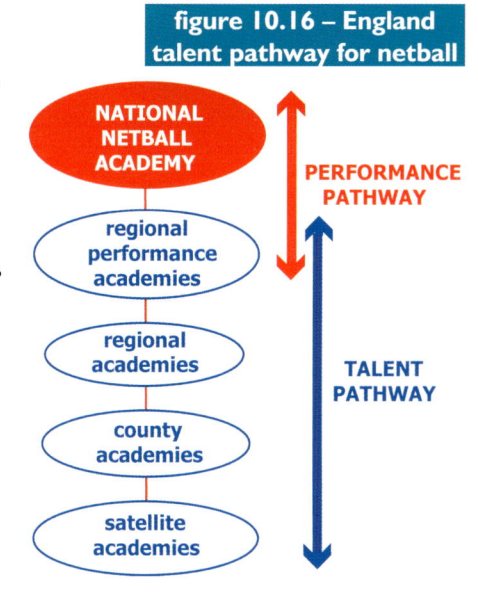

SECTION 6 CHAPTER 10 — DEVELOPMENT OF ELITE PERFORMERS IN SPORT

Rowing and Start

There are a number of **Start centres** around the UK that are hosted by the local rowing club and provide a training base for athletes. Each Start centre employs a full time professional coach who is responsible for the recruitment and development of athletes. As part of this development all Start rowers attend regular **training** and **testing** camps to monitor their **progression**.

Potential candidates need to match the **physical criteria** required for rowing: **females** need to be 5'10 and taller and aged between 14-22 years old, and **males** 6'2 and taller aged between 14-20 years old.

Graduates of Start, including Helen Glover, Alex Gregory and Heather Stanning have gone on to win Olympic, World and European medals. Website application is easily accessible: https://www.britishrowing.org/go-rowing/why-row/competition/talent-id/

Practice questions

1) Which one of the following is a national governing body of sport?
   a. Street Games.
   b. British Olympic Association.
   c. Talent Identification programme.
   d. British Athletics UK.

2) Which one of the following is not an EIS Performance Pathway?
   a. Pathway Analytics.
   b. Pathway Education.
   c. Pathway Screening.
   d. Pathway Strategy.

3) Which phase of talent identification assesses young talented athletes who have already encountered organised training?
   a. identification of talent stage.
   b. development stage.
   c. testing and selection stage.
   d. intermediate stage

4) From the following choices identify the main role of national governing bodies?
   a. to govern their sports through the common consent of their sport.
   b. to establish rules.
   c. to select individuals for funding.
   d. to pick teams for international competition.

5) The Gold Event Series is:
   a. part of the Grand Prix Diamond league.
   b. part of the World Class Performance Programme.
   c. a talent identification programme.
   d. a UK Government plan to host major international sporting events.

6) What are the four key aims of Sport England? — 2 marks

7) Identify and explain three key issues to implementing a successful nation wide athletic development programme. — 3 marks

8) There are two methods of talent identification: natural selection and scientific selection. Define and explain positive and negative aspects for each method. — 6 marks

SPORT AND SOCIETY

Practice questions

9) Describe the administrative system (institutes of sport) underpinning elite sport in the UK and account for its structure. — 4 marks

10) Briefly identify and describe what you think UK Sport is doing to satisfy the needs of elite British performers. — 4 marks

11) a) One of the key roles of National Governing Bodies is to produce a Whole Sport Plan. Outline the key features of a Whole Sport Plan. — 3 marks

    b) Select a sport and explain how this NGB has implemented a Whole Sport Plan. — 3 marks

12) Early identification of talented individuals is considered increasingly important. Discuss the personal factors required to support progression from talent identification to elite performance. — 8 marks

13) What does TASS stand for and how does it help to develop sporting talent? — 3 marks

14) Discuss the role of National Agencies in the development of an elite performer. — 8 marks

15) The UK World Class Programme that supports elite athletes, relies on the services of the three main areas of sport science, namely physiology, sport psychology and biomechanics. Discuss the ways in which an elite athlete can use these services to improve his or her sporting performance? — 15 marks

16) Describe a talent identification programme implemented by a UK governing body of sport. — 5 marks

17) The modern Olympic Games have changed in nature and size since the 1896 Athens Olympic Games. Explain the social factors and the support programmes in the UK that encourage the development of elite athletes and increase the chance of winning medals. — 15 marks

18) Identify the roles of government and lottery funding in the development of elite performers within the UK. — 6 marks

Answers link: http://www.jroscoe.co.uk/downloads/a2_revise_pe_aqa/AQAA2_ch10_answers.pdf

SECTION 6 CHAPTER 11 — ETHICS AND VIOLENCE IN SPORT

CHAPTER 11: Ethics and violence in sport

Ethics in sport

Amateurism

The term amateur comes from a French derivation of the Latin word '**amator**', defined as 'lover of'. In practice, it means a person engages in an activity for **pleasure** and feelings of **worthiness** rather than for financial benefit or professional reasons.

In 19th century Britain, rational sport was initially an exclusive development by the male upper and middle class and is normally described as the Gentleman Amateur period. Gentlemen members of the middle and upper classes were usually products of the English public school system that promoted an active policy of **athleticism** (goodness, manliness, restraint and discipline) perceived as character building qualities needed by the sporting gentleman amateur.

> **STUDENT NOTE**
>
> There is a section on Amateurism in 19th century Britain in AS/A1 Revise PE for AQA ISBN 9781901424850, page 95 onwards.

Amateur sports are sports in which participants engage largely or entirely without **remuneration**. The whole subject of remuneration was controversial in 19th century Britain, when sports such as cricket paid leading amateurs **more in expenses**, than any lower class paid professionals (figure 11.1).

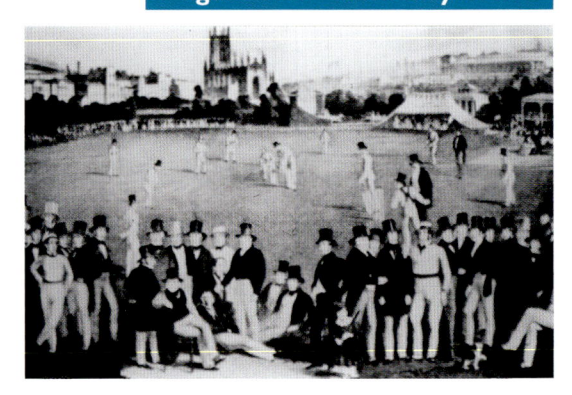

The elite amateur **Oxbridge sportsmen** initially took their games to members of their own social group, forming games clubs and sports associations and eventually National and International Governing Bodies. These clubs and sports associations were amateur and excluded the lower classes who only had popular festivals and professional opportunities to participate in sport.

figure 11.1 – cricket by 1851

Amateur games and sport became **codified** and **regulated**, **regular**, **respectable** and **rational**, and were refined to meet the supposed high moral standards that were accepted as the amateur code of conduct. For example, the FA was formed by these gentlemen and the early soccer sides (such as Sheffield Wednesday) were all gentlemen.
The FA Cup was won by old student clubs or urban gentlemen's clubs. Similarly, the early Athletic Clubs admitted middle class gentlemen who established and developed amateur athletics and gymnastics associations.

From the end of the 19th century and up to the 1990s in some sports (for example tennis, rugby union and athletics), amateur and professional sports developed **separately**.
The **middle classes** were **administrators**, **agents** and **promoters**, the **working classes** were **participants**, and the **upper classes** were **sponsors** or **patrons**.

Examples of the **attitude of administrators** to performers included:
- The definition of amateurism in athletics, which excluded the possibility of earning any money through sport until the 1980s.
- The exclusion of rugby league (and therefore potentially professional) players from any part in rugby union until the 1990s.

Sporting amateurism was a zealously guarded ideal in the 19th century, especially among the upper classes, but faced steady erosion throughout the 20th century with the continuing growth of professional sport, the role of the media, monetary gain and commercialism.
It is now strictly held as an ideal by fewer and fewer national governing bodies, even though some of them maintain the word amateur in their titles.

SPORT AND SOCIETY

Amateurism

By the early 21st century the Olympic Games and all the major team sports had accepted **professional** competitors even though the Olympic Games still retains these ideals of amateurism in its Olympic **creed**, **charter** and **oath**.

However, there are still some sports which maintain a distinction between amateur and professional status with separate competitive leagues. The most prominent of these are golf and boxing. In particular, only amateur boxers (figure 11.2, Nicola Adams, double Olympic Champion, now turned professional) could compete at the Olympics up to 2016.

figure 11.2 - Nicola Adams, Olympic champion

The Olympic Oath

Written by Baron **Pierre de Coubertin**, founder of the modern Olympic Games, the oath is a solemn promise made by one athlete from the host nation at the Opening Ceremony of each Olympic Games.

'**In the name of all the competitors, I promise that we shall take part in these Olympic Games, respecting and abiding by the rules which govern them, committing ourselves to a sport without doping and without drugs, in the true spirit of sportsmanship, for the glory of sport and the honour of our teams**.'

The Olympic Oath is an oath of **sportsmanship** and **fair play**. By swearing the oath, competitors vow to respect all the rules that govern the Olympic Games and abide by them in the true spirit of sportsmanship.

figure 11.3 – Usain Bolt, millionaire superstar

The Olympic Games remain unique as a sporting festival representing the pinnacle of sporting achievement alongside its associated spirit of fair play and sportsmanship. It pitches the true amateur against millionaire superstars, such as Andy Murray and Usain Bolt (figure 11.3).

When athletes try everything from head-butts to kicking, and taking drugs to edge out an opponent, the spirit of the Games is questioned and the darker spirit of the Olympics is revealed. In some instances physical intimidation and violence, as well as time wasting, have become all-too routine features of increasingly intense sports contests.

At Beijing 2008, Chilean tennis player **Fernando Gonzalez** caused outrage when he refused to own up to a shot clipping his racket at a crucial stage in his semi-final with James Blake. Gonzalez claimed the point and went on to win a silver medal.

At the Seoul Olympic Games of 1988, **Ben Johnson** was disqualified and labelled a drug cheat 3 days after winning the 100 metres. Johnson's blood and urine samples contained the steroid stanozolol.

In 2016 over 100 Russian athletes were banned from the Rio Olympics after proof of a **state-run doping** programme. So those athletes who use the performance enhancing drugs (PEDs) but are never tested and caught, are cheating the system.

Many sports writers and ethics professors have proposed lifting the ban on steroid abuse in the face of constant rule breaking. If there is no way to level the playing field and stop PED abuse, they reason, why not allow it and regulate it for safety?

Such **win-at-all-costs** sentiments are against the Olympic Oath and stretch the rules to their absolute limit.

The Olympic Oath

SECTION 6 CHAPTER 11 — ETHICS AND VIOLENCE IN SPORT

Sportsmanship

The idea of **sportsmanship** (figure 11.4) is not just what you play, but how you play in a sport. If the sporting activity involves competition, then it should always be performed with a spirit of sportsmanship. Sportsmanship involves conforming to the **rules** and the **spirit** and **etiquette** of a sport, and is known as the **contract to compete** concept (based on the Victorian ideas within the spirit of '**fair play**').

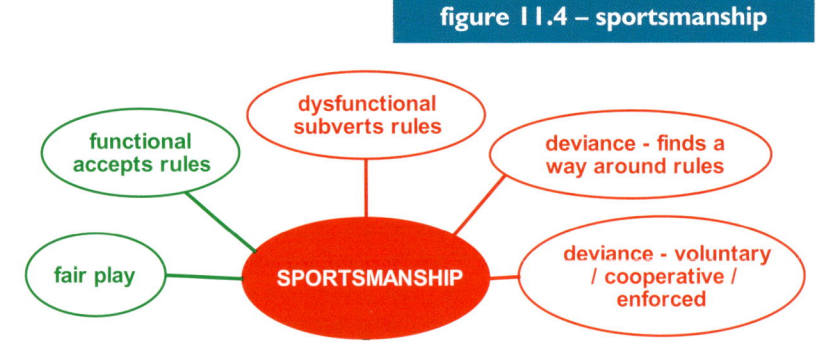

figure 11.4 – sportsmanship

- functional accepts rules
- dysfunctional subverts rules
- deviance - finds a way around rules
- fair play
- SPORTSMANSHIP
- deviance - voluntary / cooperative / enforced

Respect for an opponent is an unwritten code within sports where participants agree to '**do their best**', '**to strive to win**', '**to play within the rules**', and to do this with a degree of sportsmanship. Playing to win is said to be a good thing as long as it is within the '**spirit of the game**'. This implies that a person should allow his or her opponent to do the same, and not be unduly upset if that opponent wins. Respect is to be given to the rules, to opponents, and to officials attempting to administer a contest.

In sport, we have problems of **violence** on the field and the use of **PEDs**. This tells us that the ethic of fair play is under attack. Without fair play, sport as a noble pastime is doomed. It is possible to look at games on the television or during school sport and test the behaviour of performers.

The behaviour will vary from the high point of players making moral decisions to the other extreme of deliberate violence against others. Fair play will exist as long as you at least accept the referee, but it's better if you accept the rules of play.

- Perhaps there can be no true sport without the idea of fair play, where the spirit in which the activity is played is more important than a '**win-at-all-costs**' attitude?
- Sportsmanship is functional if the rules of a game or sport are accepted, or the decisions of a referee or umpire are accepted, and dysfunctional if a performer has no regard for others or deliberately subverts the rules of a game in order to gain advantage.
- Sportsmanship behaviour is still evident today, even within professional sports. For example, admitting fouls and shaking hands at the start of and end of a sporting contest (figure 11.5).

figure 11.5 – sportsmanship reigns

Encouraging sportsmanship behaviour
- Rigorous **drug testing**.
- Use of **technology**.
- **Punish** foul play using fines and sin bins.
- NGBs addressing required **rule changes**.
- **Awards** such as the **Fair Play Awards** are awarded to individual in recognition of remarkable acts of fair play or outstanding careers conducted in the spirit of fair play.

Gamesmanship

Gamesmanship (figure 11.6) is the term which describes behaviour **outside the rules of a sport** or game which aims to gain advantage over an opponent, and has been defined as: '**the intention to compete to the limit of the rules and beyond if you can get away with it**'.

Some professional performers and coaches maintain that '**you get away with what you can**', an admission that potential rewards, millions in sponsorship and wages, can outweigh moral considerations. Gamesmanship is driven by a '**win-at-all-costs**' attitude and shows no regard for the well-being of the opponent.

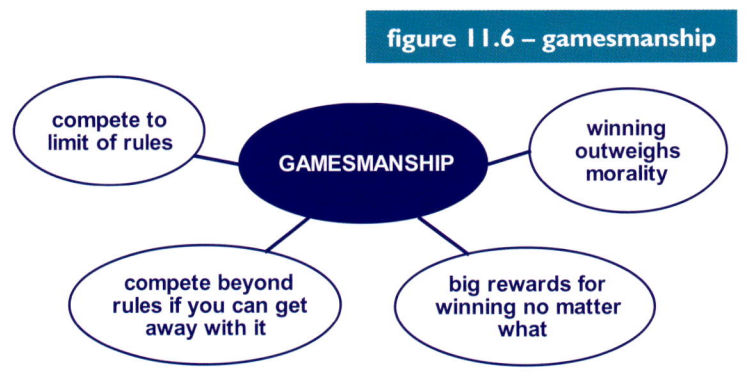

figure 11.6 – gamesmanship

- compete to limit of rules
- winning outweighs morality
- GAMESMANSHIP
- compete beyond rules if you can get away with it
- big rewards for winning no matter what

SPORT AND SOCIETY

Gamesmanship

Examples of gamesmanship are:
- A boxer or fighter thumbing the eye of an opponent.
- A soccer player deliberately fouling an opponent with the aim of getting him or her off the pitch.
- A rugby player stamping on an opposing player.
- A cricket team 'sledging' their opponents when batting – extreme verbal banter – destroying confidence and concentration.

Win ethic – win-at-all-costs

- The win ethic is also known as the **Lombardian** ethic that is heightened by the needs of **professionalism** and a society that only acknowledges the winners.
- The Lombardian ethic is based on a statement '**winning isn't the most important thing-it's the only thing**', made by **Vince Lombardi** (figure 11.7), a famous American football coach.
- This suggests that **outcomes** over-ride the process of participating.
- The win ethic sits at the heart of sport in the USA.
- Elitism is at the heart of most sporting activity, and is, in effect, a programme of excellence as exemplified by Sport England's World Class Podium programme where medals success, at major global sporting events, count towards NGB funding.
- The win ethic rejects the Olympic ideal that taking part is most significant and fair play as an essential component.
- The win ethic almost totally controls the professional sport scene, and remains a central philosophy in most athletic departments in schools.
- The win ethic is reinforced by the media, the hiring and firing of coaches and managers, a no drawn games philosophy and a high level of deviancy.
- Perhaps this win-at-all-cost culture is the reason why more children than ever before are choosing not to participate in youth sports.

figure 11.7 – Vince Lombardi, head coach of the Green Bay Packers 1959

Positive and negative forms of deviance and the performer

Deviance

The term deviance describes behaviour in which people find a way around the rules, however they are framed and can be institutional, group specific, or individual.

Deviant behaviour could be one of three possibilities:
- **Voluntary**, the performer decides to take drugs.
- **Cooperative**, the performer decides to take drugs, because all his friends are.
- **Enforced**, an East German swimmer took drugs provided by her coach.

Deviance in sport concerns the **intention to cheat** as part of deviant behaviour, and includes **aggression** and **violence** among competitors and spectators, as well as the issue of **doping**.

In **sociological terms**, deviance means the variation of behaviour from the norm (what is normal). This can be upwards (positive) or downwards (negative) deviance. Positive deviance is when someone will over-conform to norms with no intention to harm or break the rules.

Negative deviance

Negative deviance involves behaviour that fails to meet accepted norms and has a detrimental effect on individuals and on society in general.

Examples of negative deviance include using PEDs, cheating within a contest, using bribes to influence the outcome of a match, fan violence or hooliganism, illegal betting on the outcome of a contest, financial irregularities in the transferring of players and player violence (figure 11.8).

figure 11.8 – player violence

Deviance 151

SECTION 6 CHAPTER 11 — ETHICS AND VIOLENCE IN SPORT

Positive deviance

Examples of positive deviance include training through injury, adopting a 'no pain, no gain' attitude which implies an 'over' commitment to sport. For example, it used to be a common occurrence within rugby union, to continue 'playing through' an injury in the interests of the team as a whole. This behaviour has largely disappeared with the advent of substitutions, but used to be the major reason for the ending of a promising career in the sport.

Causes of deviant behaviour

- NGBs may **feel less able** to punish players due to their commercial interests.
- Fear of the offending player taking them to **court**.
- Deviant behaviour may have become more **socially acceptable**.
- Individuals lack **moral restraint** to maintain an acceptable code of conduct.
- The **fact of winning** may have more value than the loss of respect or punishment that may occur.
- **Rewards** are great and so individuals may be prepared to take **risks**, particularly true of positive deviance.

Violence within sport

Player violence

This issue arises when **acceptable aggression** (assertion) in sport becomes **violence**.

Violence is normally where aggression goes beyond the agreed codification in that game or activity. There is an additional dimension, in that **acceptable aggression** in the activity may not match up with the **laws of the land** and so players can misunderstand their legal position.

Figure 11.9 summarises the issues affecting player violence.

Physical aggression and an unacceptable level of verbal abuse may be identified as part of player violence:

figure 11.9 – aggression and violence in sport

PLAYER VIOLENCE: unacceptable aggression, acts against the law, drugs, gamesmanship taken too far, hyping-up, presence of spectators

- The presence of **spectators** can **increase player arousal**.
- Many games require players to be **hyped-up to p**erform at their best, making aggression and outbreaks of violence more likely.
- More recently, the use of **drugs** may have increased this tendency.

- On the other hand, some sports require **calmness** and **focus**.
- For example, darts, snooker, dance and gymnastics, and players in these sports are less likely to be violent.
- **Gamesmanship**, aimed at putting an opponent off, can be equally unacceptable.

Aggression by sports performers is a part of their sporting life. The need to be **competitive** and the **frustration** felt at failure can lead sportspeople to be violent as an extreme expression of this aggression. The level at which aggression becomes violence varies according to the activity.

For example, **boxing** involves punching an opponent, which would be violence in any other sport. In this case, it is argued that the essence of boxing is 'the art of self-defence' and that boxing has its own code of acceptable behaviour with a referee to see that this is observed, as well as the safety precaution of gloves. There is also a difference here between amateur and professional boxing, and between junior and senior competitors.

This rules difference also is relevant to a variety of other activities and games, such as tag rugby with young children.

SPORT AND SOCIETY

Causes of player violence in sport

The **causes of violence** among players are summarised in figure 11.10.
- The **crowd** response to player activity (chanting, booing, name calling) can affect player tendency to violence.
- The **confrontational nature** of most top professional games (the gladiatorial influence) can increase the tendency to violence.
- The popular nature of some sports can lead to **player expectation of violence** as part of the game **culture**.
- The presence of a **large number of spectators** and the significance of victory can increase the emotion of a sporting occasion, and again make violence more likely.
- The **failure** of sports administrators to adequately **punish** players who are persistently violent can cause players to cynically commit further violent offences on the field.

figure 11.10 – causes of player violence in sport

Strategies for preventing violence between players

The solutions lie in the **code of behaviour** being part of the **tradition** of the activity from school onwards and the quality of **control by officials** during a game, and the efficiency of the administration of sanctions by NGBs on offending players.

Officials
- Officials should include an **explanation** of their action (figure 11.11).
- The use of the **television match official** (TMO - fourth official) during the match, advising the on-field referee, on close calls and post match video evidence, such as the Rugby League '**on report system**' that can be used by referees to review controversial play.
- The use of deterrents, such as **sin bins**.

Managers and captains
- Establish a clear **code of conduct** and expectation.
- Understand individual player's level of arousal and train players to **manage their own arousal** levels.
- Where possible ensure that **players**, who have a low flash point, are kept away from **high stress** situations.
- **Avoid** an attitude of **winning-at-all-costs**.
- Discuss **stress appropriate behaviour** during team talks.

figure 11.11 – is it worth arguing with the referee?

NGBs
- **Punishments** by controlling bodies should be seen to be **fair** and **consistent**, and should therefore fit the offence.
- Recognise players with a good disciplinary record as **role models**.
- The use of **educational campaigns** and awards, such as the Fair Play Awards that reward clubs with good disciplinary records.
- Train officials in **player management**, such as how to defuse situations between players.
- NGBs like to deal with violence themselves, but increasingly are getting more involved with the **legal system** (page 164).

But the most essential element is the **attitude** of each player.

Player violence 153

SECTION 6 CHAPTER 11 — ETHICS AND VIOLENCE IN SPORT

Spectator violence

Spectators get very **emotionally involved**, desperately wanting their side to win.

A crucial feature of football followers is their **identity** with the team they follow. They refer to members of their team as 'us' and 'we', and members of the opposition as 'them and 'they'. This leads to the **emotional attachment** which can often be directed at opposition players on the pitch, and also at opposition supporters.

This can lead to **violence in the stadia** and on the streets, but can also involve **extreme verbal abuse**. In such instances the law is probably being broken, but access by the stewards and the police is not possible because of the crowd effect. The facilities of a stadium, in respect of the **mixing of the fans** of opposing teams, can be a cause of spectator violence particularly in **professional soccer**.

figure 11.12 – Russian and England supporters brawling during Soccer Euro16

Hooliganism

The dominance of a youth culture, where gangs identify with a professional football club and are prepared to fight an opposition group in a chosen place, is a frightening extension of soccer hooliganism. Hooliganism is **anti-social** or **aggressive**, **violent** and **destructive** behaviour by troublemakers, typically in a gang.

Acts of hooliganism (figure 11.12) often overspill and impact local surroundings such as shops and bars, as witnessed between Russian and English football supporters in the 2016 European Championships in France. Although there is a strong working class peer group culture associated with soccer, this has, occasionally, involved middle class male groups. The media can encourage confrontational situations by highlighting players' comments about opponents and giving these hooligan gangs publicity.

But spectators certainly need to recognise that no matter how much they get worked up, their violence is measured in legal terms.

Causes of spectator violence in sport

There are numerous causes in what is naturally an antagonistic and often frustrating situation. For example, the tendency towards violence by a supporter group is linked to whether or not their team is winning. Supporters of a winning team are more likely to be benevolent and good natured, whereas supporters of a losing team can be violent, particularly in 'derby games'.

Spectator violence has been explained as a form of **social deviance** and it is caused by:
- Being in a crowd, where there is **confinement** and poor crowd control.
- **High emotion**, **diminished responsibility** and the likelihood of **shared aggression**.
- Consumption of **alcohol** exacerbates these problems.
- There is also an element of **depersonalisation** that a crowd gives an individual, where it is 'easy to be lost in a crowd'.
- **Poor officiating**.

In the case of hooliganism, the question arises as to whether these are **hooligans at football** or **football hooligans**.

In the case of the former, the solution lies in the **conditions and control** needed to prevent this anti-social behaviour. If, however, football makes them behave as hooligans, then one must look at the **behaviour of the players** and the causes of frustration.

SPORT AND SOCIETY

Strategies for preventing spectator violence
Measures (figure 11.13) which have been taken to reduce the chances of spectator violence are:
- **Segregation** of home and away supporters.
- The introduction of **all-seater stadia** (outcome of the Taylor Report (page 166)
- Increase the '**family**' concept.
- Increase the number of **stewards** and police.
- Ensure that **alcohol** cannot be bought or brought into grounds.
- More responsible **media** reporting.
- Detect trouble by using **CCTV**.
- In addition, campaigns like '**kick racism out of football**', sponsored by major soccer clubs, player and Governing Bodies, can defuse unacceptable racial aggression.
- **Legal intervention** that punishes offenders.

figure 11.13 – preventing spectator violence

Practice questions

1) We often talk about sports performers playing fairly.
   Which of the following options best describes gamesmanship?
   a. playing within the written rules.
   b. it's not whether you won or lost that matters, it's how you played the game.
   c. the intention to compete to the limit of the rules and beyond if you can get away with it.
   d. fair, generous and polite behaviour, especially when playing a sport or game.

2) Which one of the following is not an example of sportsmanship-like behaviour?
   a. respect for an opponent.
   b. win-at-all-costs attitude.
   c. punish foul behaviour.
   d. use drug testing procedures to eliminate cheats.

3) The win ethic is evident in modern day elite sports. Which one of the following is an example of this ethic?
   a. outcomes over-ride the process of participating.
   b. allow everyone to compete on a level playing field.
   c. play within the spirit of the game.
   d. lend a player to the opposition team who have arrived with one player short.

4) An example of positive deviance is:
   a. using bribes to influence the outcome of a match.
   b. continue playing through an injury.
   c. using performance enhancing drugs.
   d. financial irregularities in the transferring of players.

5) Which one of the following is not a strategy for preventing player violence?
   a. officials should include an explanation of their action.
   b. the use of educational campaigns and awards, such as the Fair play Awards.
   c. train officials in player management stress techniques.
   d. referee ignores a confrontational incident during the match.

6) Explain the concept behind the Olympic Oath and discuss its relevance to contemporary Olympic Games. 4 marks

7) Explain the terms positive and negative deviance giving examples in a sporting context. 4 marks

SECTION 6 CHAPTER 11 — ETHICS AND VIOLENCE IN SPORT

Practice questions

8) The development of rational recreation was very much the result of Britain becoming an industrialised society.

   a) Using figure 11.14, explain the characteristics of an AAA Athletics Meeting.   4 marks

   b) Describe amateurism as it concerned Track and Field Athletics towards the end of the 19th century.   4 marks

figure 11.14 – the AAA championships 1870

9) Sportsmanship and gamesmanship are two opposites. Explain the differences between the two in a game of your choice.   6 marks

10) Explain what is meant by the term 'a contract to compete'. Describe the ways in which gamesmanship breaks this code.   5 marks

11) Give reasons for spectator violence at professional association football matches.   5 marks

12) Hooliganism has affected football over the past 40 years. Define the term hooliganism and discuss the reasons why it might occur. What steps have been taken to reduce the incidents of hooliganism in Premiership soccer.   15 marks

13) Discuss the suggestion that there has been a decline in sportsmanship since the late 19th century and outline strategies that the sporting authorities have used in an attempt to maintain high standards of behaviour.   15 marks

Answers link: http://www.jroscoe.co.uk/downloads/a2_revise_pe_aqa/AQAA2_ch11_answers.pdf

SPORT AND SOCIETY

CHAPTER 12: Drugs in sport, sport and the law, and commercialisation

Drugs in sport

The reason sportspeople take drugs (**performance enhancing drugs** or PEDs) or other nutritional ergogenic aids is to attempt to gain an advantage over other competitors or players.

Some drugs are **against the law** and others against sporting regulations, but young people can be attracted to these unethical and dangerous substances because their heroes and role models are presumed to have taken them.

- Thus taking drugs ceases to be only a personal decision.
- This is part of the win ethic, the willingness to win at all costs, or simply a desire to excel in something as an unbridled ambition.
- The International Olympic Committee and International Sports Authorities view drug taking as **cheating**, and it is deemed totally unacceptable for the unscrupulous to be allowed to take unfair advantage. Let's not forget the Olympic oath sworn on behalf of all participant States.

Performance enhancing drugs (PEDs)

A performance-enhancing drug (PED) is any substance taken by athletes to **improve performance**. Doping refers to **the use of banned athletic PEDs by athletic competitors**.

In the past 20 years, drug taking has become a very common part of top class sport.

A recent high profile case has involved more than 1,000 Russian athletes (competing in summer, winter Olympic and Paralympic Sports and other global events across over 30 sports) who were involved in the manipulation of concealed positive doping tests and benefitted from a state-sponsored doping regime dating back to 2011. The Russian Olympic team corrupted the London Olympic Games on an unprecedented scale and was involved in the ongoing use of prohibited substances, wash out testing and false reporting, supervised by the Russian Anti Doping Agency (RUSADA).

Drugs are **easily available** and a summary of the reasons that sportspeople should not take these substances are shown along with the reasons that people take these drugs (figure 12.1).

Some drugs are **against the law** and others against **sporting regulations**, but young people can be attracted to these unethical and dangerous substances because their heroes and **role models** are **presumed** to have taken them.

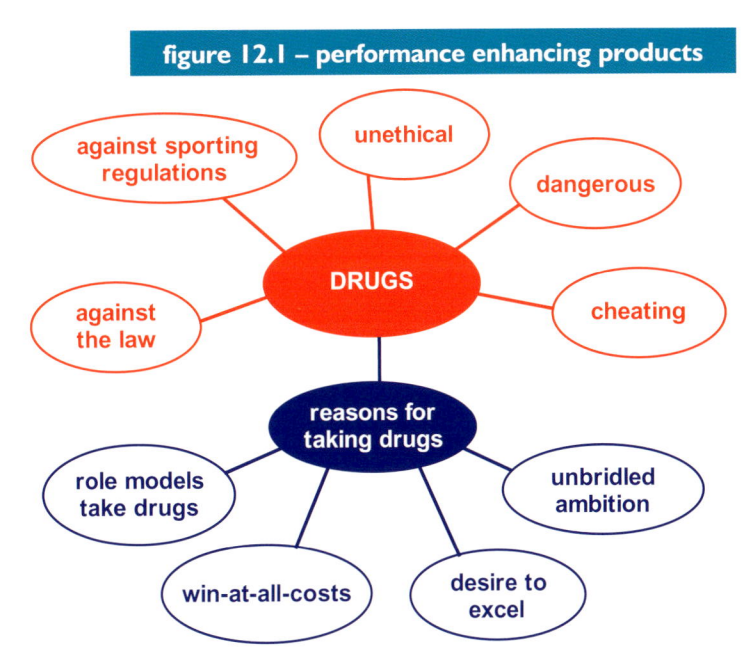

Social reasons to aid performance

A major social reason for drug taking is the belief that **everyone else is doing it**. This belief makes drug taking acceptable and reinforces the **win-at-all-costs** attitude that success cannot be achieved without drugs and that the benefits of winning are greater that the risk of being found out.

figure 12.1 – performance enhancing products

SECTION 6 CHAPTER 12 — DRUGS IN SPORT, SPORT AND THE LAW, AND COMMERCIALISATION

Social reasons to aid performance

Drugs change the conditions of winning. Such forms of behaviour not only contravene the **spirit of fair play**, but indicate the willingness to **cheat** and to **hurt others** in the interests of victory and a **violation of the rules** that surround the legal and moral arguments.

Let's not forget the **Olympic oath** sworn on behalf of all participant States: 'In the name of all competitors, I promise that we shall take part in these Olympic Games... without doping and using drugs in the true spirit of sponsorship'.

Athletes are vulnerable and socially influenced by:

- **Media coverage**: in their attempt to sell newspapers the media tend to give extensive coverage to **doping scandals** within sport.
- This may give the athlete a misleading impression of the extent to which PEDs are used in sport.
- **Peer pressure**: athletes may directly observe or hear of the practices of fellow athletes who use PEDs and may be offered drugs by their fellow competitors or team members.
- There is a perceived suspicion that rivals are using something (PEDs?) that assists them in meeting the physical demands of intense training and competition.
- **Support team pressure**: family members and coaches may instil additional pressure on athletes to improve performance by any means available.
- It has been suggested that governing bodies '**turn a blind eye**' to some drug takers in order to benefit from the commercial benefits that result from success.
- **Deterrence**: there are few deterrents that discourage an athlete from taking illegal drugs as drugs are readily available in gyms, over the counter and on the internet.
- **Fame, salaries and sponsorship deals**: also tempt athletes to **cheat**. But when found out, professional sports careers can be shattered as was the case for Maria Sharapova (figure 12.2) after failing a drug's test in 2016 was given a two year ban. In 2017, Maria was able to resume her professional career.
- Nike and Tag Heuer cut ties with Maria Sharapova. Up until that point Maria was the world's highest paid female athlete.

figure 12.2 – Maria Sharapova, ups and downs

Psychological reasons to aid performance

- **Beta blockers** help to decrease anxiety and steady the nerves.
- **Anabolic steroids** increase arousal and aggressive tendencies, traits that are needed in sports such as weightlifting and contact team sports, such as rugby.
- **Stimulants**, such as amphetamines, increase mental alertness, concentration, motivation and confidence.
- **Perception of pain** is dulled, thus enabling an athlete to work harder and longer.
- There is the fear of '**not making it**'.
- **Motivation**: athletes are driven to succeed as a result of **internal** and **external** motivation.
- **External rewards** are central to competitive sports and are immense, where athletes receive publicity, awards, money and sponsorships for their sporting achievements.
- **Taking illegal drugs** is one way to achieve this success.

> **STUDENT NOTE**
>
> There is a long list of banned substances. The AQA A level syllabus considers erythropoietin (EPO), anabolic steroids and beta blockers. Table 12.1, page 159 outlines the facts for these doping substances.

SPORT AND SOCIETY

Physiological reasons to aid performance

Table 12.1 – the categories of substances used in top level sport today

type of substance	known ergogenic effects	known health risks
stimulants example: amphetamines	increases alertness, reduces fatigue, increases competitiveness and hostility	can drive competitor beyond safe boundaries can cause lasting tissue and organ damage as well as masking injury are addictive, known to cause death
anabolic steroids steroidal androgens (male sex hormone) related to naturally occurring hormone testosterone example: THG tetrahydrogestrinone stanazolol	increases synthesis of protein within cells increases fat free mass, strength and power for aggressive sports such as American football or wrestling reduces recovery time between sessions increases muscle strength and bulk, promotes aggressiveness	excessive aggressive behaviour outside the activity testicular atrophy in men masculinisation in women liver damage cardiovascular diseases causes acne causes pituitary failure
rEPO recombinant erythropoietin cloned through genetic engineering **taking rEPO is a form of blood doping**	mimics body's naturally occurring hormone EPO that stimulates red blood cell production to increase oxygen transport and therefore increase aerobic capacity, performance, and aids recovery in endurance based activities such as long distance cycling (Tour-de-France) and marathon running	major risk of thrombosis (blood clot) and heart failure due to increase in blood viscosity reduces resting heart rate to dangerously low level during sleep reduces production of naturally occurring hormone EPO
beta-blockers a class of hormonal drugs	blocks transmission of neural impulse from sensory nervous system to reduce heart rate and blood pressure this has a calming effect by steadying nerves and reducing tension used in target sports such as archery, golf, snooker	dangerously low heart rate could lead to heart failure

Positive and negative implications of drug taking to the sport and the performer

figure 12.3 – regular injections to short-term success

Athletes don't take drugs to level the playing field, they do it to get an **advantage**. A vicious cycle of upping dosages to get a **bigger advantage** happens.

- The pay-off is now **fame, image and money** and the long term health consequences are minimised (figure 12.3).
- PEDs can cause **impotence, worsening acne, balding, 'steroid rage'**.
- **Females** acquire masculine traits such as a **deep voice, facial hair** and **breast reduction**. PEDs can also **stunt growth** in adolescents.
- More serious side effects include heart and **liver damage**, and an increased risk of blood clots.
- The risk of being caught is reducing. As undetectable drugs become more available, more athletes will choose to cheat.

Implications to the sport and the performer of drug taking

SECTION 6 CHAPTER 12 — DRUGS IN SPORT, SPORT AND THE LAW, AND COMMERCIALISATION

Positive and negative implications

Over the years there have been allegations of **doping in the Tour de France**. Lance Armstrong won seven Tour de France titles, because **blood doping** is the difference between being really, really good and being world class. When Armstrong finally admitted to blood doping, he actually said that he had to cheat just to be competitive at the top of the sport.

Other high profile drug cheats include the infamous sprinters Ben Johnson, Marion Jones and Dwayne Chambers.

Athletes are allowed to use powerful drugs that deal with **health conditions**, such as asthma, providing they have a **therapeutic use exemption** (TUE) certificate. Recently Sir Bradley Wiggins (figure 12.4) has come under sustained fire from the media for using a prescribed drug called **corticosteroid** to deal with his chronic asthma and allergies. He says that he does not obtain an unfair advantage over his rivals. However, this drug can rapidly reduce an athlete's weight whilst maintaining power.

figure 12.4 – Sir Bradley Wiggins

The dilemma here is that, on the one hand inclusive sports participation should be encouraged, but on the other hand this can facilitate drug abuse via the backdoor which is an unintended and undesirable consequence. As a result, WADA is considering a blanket ban on corticosteroids.

Drug cheats can often tarnish a **sports image** and call into question the **validity of results** in competition. **Public respect** for all sports professionals suffers if there are frequent drug scandals. It becomes **harder to believe** that all athletes aren't cheats. That may cause all victories to be viewed with suspicion. This is hardly fair on the honest athletes, and it's no fun for the spectators either.

Uncovered drug cheats risk losing their **reputation**, professional **earnings**, long-term **career prospects**, as well as negatively impacting on their **social and psychological well-being**.

The essence of sport exemplifies values such as fair play, honesty, health and excellence in sport. The challenge is for role models, parents and coaches to influence these positive values.

Strategies for elimination of performance-enhancing drugs in sport

The impact of illegal drug abuse in sport has led to the development of random drug testing programmes under the supervision of WADA (the **World Anti-Doping Agency**), set up in 1998 and tasked with enforcing (figure 12.5) the international regulations on doping or drug taking.

WADA aims to bring together governments, the IOC, international governing bodies and national governing bodies to sort out difficulties by athletes performing on the international stage. WADA is tasked to get all international governing bodies and national governing bodies to adopt and implement its **World Anti-Doping Code**.

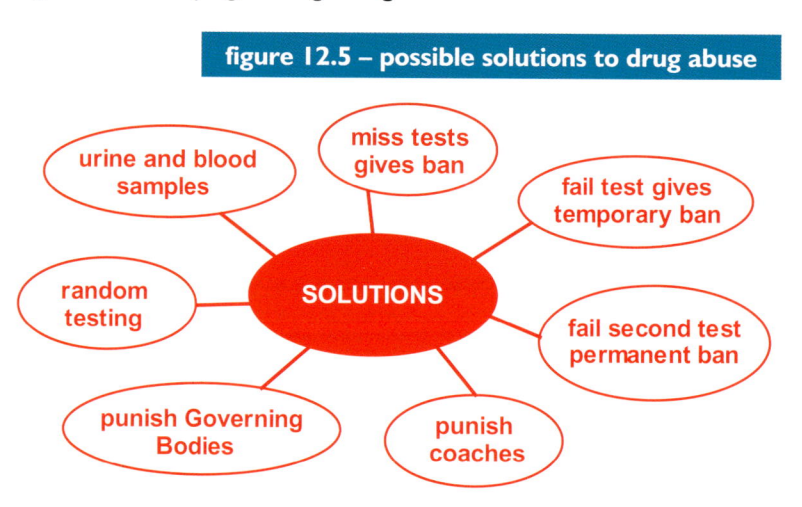

Under WADA's World Anti-Doping Code, athletes are required to state 3 months in advance their locations for one hour per day, 7 days a week. This is the time during which random testing could take place. This is called the '**whereabouts rule**' - a system designed to support out-of-competition testing and regarded as a fundamental part of an anti-doping programme.

figure 12.5 – possible solutions to drug abuse

SOLUTIONS:
- urine and blood samples
- miss tests gives ban
- fail test gives temporary ban
- fail second test permanent ban
- punish coaches
- punish Governing Bodies
- random testing

SPORT AND SOCIETY

Strategies for elimination of performance-enhancing drugs in sport

This rule has evoked anger from tennis players including Andy Murray, Rafael Nadal and Roger Federer, who feel that the European Union privacy law has been breached.

Random drug testing, (particularly out of season) ensures that athletes are discouraged from cheating the system. This includes missing these random tests under the whereabouts rule. Christine Ohuruogu (Olympic and World 400m track champion) missed three random tests and in 2006 received an automatic one year ban. This was in spite of her passing many other tests during the period when this was happening.

The major problem for WADA is to **police** the globe when some national governing bodies do not do out of season random testing.

In 2016, WADA initiated a major **retesting programme** on global sport. The anti-doping laboratory in Lausanne holds stored urine and blood samples (up to 10 years) that can be retested with improved technology to catch drug cheats who escaped detection at the time. 31 unidentified athletes in six sports have been caught during retests from the 2008 Beijing Olympic Games.

UK Anti-Doping Organisation

UK Anti-Doping (UKAD) is the UK's National Anti-Doping Organisation and is an active participant in the global fight against doping and recognises the need to take an international approach with partners such as WADA.

It is responsible for ensuring sports bodies in the UK comply with the National Anti-Doping Policy. UKAD coordinates the UK's intelligence-led risk based testing programme across more than 40 sports and is responsible for the collection and transportation of samples to a WADA accredited laboratory (figure 12.6).

In season, testing normally takes place after competitions or matches.

UKAD aims to instil a culture of clean sport by ensuring that all athletes and athlete support personnel understand and practise the **values of clean sport** and the **dangers** of physical, psychological and moral issues associated with illegal drug usage.

figure 12.6 – accredited laboratory

Initiatives, such as **100% Me**, educate athletes throughout their careers by providing anti-doping advice and guidance that embrace key values such as hard work, determination, passion, respect and integrity, associated with clean, fair competition.

figure 12.7 – Diane Modahl

Drug testing and its pitfalls

Great care has to be taken when testing takes place. Britain's Diane Modahl (figure 12.7) failed a test in 1994 just prior to the Commonwealth Games of that year. It was later discovered that her urine sample had undergone changes while being stored in the testing laboratory and she was cleared of the doping offence. She then sued the British Athletic Federation for their mishandling of the situation. This led to the eventual bankruptcy of BAF and the destruction of Diane's athletic career. Although she was reinstated, she was unable to regain the fitness and excellence needed to compete at elite level.

In the news (in 2017) is the FBIs investigation into Mo Farah's coach, Alberto Salazar, who is alleged to have abused medicines and used prohibited infusions to boost the testosterone levels of his athletes. Mo Farah (double double Olympic Champion) denies breaking anti-doping rules.

Drug testing and its pitfalls   **161**

SECTION 6 CHAPTER 12
DRUGS IN SPORT, SPORT AND THE LAW, AND COMMERCIALISATION

Drug testing and its pitfalls

There are several **benefits** that come out of law-enforcement involvement:
- It can force people to talk.
- If people don't talk, this can give the impression that they are not a good people.
- It can dig deep into personal information, for example, uncovering illicit bank accounts.

In 2014 Rhys Williams and Gareth Warburton (Welsh International athletes) were sponsored, promoted and took an energy drink that unknowingly contained anabolic steroid metabolites. Both athletes served one year bans and then later were cleared by UKAD.

What are the consequences of drug use?

Currently each case of drug use is considered individually. There are rules and regulations that guide the punishments for drug use, but as in the legal system, each case gets a different consequence depending on the circumstances. Often the consequences include **suspension** or **expulsion** from the sport, **fines** and **stripping** of awards and titles won and **repayment** of earnings.

Limitations of drug testing

The use of drug testing in sport does have limitations in its use, which some people use to debate its place in sport. These include:
- Not all drugs can be tested for. **New drugs** are created all the time, and until they are created, tests cannot be developed for them.
- During testing, the athlete is **exposed** (nudity) before the tester - athletes have to be **observed** where urine samples are taken.
- This stringent procedure was enforced after two male winners in the Athens Olympic Games were found using prosthetic **(false) genitals** and a hidden storage bag for production of their samples.
- **New prohibited lists** are developed each year, which athletes need to know and follow as they are currently held responsible.
- Testing is **expensive**.

Arguments for and against drug taking and testing

The positive and negative implications to the sport and the performer regarding drug taking have been discussed throughout this chapter. Table 12.2 (page 163) summarises the arguments for and against drug taking and testing.

Anti-doping rules often lead to complicated and costly administrative and medical follow-ups to ascertain whether drugs taken by athletes are legitimate therapeutic agents or substances which violate the definitive WADA rules and are not allowed.

In the meantime, clean athletes, who are up graded to podium medal status as result of cheats who have been stripped of their titles, could wait many years before this process is completed.

SPORT AND SOCIETY

Table 12.2 – summary of arguments for and against drug testing and drug taking

For drug testing and eliminating drug taking	Against drug testing, and allowing drug taking
athletes are role models and young people seek to emulate sports stars	strict more expensive tests have been introduced that may not be affordable for third world countries to use
testing protects athletes reputations and produces positive role models	a strict test returns more false positives (a test result that seems to detect a drug which isn't there)
drugs are not natural	the labelling of some supplements may not be complete or accurate, and some safe supplements may contain traces of prohibited substances athletes can protest that these secondary chemicals may be the products of another bodily process
creates a deterrent for athletes who may consider using drugs to cheat in sport	drug testing does not always catch athletes, and is often having to develop new testing methods for the new drugs being released retesting of stored samples is a very expensive process
anti-doping programmes seek to preserve what is intrinsically valuable about sport (values such as fair play and equity) often referred to as 'the spirit of sport' and the essence of Olympism	the whereabouts rule is time consuming and is perceived as an infringement of human rights
drug taking is illegal, a form of cheating, is unethical and immoral	public respect for all sports professionals suffers if there are frequent drug scandals it becomes harder to believe that all athletes aren't cheats and may cause all victories to be viewed with suspicion
discredits negative role models and reinforces the message to stay clean	false accusations can have an adverse effect on an athlete's career - even if she or he is later proven innocent the loss of earnings is usually significant
promotes health and safety and avoidance of the physical side-effects associated with taking PEDs	drug taking is a short-cut to realising potential, even if athletes risk their health and their athletic careers
the detection methods are accurate and reliable	a stricter test returns more false positives (a test result that seems to detect a drug which isn't there)
TUE certificates protect athletes who suffer from general illnesses/allergies and injury rehabilitation	regulated scientific research in producing safer PEDs, could reduce health risks and recovery it is hard to identify those athletes who are awarded TUE certificates who inadvertently physically benefit from such prescriptions
rewards athletes for their ability, training and efforts, and preserves what is intrinsically valuable about sport	elite athletes gain unfair advantage from training methods such as altitude training and the use of hypobaric chambers, so why not include PEDs?
alternative legal methods can enhance athletic performance, such as altitude training and nutritional supplements, for example, creatine	testing is made more difficult because some drugs are broken down quickly inside the body to produce secondary substrates
public perception could be that a PEDs reduce the role of skill and replaces it by chemically induced brute strength and endurance, and as a result may lose interest in the sports in which it is used the harm would be primarily financial	false positives, if leaked to the media, are bad publicity it is sometimes hard to prove one way or another could lead to the demise of professional leagues
drugs are bad for business and commercial organisations do not donate their money out of the goodness of their hearts they do it to attract further business	if everyone took PEDs, spectator entertainment and standards in performance would increase and with it a level playing field and more income

Arguments for and against drug testing

SECTION 6 CHAPTER 12 — DRUGS IN SPORT, SPORT AND THE LAW, AND COMMERCIALISATION

Sport and the law

Whilst it would be nice to believe that individuals who participate in sport always adhere to the rules, there are many who try to gain personal advantage from the sports they play.

Thus, in recent years, sporting laws have become more and more common. Elite sport has become more commercialised and more exposed in the media so any inappropriate behaviour is more likely to attract the attention of law enforcing agencies.

Sport is seen by the law as a special area whereby the law and legal systems does not directly interfere with the specific rules in relation to that particular sport. The International Governing Body (IGB) of a particular sport will be the regulator which develops the laws of the game of that sport. These will then be expected to be regulated in the various countries by the NGBs who regulate the various clubs which play in that particular country.

Sport legislation and the performer, officials, coaches and spectators

Figure 12.8 outlines the areas in which the law may impact on sport.

Player's contracts: the **contract to compete** is an unwritten code governing how to strive to play fairly, within the rules. It determines how a player should behave during a game, covering fair play, sportsmanship, respect for rules and officials and trying their best. Acceptance of this contract involves an expectation of how the opposition will play.
Over time a negative impact has invaded sport involving **gamesmanship**, **win-at-all-costs** attitude and **drug usage**.

figure 12.8 – sport and the law

SPORT AND THE LAW: eliminate discrimination, control violence, player rights, spectators, coaches, players vs officials, fair competition, player contracts

Fair competition can be related to teams/player's actions surrounding a game, and it is important that teams start on a level playing field. If this does not occur, the responsible team should be made accountable for their actions.

Professional **player's contracts** are concerned with ever-increasing wages in professional sports.
- Players hire agents to represent them in negotiations of multimillion pound player contracts, trades and promotional deals.
- It is important that players have **legal documents** which ensure wages and sponsorship deals are correctly paid.
- Equally, clubs require such documents in order to ensure players meet the demands laid out within their contracts.
- EU law has played a leading role in the governance of football since the landmark **Bosman ruling** (1995) a decision concerning freedom of movement for workers which banned restrictions on foreign EU players within national leagues.

Players' rights are related to players' contracts. It is now legal for players to leave a professional soccer club for no transfer fee once a player's contract has expired, thereby ensuring employment protection. Players outside the EU need a work permit.

Controlling violence is relevant to actions made both off and on the field of play. For example, players injuring other players with deliberate intent, hooliganism and crowd control. Most violent actions on the field of play are dealt with by the NGB officials who impose penalties such as **red carding**, **yellow carding**, **sin bin**s and **match bans**. When violence in sports is punished, there is a low likelihood of the same violence being repeated.

SPORT AND SOCIETY

Sport legislation

In **contact sports**, such as football or rugby, all participants owe a **duty of care** to one another. In order to show a breach of that duty, conduct must be reckless and fall below the standard required of a reasonably skilful and competent professional player. It must be an act that is **more serious** than an error of judgement.

Thereafter, the injury suffered must be foreseeable. For example, it must be the type of injury that one would expect from a foul or tackle.

Given that, the test for **negligence** in the sporting world is a high threshold to meet, since the injured party must gather as much evidence as possible to support his or her case. In some instances, players may also seek compensation from a negligent referee.

The worrying result of **fiercer professional competition** in the 21st century, particularly in rugby union and football, is an increase in **on-field violence**, the growth of which can be explained by:
- Pressures exerted by media scrutiny.
- Obsession with winning brought about by the greater availability of large prizes.
- Failure of NGBs to develop an adequate framework of regulation and control.

In 1995, Duncan Ferguson was the first British international football player to be jailed for assaulting a fellow professional on the field of play.

Court of Arbitration for Sport

The **Court of Arbitration for Sport** (CAS) was established to settle disputes related to sport through arbitration. See below some examples of their work.

- In July 2016 the CAS confirmed that the Russian Olympic Committee (ROC) could not enter track and field athletes for the 2016 Rio Olympic Games, with the exception of those cleared by the IAAF under the new competition rules regarding 'neutral athletes'.

- Dwain Chambers (GB sprinter, figure 12.9) completed a 2-year ban in 2003 for taking tetrahydrogestrinone (THG). He returned to competition and although qualified for the 2008 Beijing Olympics, the British Olympic Committee (BOA) barred him from selection under its bye-law 25 because of the serious nature of his doping offence. CAS overturned the Olympic ban on the grounds that it was not compliant with the WADA code of conduct, and Dwain did compete in the Olympics.

figure 12.9 – Dwain Chambers

CAS is able to fine, suspend or ban athletes from their particular sport and resolves disputes ranging from commercial (sponsorship) contracts to appeals against national or sports organisation disciplinary sanctions.

The **elimination** of **discrimination** concerns an extremely important type of law. It is illegal for any club to disallow an individual to become a member of an institution on the grounds of colour or race. Racism in football grounds has been largely stopped as a result of the policy of '**Let's Kick Racism out of football**'.

Spectators

Spectators must act within the law. **Hooliganism** (prevalent in football) is characterised by **unruly, violent and aggressive behaviour by overzealous supporters**. **Video monitoring** has been installed in most football grounds so that police can monitor crowd movement. All manner of legal means and policing tactics have been tried to control hooliganism, including deterrent sentencing, legislation such as the **Football Offences Act (1991)** and the creation of the **Football Intelligence Unit**.

> **SECTION 6**
> **CHAPTER 12**

DRUGS IN SPORT, SPORT AND THE LAW, AND COMMERCIALISATION

Spectators

The UK **Crown Prosecution Service** (CPS) has the right to prosecute players and spectators for violence in football grounds as well as outside as witnessed during the European Football Championships held in France in 2016.

Frequently, incidents result in **recriminations** against local police forces, which are accused of targeting, provoking or otherwise mistreating fans. Very occasionally intervening police actions have a disastrous impact on spectator sport.

Hillsborough

For example, the Hillsborough disaster of 1989 was a human crush at Hillsborough football stadium in Sheffield resulting in 96 deaths among spectators. Bereaved families were paid an average of £3,500 each, whilst 16 traumatised policemen received a total of more than £1.5million.

The legislation arising from the Hillsborough disaster is a major example of how responsibility in sport is now answerable to **international law** and no longer contained within the jurisdiction of a specific club or sport.

The **Taylor Report** found that the main reason for the disaster was the failure of police control and not unruly spectator behaviour that initially was thought to have been the cause of this tragedy and initiated the Hillsborough Justice campaign (figure 12.10).

figure 12.10 – Hillsborough

The Taylor Report had a deep impact on **spectator safety standards** for stadiums in the UK. Perimeter and lateral fencing was removed and many top stadiums were converted to be all-seated. Most football clubs refurbished or rebuilt (partly and in some cases completely) their stadiums, while others built new stadiums at different locations, and in doing so improved spectator safety.

Coaches

- **Coaches** need to be aware of their legal responsibilities, especially with respect to the advice they give their athletes and the way they manage and supervise participation in sport.
- Coaches should have appropriate insurance that covers both **public liability** and personal accidents.
- Many governing bodies include **insurance** as part of their affiliation fee.
- Coaches have an **ethical and legal** responsibility to educate and protect their athletes from all forms of **abuse** such as drug, emotional and physical abuse.
- In 2017 revelations of historical **child sexual abuse** in premier football academies hit the media. Former football coach Barry Bennell was charged with eight separate offences of sexual assault against an under 16 year old boy.

Officials

Rule enforcement is usually down to the officials who are responsible for ensuring that players abide by the written rules of a sport or game.

- If players fail to do this, then officials have the duty and power to **punish** players as necessary.
- For example, David Beckham was sent off during the 1998 World Cup Argentina game when he deliberately kicked another player.
- Referee responsibilities are no longer in the sole control of governing bodies of sport, but open to an **interpretation by law**.
- The **referee, linesman and camera recordings** interlock to police the game.

SPORT AND SOCIETY

Officials

- Officials have a **duty of care** towards their players and can be prosecuted if a player is injured through poor referring.
- For example, the case of Smolden v Whitworth (1991), in which a young rugby player was permanently paralysed when a scrum collapsed during a bad-tempered game.
It was later ruled that the referee had not acted with competence, and thus was **liable** for the player's injuries.
- In a lot of cases sports injuries can be serious and may result in the victim experiencing a **loss of earnings** or some other **financial losses** in addition to the **physical pain** caused by the injury.
- **Match fixing**, **bribery** and **conspiracy to bribe** can be prosecuted if found guilty.
- FIFA, football's world governing body, has been engulfed by claims of widespread corruption since summer 2015.
- FIFA's president Sepp Blatter has always denied any wrongdoing, but in September 2015, he too was made the subject of a Swiss criminal investigation, launched alongside the original US inquiry into these allegations.

Despite the **autonomy of sporting rules**, it is clear that they are not exempt from the **scrutiny of the courts** and must currently comply with European law. If legal challenges are brought, it is likely that the governing bodies will seek to justify their rules by reference to the legitimate aims of competitive sport and the continued development of young athletes.

Impact of commercialisation on physical activity and sport

> **STUDENT NOTE**
>
> This segment is introduced in AS/A1 Revise PE for AQA ISBN 9781901424850. Chapter 8, page 113.

The so-called **'golden triangle'** (figure 12.11) links **sport**, **sponsorship** and the **media**.

These three elements provide the bases for commercialism in sport.

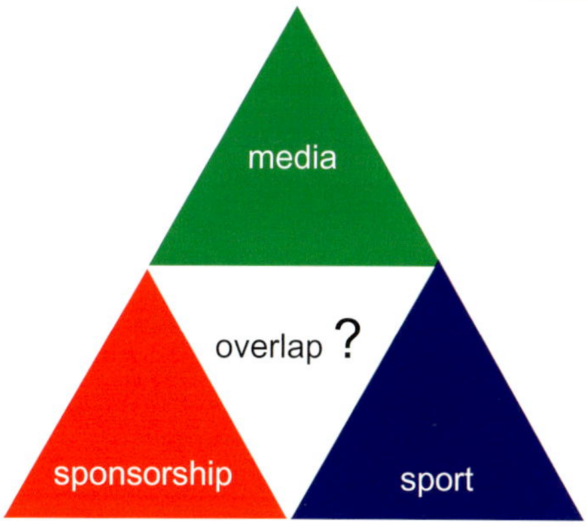

The **media** now includes:
- Television (terrestial or satellite).
- Newspapers (broadsheets or tabloid).
- Magazines.
- Radio.
- The internet (access by mobile devices).
- Social media (particularly twitter and facebook).

figure 12.11 – the media golden triangle

A **sponsor** will expect to promote its products by using a performer's image in return for financial support. A contract will be commercial and dependent on the star status of the sportsperson. If the status falls, so might the sponsorship. An example of this is Tiger Woods and his portrayal by the media after his 2009 personal difficulties. These difficulties had nothing to do with his status as world leading golfer, but caused several sponsors to withdraw support.

The media use their power to sell products with players acting as clotheshorses. This can put fashion and behaviour before performance.
An example of this is the range of clothing worn by Rafael Nadal, down to the 'Rafa' logo on his tennis shoes. Presumably he has to wear this gear regardless of whether or not it would be the best equipment for the job.

SECTION 6 CHAPTER 12 — DRUGS IN SPORT, SPORT AND THE LAW, AND COMMERCIALISATION

Commercialisation

Commercialisation creates employment opportunities in media, coaching, sport and event management, as well as stimulating businesses related to sport and benefitting the economy overall.

The following tables (table 12.3 and 12.4) set out the positive and negative impact on different aspects of sport (the performer, the coach, an official and the audience), of commercialisation, spoonsorship and the media.

Table 12.3 - positive and negative impact of commercialisation, sponsorship and the media

positive impact on sport	negative impact on sport
the elite performer	
increased income from sponsorship in return for using or wearing the sponsor's goods	sponsorship and the media can be over-demanding of a performer requiring interviews at inconvenient times
the media can increase the awareness of the public of the skill, excellence and peronality of the performer (a role model)	increased pressure on a performer to obtain or change lucrative contracts for playing
improved facilities for training, coaching, TID and competition available through increased funding for a sport	the media tend to sensationalise lifestyle and non-sporting life choices by a performer instead of sporting excellence
increased participation level due to exposure of major event, people want to have a go at a new sport (eg rugby after World Cup victory in 2003)	there are inequalities of coverage (minority sports don't get much exposure), thereby performer cannot attract sponsorship
media led developments lead to more variations to sport (eg twenty20 cricket - summer season for Rugby League) leading to greater opportunities for income to the performer and financial gain to the sport	exposure of deviance (fighting, diving to cheat, arguing with officials) lowering role model status caused by 'win at all costs' attitude in media
increase of profile of performer and the sport	elite performers are often treated as commodities
unprecedented earning power for male athletes in most popular sports and for females in a more limited number of sports	psychological pressure on high profile athletes through excessive media attention
performers can concentrate on training without financial worries	performers are under pressure to perform when injured
positive role models encourage mass participation	
the coach	
can award contracts to performers which in professional sport gives him or her control over everything to do with playing strategy	sponsorship and the media pressure can be over-demanding of a coach
sponsorship can include coaches and enable travel to support performers at coaching camps and major events	an imbalance of salaries paid to coaches/managers of top professional clubs, such as soccer, and professional coaches/managers employed in amateur sports
an official	
media led developments lead to more variations to sport (eg twenty20 cricket - summer season for Rugby League)	NGBs lose control of a game, rule structure, timing of games and breaks are adapted to suit TV or sponsors
major help with decisions, the fourth official can review incidents (including scoring) on repeat TV	media can control location of events and kick-off times, technology (HawkEye, 4th official) not always available at lower level of competition
increased profile for full time professional officials, eg the tennis gold badge umpires	may have to call time out for advertising, for example NBA basketball
technology takes the pressure off officials when decisions are close	officials may become too dependent on technology

SPORT AND SOCIETY

positive impact on sport	negative impact on sport
the audience	
increased investment improves quality of facilities, acquiring top players and entertainment eg cheer leaders to attract bigger audiences	excessive advertising could interrupt the viewing experience
certain sports (soccer, rugby, cricket, golf and tennis) are ring fenced into terrestial or free to view TV for primary events, therefore maintaining large audience for high status events (test matches, Wimbledon, cup finals etc.	pay-to-view TV can make some sports events expensive to watch
sports channels available (at a cost) for specific events	low attendance at events which are fully covered on TV
media led developments lead to more variations to sport (eg twenty20 cricket - summer season for Rugby League) leading to greater opportunities for fans and more exciting games	there are inequalities of coverage (minority sports don't get much exposure), thereby sports fans for that sport cannot see their favourite sport
technology, such as video screens and HawkEye for replays and match statistics, increase excitement, awareness and knowledge of the sport	more breaks in play can disrupt audience experience
commercial products are readily available for the spectator	player kit merchandise is regularly changed and disfavoured by some supporters due to expense
if the performers are able to work better with sponsorship, entertainment levels should rise	event schedules are planned to maximise viewing figures and so may not be timely for the arm chair spectator or athletes
	tickets to major sporting events are expensive

Table 12.4 – **positive and negative aspects of media coverage of sport**

positive aspects of media coverage	negative aspects of media coverage
players or teams gain revenue from sponsors	sponsorship companies usually only focus on high profile players or teams
sponsorship can provide teams with improved facilities and/ or equipment	sponsors can control event timings to suit peak-viewing times
teams or players gain publicity and promotion	players or teams can be restricted as to what products they can use
sponsorship can elevate new sports into the limelight via media publicity	sports can be overrun with sponsors – thus losing the nature of the game
more money for grass-roots teams	NGBs forced to alter rules to make games more exciting - in order to generate sponsorship interest
	more exciting events given priority over other sport
raises profile of the sport	leads to a squeeze on amateur sport
	media will not support minority sports, or low profile sports such as badminton with less identifiable role models

Commercialisation

SECTION 6 CHAPTER 12
DRUGS IN SPORT, SPORT AND THE LAW, AND COMMERCIALISATION

Practice questions

1) Deciding which drugs are true performance aids and which drugs should be banned is often difficult because:
   a. medical researchers lack the technology to study the drugs that athletes use.
   b. athletes often use new substances before scientists have studied them.
   c. drug companies outlaw research on performance-enhancing substances.
   d. NGBs have abandoned all efforts to control drug use in sports.

2) The physiological effect of anabolic steroids within the human body is to:
   a. extend endurance in aerobic activities.
   b. increase blood volume and red cell mass.
   c. increase muscle size.
   d. act as a buffer within the human body.

3) Which one of the following statements does not describe how sports governing bodies perceive violence?
   a. it elicits strong feelings among fans.
   b. sports are conducive to violent behaviour and aggressive conduct.
   c. practically every sport that features contact or collision either tolerates or promotes violence.
   d. being a fan is a relatively safe experience.

4) Which one of the following is not a key component of the contract to compete?
   a. give 100% effort.
   b. abide by the unwritten rules.
   c. respect officials.
   d. use gamesmanship during play.

5) Which one of the following strategies could be employed by officials to help reduce the likelihood of on-field aggression and violence amongst players?
   a. players could be made more aware of the concept of fair play.
   b. violent incidents could be ignored.
   c. use on-field aggression to increase the thrill and hostility amongst fans.
   d. avoid taking action due to the pressures of the media.

6) rEPO is an illegal drug taken by endurance athletes such as marathon runners and long distance cyclists.
   a) What is EPO? 2 marks
   b) How does rEPO benefit an endurance athlete? 3 marks
   c) What health dangers might there be in making use of rEPO to improve endurance performance? 2 marks

7) Under what circumstances might beta blockers be used as ergogenic aids? 3 marks

8) Certain sports people have been banned from sport for using illegal substances.
   a) What advantage does the use of anabolic steroids give to the performer? 2 marks
   b) What is a 'masking' agent and why is it significant? 3 marks

9) Discuss why sports people might wish to use banned substances. In your answer identify the hazards of taking such substances. 5 marks

10) Discuss the problem of illegal drug-taking in sport. Focus your answer on one performance-enhancing drug. 15 marks

SPORT AND SOCIETY

Practice questions

11) In 1998, the head of the IOC (Juan Antonio Samaranch) told a newspaper that 'substances that do not harm to an athlete's health should not be banned and should not be considered as a case of doping'. Discuss this statement. — 15 marks

12) What social issues can encourage a performer to take drugs? — 4 marks

13) What are anabolic steroids, how do they help sport performance and what are their associated health risks? — 5 marks

14) Suggest three ways in which national governing bodies are attempting to discover, punish and prevent the use of performance enhancing drugs. — 3 marks

15) Explain the difference between sport law and national law and discuss how it has changed. — 6 marks

16) Explain what is meant by 'a contract to compete'. Describe ways in which gamesmanship breaks this code. — 7 marks

17) Explain using one example, how each of the following people interact with the law in sport.
   a) Performers. — 2 marks
   b) Officials. — 2 marks
   c) Spectators. — 2 marks

18) How might a performer break the contract to compete during a sporting contest? — 3 marks

19) Discuss the continued relevance of the contract to compete for elite performers in today's society. — 6 marks

20) Many elite sports are now commercialised and seen as a form of entertainment. Discuss the suggestion that an increase in commercialisation of sport has been beneficial for performers and sport. — 8 marks

Answers link: http://www.jroscoe.co.uk/downloads/a2_revise_pe_aqa/AQAA2_ch12_answers.pdf

SECTION 6 CHAPTER 13: THE ROLE OF TECHNOLOGY IN PHYSICAL ACTIVITY & SPORT

CHAPTER 13: The role of technology in physical activity and sport

> **STUDENT NOTE**
>
> The syllabus content for understanding of technology for sports analytics is discussed, in part, in AS/A1 Revise PE for AQA ISBN 9781901424850. Chapter 11, page 146 onwards defines key terms used in sports analytics. Chapter 15, page 198 onwards, discusses the types and roles of technology in sport, including video and analysis programmes, testing and recording equipment, the use of GPS and motion tracking software and hardware, and maintaining data integrity.

Functions of sports analytics

Sports analytics is the provision and understanding of feedback to performers and coaches in an attempt to get a positive change in performance using a variety of data collection. It is also used to provide extensive data information for keen spectators.

Sports analysts (figure 13.1) are involved in **talent identification**, **player recruitment**, **nutrition**, and **rehabilitation** from injury. Video and data, captured or displayed on iPads and other devices, are used to give real-time **feedback** to coaches during a sports performance.

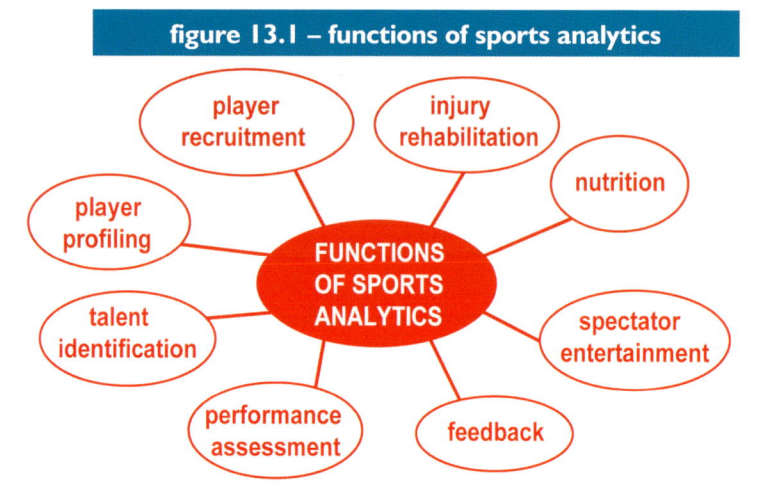

figure 13.1 – functions of sports analytics

FUNCTIONS OF SPORTS ANALYTICS: player recruitment, injury rehabilitation, nutrition, spectator entertainment, feedback, performance assessment, talent identification, player profiling

The **information** they provide and the insights they bring can give a team a truly **competitive** edge. As well as providing fans with useful statistics for after game banter, data also helps team players and individual athletes to improve their individual performance and fitness.

Analytics data can have a valuable impact for the **assessment** of performance, when it provides objective information that sits alongside other sources of information provided, for example from scouts who have an innate understanding of the game.

The most important aspect that coaches and players need to consider when selecting and using sports analytics software is that the raw data can be **trusted**, is **reliable** and that it has a **meaningful** impact on the individual and team performances.

Today's national governing bodies and clubs are better at selecting appropriate analytics data and then **fine tuning** it to their specific needs. This needs constant **collaboration with industry** that develops these bespoke products.

The future of sports analytics is to drill down new information, for example, psychological and sociological **profiling** that would give insight into individual aspects such as personality and decision making processes, resulting in meaningful KPIs (**Key Performance Indicators**).

The danger is that clubs and the individual could be swamped and overwhelmed by the sheer volume of data that could have a negative impact on performance.

The use of analytics in the monitoring of fitness for performance

> **STUDENT NOTE**
>
> There are a number of GPS trackable technologies that monitor fitness for performance, such as GPSports, described in AS/A1 Revise PE for AQA ISBN 9781901424850, Chapter 15, page 201 onwards.

SPORT AND SOCIETY

The use of analytics in the monitoring of fitness for performance

Data tracking software is available for smartphones and tablet devices. For example, **Instant Heart Rate** is the most accurate Heart Rate Monitor app for any smartphone.

Much of the value in sports analytics comes from being able combine information such as GPS or accelerometer data from matches or from training sessions (not all sensors are allowed during competitive games) with information from other parts of a player's training regime, including gym sessions.

Combining information from gym sessions, training and match-day play helps coaches and physiotherapists to fine-tune training programmes, and optimise recovery and rest times. It can even feed into match day decisions, as to when to replace (rugby) or substitute (football) a player, and help coaches to adapt formations and tactics based on data gathered about opponents' teams.

The use of analytics in skill and technique development

> **STUDENT NOTE**
>
> Using software such as Quintic and Dartfish split screen (comparative and multiple image software playback packages), a coach can highlight technical aspects of play/performance over actual footage of the individual, as discussed in AS/A1 Revise PE for AQA ISBN 9781901424850, Chapter 15, page 198 onwards.

Such **visual feedback** can be used when planning future changes in technique and over time, the coach and performer can assess if technical improvements have been made.

By using **qualitative** and **quantitative** analysis, technique can be changed, reinforced and refined.

For example, running kinematics motion analysis technology (figure 13.2) biomechanically analyses the positions, angles, velocities and accelerations of body segments and joints.

This information can be used to compare performer's technique to that of an elite performer, who is assumed as being more biomechanically efficient.

figure 13.2 – running kinematics, Loughborough University Sports Technology Institute

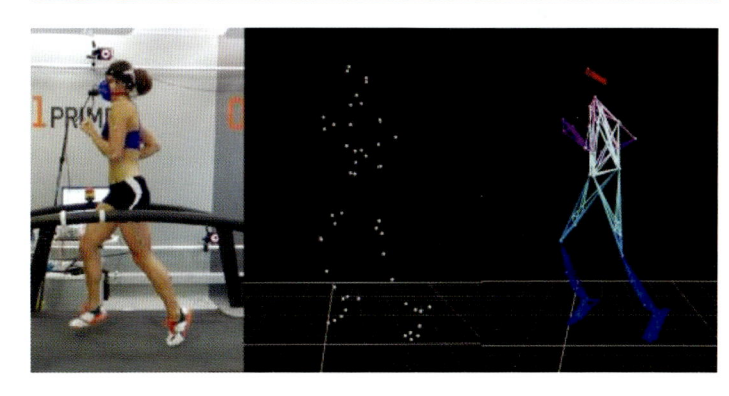

When an individual learns a new motor skill, skill progressively revealed in such software technology will determine whether the **technique** is correct or not or can be improved.

Another use of analytics in skill and technique development methods is based on **modelling** and **computer simulation** which has the potential for focusing on the whole skill development.

For example, **predictive technique analysis** encompasses these developments and offers an attractive interface between the scientist and coach through visual animation methods. Predictive techniques attempt to answer the 'what if...' questions.

For example, exploring the effect of reducing the angle to the horizontal of ball release of a basketball player (who consistently misses free throws).

SECTION 6 CHAPTER 13 — THE ROLE OF TECHNOLOGY IN PHYSICAL ACTIVITY & SPORT

The use of technology in injury prevention

Vibration technology

Vibration technology is a method of **athletic rehabilitation** training that uses a vibrating piece of equipment to cause **oscillations** in muscle tissue. It is intended to improve strength, power and flexibility. The vibrational oscillations can be altered in both size and frequency and have the option of offering heat therapy at the same time. Hence the physiological stimulus can be changed with associated therapeutic benefits which:

- Work voluntary muscles.
- Stimulate circulation.
- Increase metabolism.
- Break down cellulite.
- Remove toxins.
- Break down the lactic acid generated during exercise.
- Reduce DOMS.
- Reduce stress.

Vibration technology is recommended for **exercise recovery**, **injury prevention** and **injury rehabilitation**.

Electro stimulation

Electro stimulation (ES) also known as **neuromuscular electrical stimulation** (NMES). It is a training technique used for injury prevention, injury treatment, toning, pain relief, muscular recovery and physical preparation.

figure 13.3 – electro stimulation

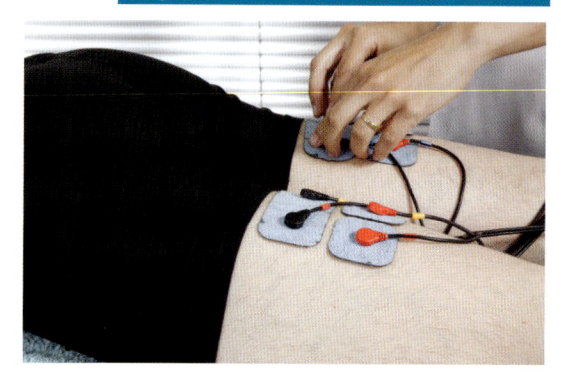

Electrodes are placed on the muscle groups such as the abdominal muscles, hamstrings (figure 13.3), calf muscles, plantar arch muscles and lower back muscles. An electric current is produced which is sent to the nerve fibres causing a mechanical response in the muscle. The current settings can vary depending on the clinical pathology requirements.

ES is thought to affect the body with associated therapeutic benefits that:
- Stimulate muscles to **contract**, by stimulating muscle fibre recruitment.
- Stimulate nerves to **decrease pain** by stimulating larger nerve fibres that can override the smaller nerve fibres that produce pain.
- Increase **blood flow** to speed healing.
- Reduce **inflammation**.
- Stimulate cells to reproduce and speed **healing**.
- Assist the **removal of lactic acid** following a training session or competition and hence reduce **DOMS**.

ES in combination with **physical activity**, serves to stimulate weaker muscles to contract and improve strength more quickly. This is often used on the quadriceps muscle group following knee surgery, or on a rotator cuff in the shoulder to stimulate strength gains.
The electrodes are placed on the muscle that is weakened and the athlete is instructed to exercise while the machine is delivering stimulation to the muscle externally.

Some research has shown that the use of ES can significantly **improve injury recovery times**. ES has been used to **strengthen muscles** following ligament and meniscal injuries especially in the acute stage of **healing** when an injury is new and **pain/swelling** is inhibiting progress or function.

ES, coupled with conventional rehabilitation exercises and therapies, is effective in improving muscle strength and function for two months after surgery. For the injured professional sports person resuming normal fitness levels as soon as possible is paramount, and so a combination of a range of appropriate therapies seems to be the best approach to take, but ES is a therapy that needs to be carefully planned and integrated within a training and/or rehabilitation programme.

SPORT AND SOCIETY

The use of analytics in games analysis

> **STUDENT NOTE**
>
> As discussed in AS/A1 Revise PE for AQA ISBN 9781901424850, Chapter 15, page 199 onwards, positional software, for example, Prozone and Hawk Eye provide valuable quantitative data such as positions and speeds of players and patterns of play for both coach and player.

The role of **feedback** is central in the performance improvement process. The provision of this **accurate** and **precise** feedback can only be facilitated if performance and practice is subjected to a vigorous process of analysis.

figure 13.4 – Andy Murray's serve pattern

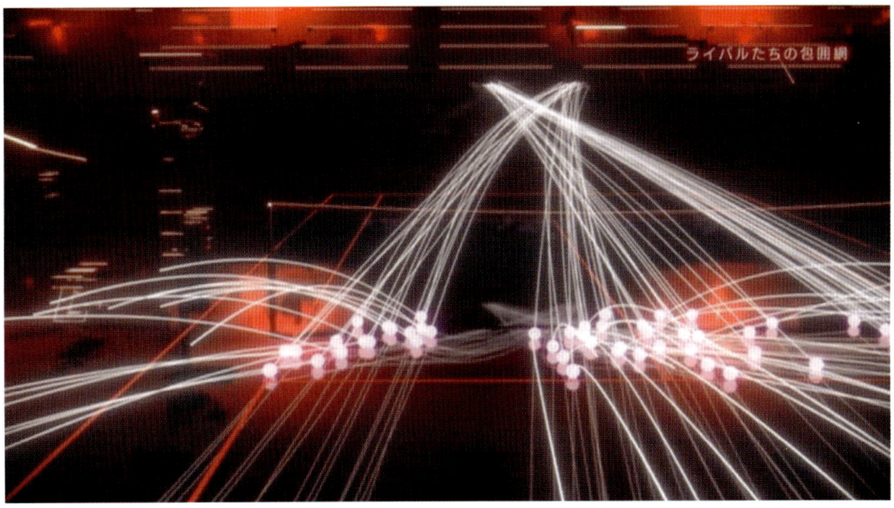

Games analytics provides **real-time feedback** so that the performer has the opportunity to make immediate adjustments. For example, a tennis set analysis (figure 13.4) provides quantitative data such as the percentage success rate of the first serve that may help the player to decide which serve to use most effectively against their opponent, during the next set. Video replay, immediately after a shot, provides qualitative feedback from which judgements can be made on shot selection.

The practical value of games analytics is that well-chosen KPIs highlight good and poor **techniques** or team **performances**. This information helps coaches to identify good and poor performances of an individual or a team member and facilitates comparative analysis of individuals, teams and players.

Poor technique is often a precursor to injury and so can be prevented when revealed and used as a result of data analysis. In addition to **biomechanical** assessments, games analytics help to support the physiological and psychological demands of sports. All information received can assist coaching staff and performers to **fine tune training programmes**, team selections and competition schedules.

The use of analytics in talent identification (TID)/scouting

Finding talent starts with a talent search. **Talent identification** (TID) is the process of identifying young talent and accelerating its progress, usually achieved by assessing a number of variables within a battery of tests.

Sports analytics provides the quantitative and qualitative data needed to create a **profile** that can be used to assess the suitability of the talented performer to the demands of the sporting activity. It is critical to **define the TID tests** when determining these key performance factors required by the sport.

Pathway Analytics enables sports to robustly measure and benchmark the effectiveness of their performance pathway using specialist diagnostic tools.

Talent identification programmes usually examine, judge and assess a performer by **watching** him or her **perform** in a competitive situation. If the player is deemed 'good enough' he or she is invited to an **academy** for a trial period.

The use of analytics in TID   175

SECTION 6 CHAPTER 13 — THE ROLE OF TECHNOLOGY IN PHYSICAL ACTIVITY & SPORT

The use of analytics in talent identification (TID)/scouting

Academies are special training centres set up by clubs to help them develop young players.

The TID system used by professional football clubs involves the use of scouts who work for or are attached to the clubs monitoring competitive matches. The criterion typically used assesses players on their techniques, balance, personality and speed.

Once recruits have entered the club system, clubs can build up a sustainable system that enables talent transfer within an aligned pathway vision (delivering tailored solutions to build sustainable programmes) that will develop talent from novice to elite performers.

This process can be supported by pathway analytics, such as the **Pathway Health Check** (PHC) devised by Sport England, which reviews the athlete's progress, fitness levels achieved and whether the athlete is transitioning well between junior and senior levels.

In contrast to soccer TID, some sports aim to identify **raw talent** as a starting point, providing physical attributes are met. For example, British Rowing TID programme identify, recruit and develop individuals with no prior experience, to become Olympic rowers through their Start programme (page 145).

Other TID initiatives include Sport England's **Talented Athlete Scholarship Scheme** (TASS) and UK Talent initiatives.

Development of equipment and facilities in physical activity and sport

Adaptive equipment for the disabled and elderly

Bespoke sporting equipment has radically changed the opportunities for disabled athletes and an ageing population to participate in sporting activities, but there is a fine balance between improving the functionality of the sport and turning individuals into robots.

The aim of researchers is to effectively match the technology with the athletes' requirements, known as **assistive** and **adaptive technology**.

Assistive technology refers to any item, piece of equipment that is used to increase, maintain, or improve functional capabilities of individuals with disabilities.

Adaptive technology covers items that are specifically designed for persons with disabilities and would seldom be used by non-disabled persons.

Given the opportunities for participation in sports for persons with a limb deficiency, the demand for new, innovative **prosthetic designs** is challenging. Made from carbon, flex-fibre, 'Cheetah Flex-Foot' blades enabled Oscar Pistoruis (figure 13.5) to break 26 world records. In 2008 he started a debate within the athletics community by petitioning to be able to compete at the Beijing Olympic Games, against able-bodied competitors.

figure 13.5– Oscar Pistorius, blade runner

Paralympic long jump champion Markus Rehm had a dream of competing at both the Rio Olympics and Paralympics in 2016. The 27-year-old set a world record of 8.40m in winning the T44 long jump event at the IPC World Championships in Doha in October 2015 a distance that would have given him gold ahead of Britain's Greg Rutherford at the 2012 London Olympics. The German track and field federation (DOSB) did not select him as it was felt that his prosthetic take-off foot and leg gave him an **unfair advantage**.

This case raises issues about **equity** of performers and performance as well as technology.

SPORT AND SOCIETY

Adaptive equipment for the elderly and disabled

Throwing frames are individually designed assistive devices which are scaffold-like chairs made of metal bars and plates welded together. The main purpose of the throwing frame is to assist in weight bearing, thus enabling a seated disabled athlete to throw.

A range of **wheelchairs** have been developed for disabled athletes, evolved to suit the specific needs of that sport, including wheelchairs for basketball, rugby, tennis, racing and dancing.

The chairs are usually non-folding (in order to increase rigidity), with a pronounced negative camber for the wheels (which provides stability and is helpful for making sharp turns), and often are made of composite, lightweight materials. Built to the individual's width, height and seating preference, the design team create a scan from the disabled athlete sitting in his chair, then create a computerised model that can be used as a template to manufacture the wheelchair.

The major barrier of this adapted technology is expense in the design and manufacturing of the wheelchairs that are often in excess of £2000.00.

Racing wheelchairs (figure 13.6) provide bucket seats, angled wheels to increase stability and a **'t' shaped frame** that gives precision steering and balance. **Specialist gloves** are used to protect the hands used in striking the push rim.

Wheelchairs, used for wheelchair **rugby** and wheelchair **basketball**, are designed to withstand heavy impacts and be easily manoeuvrable. **Tennis** wheelchairs have extended wheels in the front that would allow athletes to reach as far out to return shots.

figure 13.6 – racing wheelchairs

Adaptive equipment for the elderly

Sporting habits decline with age and mobility. Today there is a wide range of assistive and adaptive technological equipment that can engage the elderly to remain active.

A **low impact pedal machine** is ideal for an elderly person who remains seated and is able to do safe and gentle pedalling that stimulates circulation in addition to exercising lower limb joints and muscles (figure 13.7).

Hiking poles offer increased support and stability on unfamiliar ground and uneven surfaces, help improve posture and increase confidence for the individual. Walking is the most popular activity within the retirement population.

Wheelchairs offer mobility to the elderly to travel and access sports centres and pursuits such as **wheelchair bowls**.
Wheelchair bowls follows exactly the same rules as for able bodied players, and so offers the opportunity of integrating ageing immobile individuals with able bodied performers.

Assistive devices can help to improve the **quality of life** for both the disabled and elderly and maintain their sense of independence.

figure 13.7 – low impact pedalling

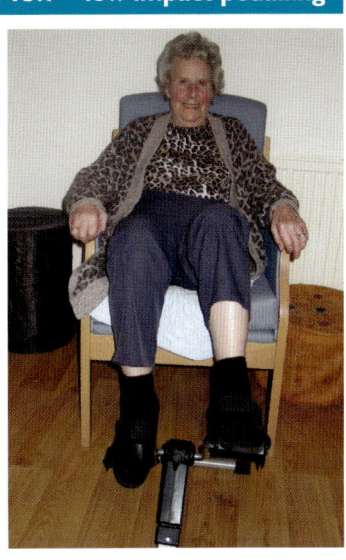

SECTION 6 CHAPTER 13 — THE ROLE OF TECHNOLOGY IN PHYSICAL ACTIVITY & SPORT

Technology and facility development - the Olympic legacy

Construction of a major Games venue often involves considerable redevelopment. For example, the 300-hectare (490 acre) Queen Elizabeth Olympic Stadium (figure 13.8) was constructed on a former industrial site at Stratford, East London and offered first class high tech facilities for many Olympic events in London 2012.

The athlete's village, a vast shopping mall and new transport links completed the physical infrastructure and a converged mobile phone, broadcast and wireless internet traffic system completed an outstanding **real-time action** and results **digital service**.

Today the Olympic legacy continues despite post Olympic austerity measures.

More recently, the Government has reaffirmed its commitment to Olympic and Paralympic success, and has also extended that ambition to **non-Olympic sports**.

figure 13.8 – facilities as a legacy

Success is supported for these sports through grassroots investment using UK shared Sport's knowledge and expertise developed from the Olympic legacy. Such initiatives require modern facilities, coaches and good digital communication channels.

Recent examples of the 2012 legacy benefits (figure 13.9) and results include:
- **Learning**: shared knowledge and lessons learned from the construction of the Olympic Park and preparing and staging the Games.
- This learning legacy provides the foundation for future host cities to use.
- Local people received **skills training** to prepare them for working on the Games, including many unemployed individuals, and these new skills can be applied long into the future.

- **Economic**: in 2012 **apprenticeships schemes** were offered in broadcasting companies including the BBC and ITV.
- Investment in infrastructure and sporting facilities that happened as a direct result of the Games.
- Since 2012, Sport England has invested in almost 1500 sporting facilities through the three facilities strands of the **Places People Play** programme.

figure 13.9 – 2012 legacy benefits

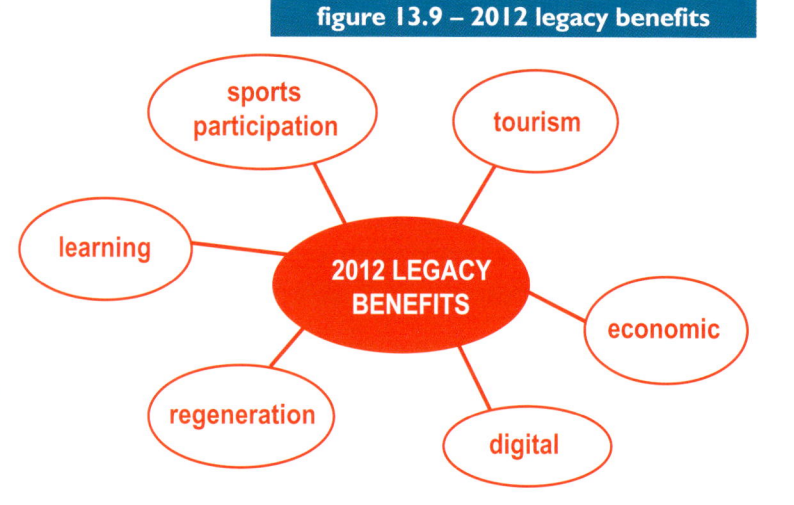

2012 LEGACY BENEFITS: sports participation, tourism, learning, economic, regeneration, digital

- **Digital**: the biggest technical London Olympic legacy involved the development of **ICT systems** needed to deliver pictures, texts, phone calls and video which created the most digitally enabled Games ever.
- BT designed and delivered the first ever converged communications network for a summer Olympics, carrying voice, data, mobile, broadcast and wireless internet traffic on one seamless, all-purpose network.
- This converged network meant improved energy efficiency, avoiding the need to build and power separate networks, and maximised the potential for its reuse after the Games.
- 60% of communications load came from devices accessing either the London 2012 mobile website or one of the mobile apps.
- This was especially driven by the real-time results that the tech team was driving to those platforms.
- Since 2012, much of this digital technology has been driven towards education.

SPORT AND SOCIETY

Technology and facility development

- **Sports participation**: post London 2012, published reports such as the **Active People Survey**, suggest that school sports participation has not been boosted, and may not be taken seriously, despite financial investment in facilities, coaching and initiatives in an attempt to increase participation levels.

- **Regeneration**: the re-opening of the Olympic Park as the Queen Elizabeth Olympic Park in July 2013 which is now becoming a world class destination for people to live, work, play and visit, hosting concerts, festivals, art installations and national and international sporting competitions, such as the World Track and Field Athletic Championships during the summer of 2017.
- The Olympic village has provided **housing** for over 800 residents and easy access to a shopping mall and public transport links.

- **Tourism**: the Games' long-term benefits on London's and Britain's tourism industry.

Multi-use playing surfaces

Most sports are now played on **synthetic** or artificial sports surfaces at both competitive and recreational levels. Hockey, netball, basketball, and athletics are almost exclusively played on synthetic surfaces (figure 13.10) at a competitive level, and other sports such as tennis, volleyball, cricket, and badminton have also benefitted from the development in sports surface technology.

figure 13.10 – artificial sports surface

3G/4G **rubber-filled** sports pitches are one of many synthetic playing surfaces that have transformed the availability, durability, and accessibility of playing facilities for school and community user groups across the country.

Multi-use games areas (MUGAS) such as 3G/4G turf technology consist of artificial grass 'blades' supported by a thin base layer of sand, and by an infill of rubber crumb. The overlaying turf has the desirable qualities of natural grass and the infill of rubber crumb acts as a shock absorber. **Moisture-retaining** underlayment provides many advantages commonly associated with natural grass turf. There is no evidence of a greater risk of injury when matches are played on artificial turf compared with natural grass.

Although the initial cost of installing a synthetic pitch could be up to £400,000, a big advantage is that **maintenance costs are low** and the all weather qualities enable sport to be played throughout the year.

A synthetic pitch cannot fully replicate the experience of playing on real turf as an artificial pitch does not offer the **true bounce of grass**. This can make difficult the issue of playing away matches on real turf.

MUGAS are great for schools and sports clubs as they offer a cost effective sport space for multi-purpose use.

Some playing surfaces are tailor-made to meet the demands of the sport. For example, tennis is played on a variety of surfaces: clay, grass, acrylic hard courts, synthetic hard courts, and carpet.

Rubberised cushioned hard courts have been developed to ease the pain of playing on a concrete court. Consisting of acrylic and a rubberized cushioning surface, this hard court playing surface (decoturf coating) is used at the USTA National Tennis Centre in New York City, home of the U.S. Open tennis tournament. This more yielding surface reduces chronic injury rates and enables professional tennis players to **extend their playing careers**.

SECTION 6 CHAPTER 13 — THE ROLE OF TECHNOLOGY IN PHYSICAL ACTIVITY & SPORT

The role of technology in sport summary tables

> **STUDENT NOTE**
> Advances in technology have had a profound positive and negative impacts on sport as discussed throughout this chapter and as summarised in the following tables.

Table 13.1 - **positive and negative impacts of sports technology**

Positive impacts	Negative impacts
electronic timing provides instant and accurate results	modern technologies, such as bespoke wheelchairs, may only be available to those athletes/countries who can afford them
force platform measures ground reaction force	modern technology can also support an unfair 'playing field' with such things as the development and use of ergogenic aids, for example, oxygen tents, where cost is an important factor
HawkEye has greatly enhanced sporting knowledge	technological aids may have a placebo effect that boots performer's confidence, as opposed to actually benefitting the performer
fibre reinforced tennis racket frames has a resulted in larger racket heads and an increase in the sweet-spot area of the racket which has increased the speed of the game	officials may become too reliant on technology systems and so lose skills such as time-keeping and the ability to make quick and marginal decisions
high tech equipment at elite level has made sport a global product benefitting sports business	

Table 13.2 - **positive and negative impacts of technology on the coach**

Positive impacts	Negative impacts
sports analytics make it possible for coaches to provide their athletes with the best possible opportunities to achieve maximal performance	coaches may become too reliant on technology and not use their intuitive coaching instincts
enables effective and informed team selections and player substitutes during a match and rest and recovery	software data may get corrupted and become unreliable
the video camera is perhaps the single most important development in coaching in the modern era of sport	as sports technology continues to evolve, will sports technology replace the coach?
software such as Dartfish, provide the coach with detailed technique analysis and the biomechanical tools that can compare and monitor skill development	using motion capture analysis is very time consuming, expensive and needs the technical understanding of how to use it to best effect
smartphones and ipads are cheap accessible technologies coaches can use to analyse real-time performances in terms of strengths/weaknesses and/or tactics/strategies	coaches need to be aware that their athletes don't become 'guinea pigs' in the experiments of the technology industry
smart equipment can be used to measure performance such as exercise stress testing and cardiovascular assessment	coaches sometimes find video difficult to use while an athlete is performing, it can be better to observe by eye and interpret rhythms and corrections from this
electronic timing devices provide the coach with specific, detailed recording of performances such as gun reaction time and lap split times	
nutrition and fitness software programmes are used elite coaches to accurately monitor and analyse an athlete's nutritional needs, and fitness levels	

Table 13.3 - **positive and negative impacts of technology on the performer**

Positive impacts	Negative impacts
development of nanotechnology (study and application of extremely small things) has created a variety of products aimed at improving and increasing athletic performance	footwear and clothing are generally chosen more for comfort and sometimes fashion and injury avoidance rather than performance enhancement
faster injury rehabilitation	protective equipment, such as helmets, can create a more aggressive playing environment
the use of hypobaric and humidity chambers can recreate competition environments	the growing use of drugs in sport has led to many high profile athletes cheating the system
sporting equipment, such as helmets and body protection, are used for example in cricket and hockey to help prevent injuries	PEDs are part of the win-all-costs ethic, and can lead to over-aggressive behaviour in addition to detrimental physiological side effects
smart clothing eg sports socks are that are absorbent, flexible and breathable and wick away sweat	
compression clothing, such body suits, increases venous return and VO_{2max} during high intensity exercise and aids recovery as the effects of DOMS is reduced	
footwear can be made to match the shape and mechanics of feet on an individual basis to make movement more efficient and improve performance	affordability is an issue unless the individual is sponsored
prosthetics have also been made for those athletes with a specific disability	prosthetics are very expensive
wheelchair devices used in sporting activities have also become more sophisticated	wheelchair devices are very expensive when tailor-made
improvements in the design of sport equipment and clothing have both aerodynamic and physiological benefits for sports performers	at what point does technology enhance performance unnaturally?
GPS and associated apps, linked to Google Earth, provide KPIs such as position, distance covered and speed of player's performance	elite athletes could see a pay decrease during salary negotiations not based on their performance, but on sports analytics data
quantitative data from GPS technology, can be used to create training programmes, monitor progression and recovery during and between training sessions, and injury prevention and rehabilitation	data analysis can be time consuming and at times overwhelming
nutrition analysis and menu planning software assess energy expenditure and dietary intake used to create meal plans to achieve performance goals	
advances in stress management techniques that can redirect attention away from failure or perceived failure	

SECTION 6 CHAPTER 13 — THE ROLE OF TECHNOLOGY IN PHYSICAL ACTIVITY & SPORT

Table 13.4 - **positive and negative impacts of technology on the audience**

Positive impacts	Negative impacts
sports are a form of entertainment, and providing new technologies such as HawkEye can increase their engagement and knowledge of the game	breaks in play, whilst replays are being judged, slows down the action and increaises the playing time and may lead to spectator frustration
the armchair audience has access to enhanced experience in the home through the use of more cameras/player cam, as a result of miniaturized video cameras	commercial adverts disrupt playing schedules for the armchair spectator
technologies can help to diffuse audience aggression and frustration, when pressure points do not fall prey to with bad umpiring decisions	commercial advertising of sports clothing may be fashion led, as opposed to what is best
a 'miked up' referee further facilitates the involvement of live and armchair fans to engage in real-time play	high tech equipment is expensive to buy for the average spectator/participant
spectator interest and excitement are enhanced by broadcasting and in-stadium replay screens scoreboards that can very quickly communicate results to an audience	some people decry the use of technology to improve sports performance but in reality it is inevitable
a wider range of sports are accessible and visible through the development of technology, for example, glass walled squash courts	the research and development of sport apparatus and apparel is an industry in itself which creates opportunity for investment and employment

Some people decry the use of technology to improve sports performance but in reality it is inevitable. The research and development of sport apparatus and apparel is an industry in itself which creates opportunity for investment and employment.

Practice questions

1) A successful training programme may be used for injury prevention.
   Which one of the following is not considered to be a preventative method?
   a. fitness training.
   b. the training cycles within a periodised year.
   c. ice baths.
   d. a balanced diet.

2) What is meant by the term talent identification?
   a. the process of identifying promising young talent and accelerating its progress.
   b. providing a learning environment that develops potential.
   c. using a variety of testing methods that profiles an individual.
   d. a monitor of progress and performance.

3) Which one of the following has a negative impact on sport technology?
   a. hypobaric chambers provide faster rehabilitation following injury.
   b. smart clothing creates an 'uneven playing field'.
   c. sports equipment can be designed for individual needs.
   d. video analysis of matches highlight strengths and weaknesses of a player's performance.

4) Which one of the following is not an example of negative impacts derived from hosting a global sports event?
   a. overcrowding.
   b. generation of civic pride.
   c. litter.
   d. noise pollution.

SPORT AND SOCIETY

Practice questions

5) Which one of the following is not a desirable legacy from the Olympic Games?
   a. residential displacement.
   b. new branding opportunities.
   c. new stadia and infrastructure.
   d. civic pride.

6) How can sports analytics assist in the development skill and technique?   4 marks

7) How can adaptive and assistive technology increase access to sport for the disabled and elderly?   4 marks

8) Identify and describe a modern technology that aids analysis and feedback for improvements in sporting performance.   4 marks

9) The London 2012 Olympic legacy is described as the longer term benefits and effects of the planning, funding, building and staging of the Olympic and Paralympic Games in the summer of 2012. Evaluate the success of this legacy.   6 marks

10) Identify the disadvantages of using technology in assisting officials in their decision making.   3 marks

11) Discuss how increased technology has helped officials in their decision making and its impact on the sporting event.   3 marks

12) Discuss how technology that can be used to improve performance?   6 marks

13) Discuss the notion that sports performers are only as good as the technology that supports them. Use examples from global sports to support your answer.   15 marks

14) Comment on how the future of sport may be affected by the developments in technology.   6 marks

15) Sports are a form of entertainment. How have contemporary technologies enhanced the entertainment value for both live and armchair spectators?   5 marks

Answers link: http://www.jroscoe.co.uk/downloads/a2_revise_pe_aqa/AQAA2_ch13_answers.pdf

SECTION 6 — AQA A LEVEL PHYSICAL EDUCATION PAPER

AQA A Level Physical Education Examination Paper

The A level examination structure consists of:

- Two papers each lasting 2 hours.
- Worth 105 marks each paper.
- Includes multi-choice, short and 15 mark extended questions.

Each paper consists of three sections:

Paper 1
- Section A: Applied Anatomy and Physiology.
- Section B: Skill Acquisition.
- Section C: Sport and Society.

Paper 2
- Section A: Execise Physiology and Biomechanics.
- Section B: Sport Psychology.
- Section C: Sport and Society and Technology in Sport.

Our answers to short and extended practice questions (located at download link www.jroscoe.co.uk/downloads/a2_revise_pe_aqa/) have been presented in bullet format to enable clear identification of the point being made.

Bullet point responses can be used when command words 'state', 'name', 'identify' and 'list' have been used. Otherwise, you must write your answers in continuous prose and paragraphs.

It is advisable to sketch out a short plan (such as a spider diagram) for the extended questions.

AQA Assessment objectives for A Level AQA Physical Education are included in the introduction to the questions and answers electronic file at www.jroscoe.co.uk/downloads/a2_revise_pe_aqa/

It is important that you use correct terminology, accurate knowledge and its application, supported by relevant examples in sufficient detail, when answering a question.

Key command words used in examination papers

Your first task when answering a question is to understand what the question is actually asking. Underline the key command words (within the question) and its interpretation, to maintain focus in your answer.

Advantages and disadvantages
Clear statement of why one condition is better that another. Would normally need justification and/or qualification relevant to the question.

Analyse
Break down into component parts and identify their characteristics.

Apply
Using the information provided, link it directly to practical and relevant situations within sport.

Assess
Judge the relevance and accuracy of information provided.

Calculate
Be able to enumerate and evaluate data in numerical form.

Characteristics
Common, agreed factors for a situation, structure or process.

Comment
Present a written evaluation of the worth of a situation in the context of sport or physical education.

INDEX

Compare
Identify similarities and or differences between two or more situations.

Consider
Look at the information given and give an opinion as to its worth in its context.

Contrast
Identify differences and draw attention to the significance of these differences.

Define/What is meant by....?
Formal and precise description frequently of a technical term/less formal by definition.

Describe
Use of quantitative or qualitative information to explain a statement or a relationship between factors. This term is maybe qualified as 'briefly describe'. Examples are frequently used.

Differences
A comparison between two states in the question. You should be precise and not be tempted to wander.

Discuss
Presentation of both sides of an argument, seeking an opinion based on knowledge and analysis with a justified conclusion.

Evaluate
Estimate the worth of something either qualitatively or numerically quantitatively.

Explain
Justification beyond simple statement or descriptions required (the why). Will frequently require examples, sometimes qualified as explain briefly. Consider number of marks allocated.

Give
Provide an answer from recall.

Identify and explain
Linking of cause/problem and effect/solution. Marks awarded only if links are made.

Interpret
To explain and translate information into a simpler form.

Justify
To explain based on evidence or detailed examples, the accuracy of a statement or opinion. The more detail the better.

List
A number of points or features, frequently only a single word. No description required.

Name
No explanation required or credited. Will normally require use of a degree of technical language. One or two words.

Outline
Briefly state a plan of a situation.

Plot, Sketch and Label
Used for graphical presentation. For a sketch, graph paper is not required. Important factors are correct labelling of axes and shape of graph. Plotting requires the use of appropriate scales on axes and accurate plotting points.

Principle
Theoretical concept underpinning a practical example.

State
Express clearly and briefly.

Suggest
More than one option available which require a justification linked to a question. Not to be answered from pure recall.

INDEX

A

AASE, advance apprenticeship in sporting excellence 142
acceleration   74, 76
accumulation of lactic acid 18
acetyl-CoA   12, 13
achievement goal theory 103
achievement motivation 102, 111
achievement motivation, situational factors 102
achilles tendonitis   57
active leisure   125
active rest   65
active stretching   60
acute injuries   56
adaptive and assistive technology 183
adaptive equipment for disabled and elderley 176, 177
adaptive equipment for the elderley 177
adaptive technology   176
adenosine diphosphate, ADP   12, 19, 23, 24
adenosine triphosphate, ATP   12, 13, 14, 15, 16, 19, 23, 24,
advance apprenticeship in sporting excellence, AASE 142
aerobic respiration   14
aerobic energy system, 12, 13, 24
afferent system   40
age effect on VO_{2max} 27
air resistance   77, 78, 93, 99
alactic component   19
altitude training   30, 31, 32, 37
amateur sports   148
amateurism   148, 149
anabolic steroids   158, 159, 170, 171
anaerobic energy systems   14
anaerobic glycolytic system   12, 15, 32
analytics in games analysis   175
analytics, sports   172
analytics, use in monitoring fitness 173
analytics, use in skill and technique development 173
analytics, use in TID and scouting 175, 176
angle   88
angular acceleration   88
angular displacement   88
angular momentum   89, 97, 98
angular momentum, conservation of   89, 97
angular motion   87
angular velocity   88, 96, 97, 98
anticipation   48, 52
anti-inflammatary fats   66
aquajogging   64
arousal   47, 121
articulatory loop   45
assistive technology   176
athleticism   126
Atkinson's model of achievement motivation 102
ATP muscle stores, 16
ATP, adenosine triphosphate 12, 13, 14, 15, 16, 19, 23, 24,
ATP-PC system   12, 14, 16, 32
attention   42, 118
attentional control   118
attentional control training   ACT, 119

attentional narrowing   119
attribution   104
attribution relationship to sports achievement 104
attribution retraining, strategies for 106
audience, impact on sport 169
audience, impacts of technology 182
authoritarian, leadership   113
autocratic behaviour, leadership 116
autocratic style, leadership   113
axes of rotation   87

B

β oxidation   12
Baddeley and Hitch working memory model 44
ballistic stretching   61
Bandura's self-efficacy   108, 111
behavioural symptoms, stress   116
benefits of outdoor education   132, 133, 135
benefits of physical education   130, 131
benefits of physical recreation   126
benefits of sport   128
Bernoulli effect   94, 95, 96, 99
beta blockers   158, 159, 170
biofeedback   120
blood lactate   21, 24, 37
blood lactate removal, rate of   22
body composition effect on VO_{2max} 27
body fluid balance and dehydration 18
braces   61
breathing control   120
buffering   21
building self-efficacy, strategies for coach 110, 112

C

calorimetry, indirect   27
capillary density   16
carbohydrate   13
cardiac risk in the young, CRY   58
cardiovascular aerobic exercise, general 59
central executive   45
central nervous system, CNS   40
centring   120
chaining   51, 52
characteristics of outdoor education 131, 132
characteristics of physical education 129
characteristics of physical recreation 125, 134
characteristics of sport   127, 134
Chelladurai continuum   113
Chelladurai, model of leadership 120, 122
Chelladurai's five types of leader behaviour 115, 116
Chelladurai's multidimensional model 115
chemical energy   12
choice reaction time   47
chronic injuries   56, 57
chunking   51, 52
citric acid cycle   13

INDEX

coach, impact on sport   168
coach, impacts of technology   180
coaches, legal responsibility   166
cognitive relaxation techniques   117
cognitive techniques to assist concentration 118, 121
cold therapy methods   64
commercialisation   167, 168, 171
commitment, development of talent 136
competitive orientation   109
components of a vector   73
compression garments   65
compression sportswear   59
compression stockings   65
computer simulation   173
concentration   48, 118
confidence   107, 112
confidence, lack of   109
confidence, relationship to attribution 109
conservation of angular momentum 89, 90
conservation of angular momentum, sporting examples 90
continuous oxygen recovery   20
contract to compete   150, 164, 171
contracts, players'   164
control of stress and anxiety   117
controllability in attribution   105
cool-down   21, 68
core stability exercises   62
coupled reaction   14
court of arbitration for sport, CAS   165
crown prosecution service, CPS   166
CRY, cardiac risk in the young   58
cryotherapy   63, 68
cue   48
cue utilisation   119

D

data tracking software   173
deamination   13
decision making   40, 41, 48
decision making, sport   128
deep vein thrombosis, DVT   65
democratic behaviour, leadership   115
democratic style, leadership   113
depletion of energy stores   18
determination, development of talent   136
developing the need to achieve, coach   103
deviance   151
deviant behaviour, causes of   152
digital, Olympic legacy   178
dislocations   56
displacement   74
DOMS, delayed action muscle soreness   21, 36, 65, 68, 174
drag   71, 78, 93
drinks, hypertonic sports   66
drug taking, positive and negative implications 159, 160
drug testing   161
drug testing, arguments for and against   163
drug testing, limitations   162

drug testing, pitfalls   161, 162
drug use, consequences   162
drugs in sport   157, 170, 171
DVT, deep vein thrombosis   65

E

eccentric-to-concentric actions 33
economic, Olympic legacy   178
education providers, development of talent 138
effective leadership   113
effector mechanism   46, 52, 53
efferent system   40
efficacy expectations   108
EIS Performance Pathways   143, 144, 146
EIS, English Institute of Sport   140
elastic band training   63
electron transport chain   14
electro stimulation, ES   174
elite level of the sports development pyramid 124, 136
elite performer, impact on sport   168
emergent leaders   113, 120
emotional arousal in self-efficacy   108
endothermic reaction   14, 23
energy   12
energy continuum   15
England Pathway for Netball   145
English Institute of Sport, EIS   140
enzymes, oxidative   31
episodic buffer   45
EPO, erythropoietin   31, 159, 170
EPOC, excess post-exercise oxygen consumption 19, 25
excellence in sport   136
excellence level of the sports development pyramid 124
excess post-exercise oxygen consumption, EPOC   19
exercise prescription, injury prevention   58
exothermic reaction   23
external factors in attribution   104

F

facilitation, homefield advantage   110
factors affecting horizontal displacement of projectiles 92
fair play   127, 130, 149, 150
fair play awards   150
false confidence   109
fast twitch muscle fibre type   16
fatigue, muscle   18
feedback data   46
feedback in information processing   40
Fiedler's contingency theory   114, 121
FIFA   141
flight path   99
fluid friction   78, 93, 99
footwear, activity specific   59
force   70, 71, 72, 77, 85, 86

INDEX

F (continued)

force, components of 72, 73
foundation level of the sports development pyramid 124
fractures 56
free fatty acids, FFA 13
friction 77, 78
friendship groups, development of talent 138
frontal axis 87
FT muscle fibres 18
future expectations in attribution 104

G

gamesmanship 150, 151, 155, 156, 170, 171
gender effect on VO_{2max} 26
general learned helplessness 106
generalised motor programmes 49
genetic effect on VO_{2max} 26
glucagon 13
glucose 13, 14, 17
glycogen 16, 17, 18, 65
glycogen phosphorylase, GPP 13
glycogen sparing 17
glycolysis 13, 15
glycolytic capacity 20
glycolytic enzyme activity 16
glycolytic enzymes 20
goal orientation 103
gold event series 144, 146
golden triangle 167
graphs of distance against time 76
graphs of speed against time 76

H

haemoglobin 26, 35
HBOT, hyperbaric oxygen therapy 63
healing 174
Hick's law 47, 53, 54
high intensity interval training, HIIT 32
HIIT, high intensity interval training 32
Hillsborough 166
homefield advantage 110
hooliganism 154, 156, 171
horizontal forces 71
hub sites, regional multi-sport 140
hydrotherapy 64
hyperbaric chambers 63, 67
hyperbaric oxygen therapy HBOT, 63
hypertonic sports drinks 66

I

IAAF 141
ice baths 64, 67, 68
imagery 122
imagery relaxation 118
immersion, total cold water 64
impulse and impact 79, 80, 81, 85
impulse and Newton's second law 79, 80
impulse, applications 81, 82, 83
incentive to achieve 102
inertia 75
inertia, moment of 88, 89, 97, 98
information processing, strategies to improve 51
initiative, development of talent 136
injury prevention 58, 59, 67, 174
injury rehabilitation 62, 174
injury types 56
input/output 40
insulin action 32
intentional attention 43
internal factors in attribution 104
interval training 20
intrinsic feedback 41
involuntary attention 43

K

kinaesthesis 41
KISS, keep it simple stupid 51
knowledge of environment 50
Kreb's cycle 13

L

lactacid component 19
lactacid oxygen recovery 20
lactate dehydrogenase 15
lactate sampling 29
lactate shuttle 21
lactate threshold 24, 37
lactic acid 19, 22, 24
lactic acid system 12, 15, 16
lactic acid, removal 21
laissez-faire style, leadership 113
laminar flow and drag 94
law, sport and the 164, 171
leader 121
leader characteristics 114, 115
leadership 113, 122
leadership styles 121
leadership, theories 114
learned helplessness 106, 112
learning, Olympic legacy 178
lifestyle funding 140
lift force 94
locus of causality 104, 105

188

INDEX

locus of control 105
longitudinal axis 87
long-term athlete development, LTAD 142
long-term memory, LTM 44, 45, 53
low arousal, homefield advantage 110

M

Magnus effect 95
managers and captains, role in preventing violence 153
mass 75
massage 65
mastery goals 103
maximum oxygen uptake, $\dot{V}O_{2max}$ 17, 22, 23, 24, 26, 28, 31, 35, 36, 37, 65
measuring RER 30
media, development of talent 138
media, impact on sport 169
medical support, EIS 141
members' characteristics within leadership 115
memory model 44
memory system 43
mental rehearsal 110, 117
metabolic accumulation 18
mitochondria 31
mitochondria, muscle cell 13, 23
mitochondrial enzymes 16
moment of inertia 88, 89, 97, 98
moment of inertia, values 89
momentum 80, 81, 83, 84, 86
momentum, conservation of 83, 84, 85
momentum, transfer of 83, 84
moral benefits of sport 128
motivation, attribution, and task persistence, link 105
motivation, development of talent 136
movement time 47
multi-use games areas, MUGAs 179
multi-use playing surfaces 179
muscle capillarisarion 22
muscle glycogen stores, restoration 21
muscle phosphagen 25
muscular hypertrophy 62
myoglobin 25, 31, 35
myoglobin, muscle 19, 20, 21, 26
myoglobin, restoration 21
myosin ATPase activity 16

N

Nach, need to achieve 102, 111
Naf, need to avoid failure 102
national governing bodies of sport, NGBs 141, 142, 146
national physical education curriculum 129
nature theory, leadership 114
NCF multi-stage shuttle run test 29
need to achieve, Nach 102, 111
need to avoid failure, Naf 102
negative deviance 151, 155

negative feedback 103
net force 71
neuromuscular electrical stimulation, NMES 174
Newton's laws of angular motion 90
Newton's laws of motion 70, 75, 76, 79, 85
NGBs, role in preventing violence 153
Nideffer's attentional styles 119, 121
non-rapid eye movement, NREM 65
nurture 136
nurture theory, leadership 114
nutrition, training 66, 68

O

objective sporting situation 109
objectives of physical education 130
objectives of physical recreation 126
objectives of sport 127, 128
officials, impact on sport 168
officials, legal responsibility 166, 167
officials, role in preventing violence 153
Olympic Oath 149, 155
Olympism 126
onset of blood lactate accumulation, OBLA 22, 24, 29
optimum motivation 48
organisations, talent identification and elite performance 139
outcome goals 103
outdoor education 131, 134, 135
output 46
over-confidence 109
Oxbridge sportsmen 148
oxidative enzymes 31
oxygen consumption 18
oxygen consumption during exercise 17
oxygen debt recovery 25

P

pain tolerance, development of talent 137
PAR-Q 32
partial pressure 30
participation level of the sports development pyramid 124
passive stretching 60
pathway analytics 143, 175
pathway education 143
pathway frontline technical solutions 143
pathway health check, PHC 145, 176
pathway strategy 143
peak anaerobic power 16
perception 42
perceptual mechanism 43, 46, 52
performance accomplishments 108
performance enhancing drugs, PEDs 157, 163, 171
performance enhancing drugs, PEDs, strategies for elimination 160, 161

INDEX

P (continued)

performance goals   103
performance level of the sports development pyramid   124
performance lifestyle   139, 140
performer, impacts of technology   181
peripheral nervous system   40
personal factors in development of talent   136
person-centred leadership   114
phonological loop   44, 45
phosphagen recovery   19, 20
phosphocreatine, PC   14, 19
phosphofructokinase, PFK   13
physical activity, concept of   124, 133
physical education and school sport   129
physical prowess, development of talent   137
physical recreation, concept of   125, 126, 133, 135
physiological symptoms, stress   116
physiotherapy   58
Pierre de Coubertin   149
planes of the body   87
player violence   152, 153, 155
player violence, causes of   153
players' contracts   164
plyometric training   33, 34, 35, 36
PMR, progressive muscle relaxation   120
positive deviance   151, 152, 155
positive reinforcement   103
positive self-talk   119, 122
power   12
predicted VO_{2max} tests   28
prescribed leaders   113
primary acoustic store   45
probability of success   102
progressive muscle relaxation, PMR   120
pro-inflammatory foods   66
projectiles   91, 92
proprioception   41
proprioceptive retraining   68
proprioceptive training   62
prosthetics   176
protein   13
protein supplements   66
protein synthesis   66
psychological reasons to aid performance   158
psychological refractory period   47, 48
psychological skills training, PST   117
psychological symptoms, stress   116, 122
pyruvic acid   13

Q

qualitative analysis   173
quantitative analysis   173
Queen's college step test   28

R

random drug testing   161
rapid eye movement, REM   65
rational recreation   156
reaction forces   78, 79, 86
reaction time   47, 52, 53
real-time feedback   175
recall schema   49, 50, 54
receptor systems   46
recognition schema   49, 50, 52
recovery from exercise   22
regeneration, Olympic legacy   179
relative sizes of forces acting on a projectile in flight   92
REM, rapid eye movement   65
rEPO   159, 170
RER, measuring   30
respiratory exchange ratio, RER   22, 27, 29, 30, 35, 37
respiratory quotient   27
response outcomes   49, 50
response specifications   49, 50
response time   47, 48, 53
rest, active   65
restoration of muscle phosphagen   19
resultant force   72, 99
rewards behaviour, leadership   116
RICE, rest ice compression elevation   57
rights, players'   164
role models, self-efficacy   110
rolling friction   78
rowing and start   145

S

SAQ, speed agililty and quickness   34
sarcoplasm, muscle cell   13, 15
scalar   70
schema theory   49, 50, 51, 52, 54
Schmidt's schema theory   49, 50
school sport   129, 133
screening   58
selective attention   42, 43, 44, 54, 118, 121,
self-confidence   107, 108
self-confidence, development of talent   137
self-efficacy   106, 107, 108, 112
self-efficacy, development of talent   137
self-esteem   107
self-serving bias   105
senses   40, 41
sensory consequences   49, 50
sensory organs   46
short-term memory, STM   44, 53
short-term sensory store, STSS   43, 44
single channel theory   48
situational factors within leadership   115
skill level, development of talent   137
sleep   65, 66, 68
sliding friction   78

INDEX

slow twitch muscle fibre type 16
social and cultural factors, development of talent 137
social learning theory, leadership 114, 120
social reasons to aid performance 157, 158, 171
social support behaviour, leadership 116
socio-economic status, development of talent 137
somatic relaxation techniques 117, 120, 121
specific learned helplessness 106
spectator violence 154, 156
spectator violence, causes of 154
spectator violence, strategies for preventing 155
spectators, hooliganism 165
speed 70, 74
speed agility and quickness training, SAQ 34
speed and velocity 74
spinning ball, Magnus effect 95
spirometry 27
sport coaches, development of talent 137
sport-confidence 107
Sport England 146
sport equity, development of talent 138
sport legislation 164, 165
sport science, EIS 141
sport, concept of 126, 133, 135, 136
sporting amateurism 148, 156
sports analytics 172, 183
sports clubs 141
sports development continuum 124, 134
sports injury 56, 67
sports participation, Olympic legacy 179
sports technology, impacts 180
sportsmanship 127, 128, 130, 149, 150, 155, 156
sprains 57, 67
sprinter and velocity 77
stability dimension 104, 112
stable factors in attribution 104
state anxiety 122
state sport-confidence 109
static stretching 59, 60
steady-state level 17
stimulants 158, 159
strains 57
strapping 61
strategy building, benefits of outdoor education 132
strength training 62
strength, development of talent 136
stress 121, 122
stress and anxiety 116
stress and performance 121
stress fractures 58
stress management 122
stressors 116, 121, 122
stretching, types of 60
supplements, protein 66
symptoms of stress 116

T

talent development 142
talent identification, TID 172, 175, 182
talent identification programmes, TIPs 142, 143, 145, 146
talented athletic scholarship scheme, TASS 142, 176
taping 61
task goals 103
task orientation 103
task-centred leadership 114
TASS, talented athletic scholarship scheme 142, 147
Taylor report 166
technique analysis 173
technology in sport 172, 183
technology, adaptive 176
technology, Olympic legacy 178
technology, role in sport 180
tennis elbow 58
therapeutic massage 68
thought stopping 119
thresholds, long-term responses 16
thresholds, short-term responses 16
TIP UK 142
TIPs, talent identification programmes 142, 143, 146
torque 88
touch 41
tough-minded, development of talent 136
tourism, Olympic legacy 179
training and instruction behaviour, leadership 115
trait anxiety 122
trait sport confidence 109
trait theory, leadership 114, 120
translatory mechanism 46
transverse axis 87
triglycerides 17
tubing 63
turbulent flow 99

U

UK anti-doping, UKAD 161
UK Sport 139, 140, 146
UK Sports Institute 140
UK Sport's world class coaching strategy 139
UK Sport's world class performance pathway 139
UK world class programme 147
uncertainty, homefield advantage 110
unstable factors in attribution 104

INDEX

V

Vealey's model of sport confidence   108, 109, 111
vector   70, 71, 72, 73, 83, 84, 85
vector components   73
vector components of velocity during flight   93
vector diagram   72, 99
velocity   70, 73, 74, 76, 80, 81, 85
verbal persuasion in self-efficacy   108
vertical forces   71, 77, 99
vibration technology   174
vicarious experiences   108
violence   170
violence within sport   152
violence, controlling   164
violence, strategies for preventing   153, 170
vision and hearing   41
visual feedback, technology   173
visualisation   118
visuospatial sketchpad   44, 45
$\dot{V}O_{2max}$ 35, 36, 37, 65
$\dot{V}O_{2max}$ tests   28
$\dot{V}O_{2max}$, maximum oxygen uptake   17, 22, 23, 24, 26, 28, 31, 35, 36, 37, 65

W

WADA   world anti-doping agency, 160
warm-up   48, 59, 68
weight   75
weight and mass   75, 84
Weiner's model of attribution   104, 111, 112
wheelchairs   177
Whiting's model of information processing   46, 53
whole body cryotherapy, WBC   64
whole sport plans and NGBs   141, 146
win ethic   151, 155
win-at-all-costs   149, 150, 151
work   12
working memory   44, 45, 46, 54
world anti-doping agency, WADA   160
world class performance programme, WCPP   144
world class podium potential, WCPP   144
World Class Programme, WCP   139, 140